The Role & Contribution Of Student Affairs in

Involving Colleges

George D. Kuh
John H. Schuh
editors

National Association of Student
Personnel Administrators, Inc.

D1372109

The Role and Contribution of Student Affairs in Involving Colleges

Additional copies of this book may be ordered from:
National Association of Student Personnel Administrators, Inc.
1875 Connecticut Avenue, NW, Suite 418
Washington, D.C. 20009-5728

Library of Congress Cataloging-in-Publication Data

The role and contribution of student affairs in involving colleges / George D. Kuh, John H. Schuh, editors. — 1st ed.
 p. cm.
 Includes bibliographical references.
 ISBN 0-931654-17-3 : $16.95
1. College student development programs — United States — Case studies. 2. Universities and colleges — United States — Case studies. 3. Personnel service in higher education — United States — Case studies. I. Kuh, George D. II. Schuh, John H. III. National Association of Student Personnel Administrators (U.S.)

LB2343.4.R65 1991	91-39503
378.1'94 — dc20	CIP

Contents

Preface

This book was prompted by three independent but complementary projects. First, in cooperation with the American Council on Education, NASPA's Plan for a New Century Committee produced *A Perspective on Student Affairs* (National Association of Student Personnel Administrators, 1987) to coincide with the 50th anniversary of *The Student Personnel Point of View* (American Council on Education, 1937). Taken together, these documents along with numerous entries to the higher education literature (Astin, 1977, 1985; Bowen, 1977; Chickering, 1969, 1974; Feldman & Newcomb, 1969; Pace, 1979) underscore the important relationship between student life outside the classroom and a high-quality undergraduate experience.

Second, during the 1988-89 academic year we studied 14 colleges and universities reputed to be among those that provide high-quality, out-of-class learning opportunities for their students. The major publication resulting from our work, *Involving Colleges* (Kuh, Schuh, Whitt & Associates, 1991), was addressed to a general higher education audience (e.g., presidents, trustees, faculty, student affairs staff). Other papers describe specific aspects of these institutions that encourage undergraduates to take advantage of learning opportunities in the college environment (Kuh, 1991a, 1991b, in press; Kuh & Lyons, 1990; Kuh & MacKay, 1989; Kuh, Schuh & Whitt, in press; Schuh & Kuh, 1991; Schuh, Andreas & Strange, in press).

The third project was the synthesis of about 2,600 studies of college student learning and development produced by Ernest Pascarella and Patrick Terenzini (1991). Predictably, a high correlation exists between the characteristics of involving colleges and the environments and contextual conditions that Pascarella and Terenzini found to be positively associated with student learning and personal development.

It is fair to say that most scholars in higher education readily acknowledge the importance of student affairs in contemporary colleges and universities. However, the role and contributions of student affairs staff in creating conditions under which students take advantage of learning opportunities have not been examined systematically by Kuh et al. (1991), Pascarella and Terenzini (1991), or the other writers who have analyzed the impact of college on students. This book is an attempt to address that void in the literature.

Purpose of the Book

This book describes how student affairs organizations, programs, services, and personnel assist an institution in attaining its educational purposes by promoting student involvement in out-of-class learning opportunities. As with *Involving Colleges* (Kuh et al., 1991), this publication draws on information collected under the auspices of the College Experiences Study. In preparing this volume, additional information was collected during 1990-91 from the seven institutions featured: Earlham College, Mount Holyoke College, Xavier University, Stanford University, Evergreen State College, Iowa State University, and the University of Louisville. These institutions represent large public and private residential universities, an urban university with predominantly commuter students, small residential colleges including a women's college, and a historically black college.

Obviously the missions, philosophies, locations, cultures, student characteristics, policies, and practices of these institutions differ markedly. These descriptions of how student affairs promotes student learning in different types of institutions provide student affairs practitioners, faculty members, other administrators, and graduate students with multiple "models." Multiple cases enhance the explanatory power of the role of student affairs in involving colleges (Glaser & Strauss, 1967) and increase the chances that examples of policies and practices from one or more of the institutions may be appropriate for consideration by student affairs professionals, faculty, and other administrators at other colleges or universities.

Audiences

The book was written with two vital NASPA constituencies in mind. Included in the first group are student affairs professionals from entry-level staff through chief student affairs officers who we hope will find ideas in every chapter that cause them to reflect on the role, philosophy, and contributions of student affairs on their campuses. The principles on which involving college policies and practices are based are transportable to many institutions represented among the NASPA membership. As a result, the vast majority of student affairs staff at four-year institutions should find something of interest. Unfortunately, resources were not available to include two-year and community colleges in the College Experiences Study. With adaptations, however, many of the characteristics of four-year involving colleges, particularly those institutions that have large numbers of part-time, commuting students (e.g., University of Louisville), may be instructive for staff at two-year institutions.

The second target group is students and faculty from graduate programs in higher education and student affairs. Because no other publication of which we are aware is similar in scope and purpose, this book should be a useful resource in a seminar in student affairs or higher education administration.

A Caveat

The editors and authors offer a caveat to the reader. The cases reported in this book reflect "snap shots" of institutions as they were studied during the 1988-89 academic year. Since that time, fundamental changes have occurred in higher education in general and at several of these institutions in particular. Readers should not be tempted to compare the colleges and universities described in this volume with their understanding of how these institutions operate today. The cases are most valuable when viewed as exemplars of good practice during the time they were studied.

Overview

Chapter One discusses the challenges facing higher education institutions and highlights the important role of student affairs in promoting student involvement in learning and personal development opportunities. In addition, suggestions are offered for how the cases and commentaries could be used in staff development or preparation programs. In Chapter Two, the five clusters of factors and conditions common to involving colleges are summarized.

Chapters Three through Nine present case analyses of the seven involving colleges listed earlier. To establish a context for understanding how student affairs programs, services, and personnel promote student learning, each case describes the institution's history, mission, and philosophy; noteworthy aspects of the campus environment and cultural properties; and selected policies and practices. Then the role and contributions of student affairs are considered. Following each case is a commentary by a scholar practitioner which analyzes the relationship between particularly salient institutional characteristics and student involvement. Policies, programs, and practices are identified that might be adapted by student affairs practitioners at similar types of institutions.

The final chapter draws conclusions about student affairs organizations and personnel at involving colleges and offers recommendations for student affairs staff desirous of developing campus environments, policies, and practices that promote student learning.

Acknowledgements

The cooperation of many groups and individuals was necessary to complete a project of the magnitude of the College Experiences Study. We are indebted to three organizations that generously shared their resources: the NASPA Institute for Research and Development (NIRAD), the Lilly Endowment, Inc., and the Education Services Division of the Marriott Corporation. We appreciate very much the assistance of students, faculty, staff, and others at all 14 involving colleges and, in particular, being permitted to describe the seven colleges and universities featured in this book in such detail.

We also thank Elizabeth Nuss, executive director of NASPA, and the NASPA Board of Directors for believing in the College Experiences Study from the beginning and especially for their support in publishing this volume. Finally, the following individuals provided invaluable assistance in collecting information during the campus visits in 1988-89 and drafting various iterations of the institutional site reports on which Chapters Three through Nine are based: James Lyons, Earlham College; Kathleen MacKay, Mount Holyoke College; J. Herman Blake and Carney Strange, Xavier University; Rosalind Andreas, J. Herman Blake, Carney Strange, and Elizabeth Whitt, Stanford University; Rosalind Andreas, Evergreen State College; and Kathleen MacKay, Carney Strange, and Elizabeth Whitt, Iowa State University.

Unsolicited Advice to the Reader

The 1990s portend to be difficult economic times for higher education. As we write, many institutions are engaged in budget drawdowns, reductions in force, reorganizations, and other cost-containment strategies (Zemsky & Massey, 1990). In such environments, student affairs organizations typically have not fared well. Such episodes often have had long-lasting negative effects on the morale of faculty and staff.

Given the present period of austerity, some readers will wonder if the themes common to student affairs organizations and personnel at involving colleges harken to an era that has passed. Some readers may conclude that the colleges and universities featured in this volume are anachronisms rather than lighthouses of contemporary American higher education. This conclusion is wrong for three reasons.

First, most of the policies and practices characteristic of involving colleges are not particularly expensive. Therefore, cost-containment mandates should not preclude efforts to encourage out-of-class learning. Second, the characteristics of institutions that maximize student learning and personal development identified by Pascarella and Terenzini (1991) are typified by involving colleges. As a result, the colleges and universities described later and in Kuh et al. (1991) illustrate different types of policies, practices, campus environments, and institutional cultures that positively affect students. Finally, a variety of state and federal initiatives have been proposed to encourage higher education institutions to address campus life problems (e.g., mandatory reporting of campus crimes, graduation rates, sanctions for illegal use of alcohol and other drugs). We do not claim that the involving colleges framework is a panacea for resolving these and other issues common to most campuses. We do believe, however, that the quality of campus life will be enhanced if educationally meaningful out-of-class experiences become an institutional priority and the focus of student energy.

The need has never been greater for student affairs professionals to create a vision of their role in promoting student learning and personal development and to passionately pursue that vision by positively shaping out-of-class learning environments. Certainly if there ever was a time for expecting students to take more responsibility for running their own affairs and for learning how to understand and live with people who are different, it is now. We urge the reader to adopt this frame of reference when reviewing the accounts of the involving colleges in this book.

George D. Kuh   John H. Schuh
Bloomington, Indiana   Wichita, Kansas

June 1991

The Authors

GEORGE D. KUH is professor of higher education at Indiana University where he teaches and conducts research at the Center for Postsecondary Research and Planning. He has degrees from Luther College, St. Cloud State University, and the University of Iowa. Kuh has been recognized for his contributions to the literature by the American College Personnel Association and the National Association of Student Personnel Administrators. His administrative experience includes work as an admissions officer, department chairperson, and associate dean for academic affairs. He was director and, with John Schuh, co-principal investigator of the College Experiences Study.

JOHN H. SCHUH is associate vice president for student affairs and professor of counseling and school psychology at Wichita State University. Previously he held administrative and faculty positions at Indiana University and Arizona State University. Schuh earned his undergraduate degree from the University of Wisconsin-Oshkosh and his graduate degrees from Arizona State University. He has received awards for contributions to the literature and professional service from the American College Personnel Association and the Association of College and University Housing Officers-International. With George Kuh, he was co-principal investigator of the College Experiences Study.

ROSALIND E. ANDREAS is vice president for student affairs at the University of Vermont. She received her undergraduate degree from Bethel (KS) College, her master's degree from the University of Kansas, and her Ph.D. from the University of Michigan. Previously she was dean of students at the University of Arizona and Oakland University. She was founding chairperson of the Commuter Programs Commission of the American College Personnel Association and has served as a member of the NASPA Journal Editorial Board. She is a member of the board of directors of Bethel College.

DAVID DODSON has been chief student affairs officer at the University of Puget Sound for ten years where he has observed closely the developments at Evergreen State College, a sister institution. Prior to coming to the Northwest, he was dean of students and professor of philosophy at Chapman College in Orange, California.

WILLIAM D. GUROWITZ recently assumed the position of vice president and dean of student affairs at Illinois State University. Prior to that he served for almost 20 years as vice president for campus affairs at Cornell University. He served as a Fulbright Fellow at the University of London during the 1987-88 academic year, looking at how students and faculty interact.

LEE E. KREHBIEL is director of campus activities and the alumni building at Berea College in Kentucky. He has undergraduate degrees from Wichita State University and the University of Kansas, and his master's degree from Indiana University. Previously he taught high school social studies and coached track. Krehbiel has given presentations at NASPA's regional and national conferences and coauthored an ERIC digest on volunteerism and a report on personal development during the college years for the New Jersey Department of Higher Education.

FRANCES LUCAS-TAUCHAR is vice president for student affairs at Baldwin-Wallace College. Previously she held administrative positions at the University of Alabama and Mississippi State University. She received her undergraduate degree from Mississippi State University and her graduate degrees from the University of Alabama. She graduated from the Harvard University Institute of Educational Management in 1989. She is actively involved in teaching The Freshman Experience and is a frequent speaker and workshop facilitator.

JAMES W. LYONS is a senior fellow at the Stanford University Institute for Higher Education Research. Previously he was chief student affairs officer at Haverford College and Stanford University. His undergraduate degree is from Allegheny College and his graduate degrees are from Indiana University. He has consulted widely, served as a member of accreditation teams for the Western Association of Schools and Colleges and the Middle States Association of Colleges and Secondary Schools, and was the 1988 recipient of NASPA's Scott Goodnight Award for Outstanding Service as a Dean.

ARTHUR SANDEEN is vice president for student affairs at the University of Florida, where he is also professor in the Department of Educational Leadership. Previously, he held administrative positions at Michigan State University and Iowa State University. Sandeen earned his undergraduate degree at Miami University and his graduate degrees at Michigan State University. He was president of NASPA in 1977-78 and chaired the committee that produced *A Perspective on Student Affairs* which commemorated the

50th anniversary of *The Student Personnel Point of View*. He is the author of two books, including the recently released *The Chief Student Affairs Officer: Leader, Manager, Mediator, Educator.*

DARYL G. SMITH is associate professor of education and psychology at the Claremont Graduate School. Previously she was dean of students and vice president for planning and research at Scripps College. She earned her undergraduate degree at Cornell University, her master's degrees at Stanford University and the Claremont Graduate School, and her Ph.D. at Claremont. She is the author of articles appearing in the *Journal of Higher Education*, the *NASPA Journal*, and the New Directions for Student Services Sourcebook series.

C. CARNEY STRANGE is associate professor and chairperson of the Department of College Student Personnel Administration at Bowling Green State University. He earned his undergraduate degree from Saint Meinrad College and his graduate degrees from the University of Iowa. Active in several professional organizations, Strange has served on the editorial boards of the *NASPA Journal* and the *Journal of College Student Development*. He is a member of the Board of Overseers of the Saint Meinrad School of Theology and College of Liberal Arts.

RODGER SUMMERS is vice president for student affairs at the State University of New York at Binghampton. Previously he was chief student affairs officer at West Chester University and North Adams State College. His other work experience includes positions in residence life, financial aid, admissions, the dean of students office, and the classroom on both secondary and university levels. Summers has been active in NASPA since 1972, having served on conference planning committees, the NASPA Monograph Editorial Board, Region II Advisory Committee as ethnic minority representative, and national chairman of the Ethnic Minority Task Force. Summers earned his Ed.D. from Indiana University, his master's degree from the University of Vermont, and his undergraduate degree in secondary education from Cheyney University.

ELIZABETH J. WHITT is assistant professor of higher education at Iowa State University. She received her bachelor's degree from Drake University, her master's degree from Michigan State University, and her Ph.D. from Indiana University. Whitt has held administrative positions in residence life and student affairs, including serving as chief student affairs officer at Doane College. She has served on the board of directors of the Association for the Study of Higher Education and is a member of the NASPA Monograph Editorial Board.

CARMEN WITT is dean of students at the University of Wisconsin-Milwaukee. She has been actively involved with the Urban 13 association of metropolitan universities and in a variety of positions at the regional and national levels of NASPA. An active contributor to university and community life, she has received several awards in recognition of her professional achievements and public service.

Chapter One

Student Involvement
The Key to Promoting Student Learning and Growth

John H. Schuh

In *Campus Life: In Search of Community,* Ernest Boyer (1990) identified six principles that provide a framework to strengthen the spirit of community on campus (p. 8). These principles speak directly or indirectly to the climate of the collegiate campus in which students learn and grow. Few would dispute the assertion that a great deal of what students learn results directly from their activities in the classroom, laboratory, library, studio, and other places where students and faculty interact as part of the formal instructional process. But others (Hood, 1984; Schuh & Laverty, 1983; Wilson, 1966) report that students learn much in settings other than those identified above.

Boyer (1987) estimated that students devote approximately 48 hours per week to attending class and studying. During a 168-hour week, taking into account that students will spend time eating, sleeping, and taking care of personal needs, perhaps 50 hours or more are unaccounted. While one may quibble about the precise number of hours students have available for other activities, the fact remains that students have substantial blocks of time that can be devoted to purposes other than attending or preparing for class. One of the most powerful ways students can spend their time is in educationally purposeful experiences outside the classroom. These experiences can range from living in a residence hall (Astin, 1985) to participating in leadership experiences (Schuh & Laverty, 1983) to working on campus on a part-time basis for pay (Astin, 1984; Herndon,

1984). The collegiate experiences of undergraduate students outside the classroom have tremendous potential to be growth producing.

Students who are involved in powerful out-of-class experiences are likely to have a much more satisfying college experience than those who do not participate. According to Astin (1985), "...the greater the student's involvement in college, the greater the learning and development" (p. 157). Additionally, persistence to graduation may well be determined, in part, by involvement (Tinto, 1987). Pascarella and Terenzini (1991, p. 520) added that, "With some exceptions... the weight of the evidence suggests that there may be a small positive and statistically significant correlation between involvement in extracurricular activities, particularly in a leadership role, and subsequent earnings."

Increasingly, student affairs professionals are asked to provide leadership in developing students' educational experiences. Rather than subscribing to the claim that their activities are "...indispensable but peripheral" (Fenske, 1980, p. 3) to the academic enterprise, student affairs staff can play a central role in developing learning experiences for students. Indeed, Boyer (1990) observed, "Student personnel administrators especially deserve high praise for their sensitive and creative work, often making decisions under difficult conditions" (p. 6).

Student affairs is not alone in the view that a student's education consists of all of a student's experiences while enrolled in a higher education institution. In his 1990 report, Boyer observed, "...As we visited campuses, it soon became clear that the academic and nonacademic could not be divided" (p. 9). Previously, Boyer (1987) had written, "We conclude that the effectiveness of the undergraduate experience relates to the quality of campus life. It is directly linked to the time students spend on campus and to the quality of their involvement in activities" (p. 191). He called for collaboration between those who are responsible for the formal learning experiences that occur in the classroom and those responsible for student life: "The goal should be to build alliances between the classroom and campus life, to find group activities, traditions, and common values to be shared" (pp. 191, 193).

Student Involvement

A brief review of the literature on college students leads one to an inescapable conclusion: Interest in educating students beyond that which occurs in the classroom or laboratory has been a recurring theme for decades. Much of the literature regarding the education of students has been concerned with "...student affairs' central, historical educational value, concern for the development of the whole student" (Rodgers, 1990,

p. 27). More recently, involvement has been seen as a means by which the whole person is educated. Let us trace these developments in the literature.

The learning and personal development of students associated with experiences outside the classroom has been a concern of many higher education professionals for at least a half century, although one can trace the education of the "whole person" back to Plato (Bowen, 1977). Affirmed many times, this issue was addressed in the seminal document, *The Student Personnel Point of View* (American Council on Education, cited in NASPA, 1989). This document asserted that "educational institutions have an obligation to consider the students as a whole" and emphasized "the development of the student as a person rather than upon his (*sic*) intellectual training alone" (p. 49). *The Student Personnel Point of View* called for research on student out-of-class life and faculty-student out-of-class relationships to learn more about the activities in which students are engaged and the role of faculty in "student personnel work" (p. 62).

The 1937 version of *The Student Personnel Point of View* was revised in 1949. The philosophy advanced by this document stated, "The student personnel point of view encompasses the student as a whole" (American Council on Education, cited in NASPA, 1989, p. 22). The 1949 version argued that the "test of the effectiveness of any personnel service lies in the differences it makes in the development of individual students" (p. 43).

Student experiences outside the classroom have been seen as a vehicle for educating the "whole person" according to the literature of student affairs administrators. Although referred to as "activities" in her book, Mueller (1961) pointed out that out-of-class experiences contribute to student growth by enhancing classroom learning, developing social interaction, providing for a profitable use of leisure time, and encouraging better values and higher standards.

The theme of the education of the whole person surfaced again in Bowen's (1977) economic analysis of higher education. He outlined the following goal for higher education: "Education should be directed toward the growth of the whole person through the cultivation not only of the intellect and of competence but also of the affective dispositions, including the moral, religious, emotional, social, and esthetic aspects of the personality" (p. 33).

On the 50th anniversary of the 1937 version of *The Student Personnel Point of View,* the National Association of Student Personnel Administrators (1987) published a contemporary statement on student affairs. One of the guiding assumptions of student affairs work in this statement is that student involvement enhances learning. The statement asserted, "Students learn most effectively when they are actively involved with their work in the classroom and in student life" (NASPA, 1987, p. 11). Lyons (1990, p. 31) elaborated, asserting that "a learning opportunity is missed every time a teacher (be it a professor, activities adviser, orientation director, or resident assistant) does something for students that students could do for themselves."

The report of the Study Group on the Conditions of Excellence in American Higher Education (1984) stimulated interest in the concept of student involvement. This committee, made up of outstanding figures in American higher education (e.g., Astin, Blake, Bowen, Gamson, Hodgkinson, Lee, and Mortimer) affirmed that student involvement was perhaps the single most important condition for improving undergraduate education. This group characterized student involvement as being manifested by those who devote considerable energy "...to studying, by working at on-campus rather than off-campus jobs, by participating actively in student organizations, and by interacting frequently with Faculty members and student peers" (p. 17).

It is significant that virtually all of the activities excerpted above from the study group's report fall into the domain higher education institutions traditionally have assigned to student affairs. This report was published over half a decade ago. Rhetorically, we wonder how many student affairs administrators seized upon the study group's report as a mandate to enlist support from our faculty colleagues, senior administrators, and members of our governing boards for developing educationally purposeful out-of-class experiences for our students?

The study group identified two principles about the conditions of educational excellence:

1. The amount of student learning and personal development associated with any educational program is directly proportional to the quality and quantity of student involvement in that program.

2. The effectiveness of any educational policy or practice is directly related to the capacity of that policy to increase student involvement in learning (p. 19).

So the study group asserted that student involvement was central to the educational experience and suggested two principles which can be used to determine if educational excellence exists in our programs. But what about empirical evidence? Several studies point to the effects of student involvement.

Benefits of Involvement

A variety of studies have detailed the benefits of student involvement. In general, involvement is positively related to satisfaction with the living environment and academic major (Kegan, 1978) and community service and post-college income (Pace, 1979). On the other hand, lack of involvement is related to higher attrition rates according to Astin (1977). Living in a campus residence, joining a social fraternity or sorority, participating in athletics, enrolling in honors programs, getting involved in ROTC, and participating in professors' undergraduate research projects all have a positive effect on persistence (Astin, 1985).

Astin (1985) concluded that involvement had significant effects on students:

> Perhaps the most important general conclusion from this elaborate analysis was that nearly all forms of student involvement are associated with greater-than-average changes in the characteristics of entering freshmen. And for certain student outcomes, involvement is more strongly associated with change than either entering freshmen's characteristics or institutional characteristics (p. 147).

Thus, the evidence seems clear: students benefit significantly from being involved in the educational process. How does a higher education institution facilitate the involvement process? The College Experiences Study sought some answers to this question.

The College Experiences Study

The College Experiences Study (CES) was undertaken during the 1988-89 academic year to determine the institutional factors and conditions that encourage students' personal learning and development through out-of-class experiences. After reviewing much of the literature regarding student involvement (e.g., Astin, 1985) and the concerns that had been raised about the undergraduate experience (e.g., Boyer, 1987), the research team sought to identify institutional factors and conditions that facilitated student learning outside the classroom. Support was secured from three funding agencies (Lilly Endowment, Inc., NASPA Institute for Research and Development, and Marriott Education Services) to underwrite the costs of the project.

We assembled a team which consisted of individuals who had experiences with a wide variety of institutions located throughout the United States and who were very conversant on the topic of student involvement: Rosalind Andreas, J. Herman Blake, James Lyons, C. Carney Strange, and Elizabeth Whitt. Two graduate assistants, Lee Krehbiel and Kathleen MacKay, completed our research team.

With the advice and assistance of 48 experts on higher education (e.g., Astin, Gamson, Pace, Reisman), 14 higher education institutions were identified for study using a modified Delphi technique. These institutions included four small residential colleges (Berea College, Earlham College, Grinnell College, and Evergreen State College); four large residential universities (Iowa State University, Miami University, Stanford University, and the University of California, Davis); four metropolitan universities (the University of Alabama-Birmingham, the University of North Carolina-Charlotte, the University of Louisville, and Wichita State University); one historically black institution (Xavier University); and one single-sex institution (Mount Holyoke College).

Members of the research team visited each campus in groups of two, three or four. Status sampling (Dobbert, 1984) was utilized to identify people for interviews for the study team's first visit to a campus. Such people as the president, chief academic officer, chief student affairs officer and his or her principal assistants, faculty, professional staff who work with students, student leaders, students, the campus historian (either formal or informal), and a member or two of the institution's governing board were interviewed. At the conclusion of our interviews, we asked the respondents to identify others who might have additional information for us (snowball sampling). In particular, we were interested in students who were not highly involved in campus life. Other impromptu interviews were conducted in residence halls, lounges, cafeterias, and recreation areas with students whom we were not formally scheduled to interview.

A second source of data was observations of various events, such as student activities, campus tours, and regularly scheduled events. Notes were recorded on observation sheets and points for clarification were identified.

Finally, numerous documents from each institution were reviewed for each institution. Included in these were the institution's catalog, viewbook, student handbook, annual report(s), organizational charts, student newspapers, and alumni magazines. Impressions and observations about the content of these materials were recorded and, again, questions about the material or points needing clarification were noted.

After completing the visit, the site team prepared a preliminary institutional report which was sent to the campus for comment and critique. Upon returning to the campus for a second visit, the team spent a substantial amount of time listening to those who read the report critique its contents and add information to it. Other people were interviewed during the second visit to clarify points from the first campus visit and to fill in content areas that had not been addressed in the first visit.

A second report was sent to each campus after the site visits had been completed. If the reviewers of the second report had any suggestions or comments about it, those were incorporated in a final draft of the report.

Team meetings were held at various stages of the project. One was held before the visits began to select the potential sites and discuss the research methods utilized in the project. After the first round of visits was completed, the team met to develop preliminary constructions of what they had found concerning the factors and conditions which encouraged meaningful out-of-class experiences for students. Another meeting was held midway through the second round of visits to discuss the progress that had been made in the second site visits. A third meeting was held after all the visits were completed to bring together what had been found and draw conclusions about the project. A final meeting was held six months later to refine our thinking about the project and identify our final thoughts about what had been learned. In addition, considerable time was invested in electronic mail and telephone communications in sharing our ideas, thoughts, and reactions to what we were learning as the result of our investigation.

Occasional papers and other documents were generated throughout the course of our study. Several of these formed the basis for additional thinking and discussion about specific topics while others were refined into position papers or manuscripts which were submitted for publication.

Additional information about the methods utilized in this project, including the Involving Colleges Audit Protocol, are discussed by Kuh et al. (1991). From this project emerged the data upon which the cases included in this book are based. Data generated from interviews, document review, and observations of student behavior support the facts of each case.

Using This Book

This book of cases can be used by two groups of people: those who are enrolled in graduate preparation programs in student affairs, higher education administration, or related subject areas and those who administer student affairs programs. There are several ways this material can be used by members of each group.

Graduate Students

In the next chapter, Kuh discusses five categories of factors and conditions that encourage student learning and personal development outside the classroom. The five categories include the following: institutional mission and philosophy, campus culture, campus environment, policies and practices, and the behavior of institutional agents. With these factors and conditions in mind, we suggest that graduate students consider the following projects:

1. Recall your undergraduate experience. Describe how the factors and conditions were present or not present on your alma mater's campus. What would you recommend to improve the quality of out-of-class experiences for undergraduates? Read a case in this book and write a paper comparing the campus described in the case with your undergraduate college. Send the report to the chief student affairs officer for comment.

2. Read a book about a distinctive college or a cluster of colleges such as Clark (1970) or Grobman (1988). Find a case in this book which describes a similar college. Compare and contrast the descriptions of the two colleges. Are there factors and conditions similar to those identified in this book discussed in some form in the book you read? Based on the book's descriptions of student life, what would you recommend to the chief student affairs officer to improve student out-of-class experiences?

3. Frequently, graduate students, as part of a class project, visit another college to learn about the structure and functions of student affairs. The next time you participate in such a visit, use the factors and conditions described in this volume to frame questions for administrators and students at the campus you visit. Perhaps you could ask such seemingly simple yet revealing questions to administrators and faculty as, "What makes this college special?" or to students, "If there was one thing at this campus that you would not want to change, what would that be?" These questions will yield a substantial amount of information about what — if anything — makes the campus distinctive. When you return to your institution, compare what you have found in your visit with a description of a similar college or university in this book. How are the institutions similar? How are they different? How could the campus you visited improve the quality of student experiences based on the case description in this book?

4. If you are an advanced graduate student and need a topic for a major research project, perhaps you and several colleagues could study out-of-class life at a nearby college. With an understanding of qualitative research methods you could conduct a study of out-of-class life as a major paper for an advanced seminar.

5. Take the discussion of college culture in this volume and compare with other books on campus culture such as Horowitz (1987) or Moffatt (1988). Conduct a study of the student culture on your campus to determine how closely it mirrors the aspects of student culture described in this volume and others.

For Practitioners

There are a variety of ways that the material in this book can be used by student affairs administrators. Some of them follow:

1. Most student affairs divisions undergo periodic evaluations. Select one type of institution described in this book similar to yours and develop an evaluation plan using elements from that institution as the basis for a self-study. What can you learn from the institution reported in the book that may be transferable to yours? Are there some ideas which could be implemented on your campus?

2. If you are preparing for a regional accreditation site visit, consider developing your self-study around the five clusters of factors and conditions that enhance student involvement which will be discussed in the next chapter. What more could you do to enhance student involvement in meaningful out-of-class experiences?

3. If you are responsible for orientation, admissions, or other aspects of the university where you work with individuals new to your college, what are the messages you communicate to prospective students? Review the case descriptions. What can you learn from these institutions about how to communicate with students new to your campus? Review your literature. Do your catalog, viewbook, student handbook, and other materials emphasize student involvement opportunities? Do you address student involvement at all?

4. As a staff development activity, have members of the student affairs division meet with faculty to discuss how links between student life and classroom activities can be strengthened. Ask faculty if they can describe what the student affairs division does. What can be learned from these cases which will stimulate more interaction between faculty and student affairs staff? Do faculty have an accurate perception of your responsibilities and your contributions to student growth? What additional collaborative projects can be identified?

5. As a staff development activity, meet with student affairs staff from a nearby institution. Use the case which most closely describes the institution you are visiting as a model. Does the institution you visit encourage student involvement? In what ways? What can you learn from the campus and take back to your own?

6. Study the case reported in this book which is most like your own. What can you learn from it? Are there things you could do differently to encourage more meaningful out-of-class experiences with students?

7. Use the case from this book which most closely resembles your campus as the basis for a retreat with student leaders. Have them react to the case. What do they find attractive? What would they like to see implemented on your campus which would improve the quality of their out-of-class experiences?

For both graduate students and practitioners: Each case includes the commentary of a person familiar with the institutional type the case represents. Do you agree with the commentator's analysis? What observations would you have made had you been commentator? What would you have deleted?

Summary

This chapter has provided a brief in support of educating the whole person by providing educationally purposeful experiences outside the classroom. This concept is not new. It has been affirmed in the literature for more than half a century, going back at least as far as *The Student Personnel Point of View*. In the past decade student involvement has been discussed in several of the most prominent contributions to the student affairs and higher education literature.

In Chapter Two the factors and conditions that encourage student learning through out-of-class experiences are summarized. The remaining chapters are case studies of how student affairs in different types of institutions promote student involvement. The cases can be used by practitioners and students in a variety of ways depending on their specific educational needs.

Chapter Two

Characteristics of Involving Colleges

George D. Kuh

As Schuh reported in Chapter One, the College Experiences Study identified institutional factors and conditions that promote student involvement in educationally purposeful out-of-class learning opportunities. This chapter summarizes the characteristics of the 14 colleges and universities included in the study. To illustrate how these concepts are operationalized, examples are provided from involving colleges not featured elsewhere in this book. More detailed examples of how the properties of involving colleges work in various types of institutions are provided in Chapters Three through Nine and in *Involving Colleges* (Kuh et al., 1991).

Factors and Conditions Common to Involving Colleges

Involving colleges share — to varying degrees — five categories of factors and conditions:

- a clear, coherent mission and philosophy
- campus environments with human-scale attributes that use their location to educational advantage
- campus cultures that value student involvement
- policies and practices consistent with the institution's mission and students' characteristics
- institutional agents who acknowledge the contribution of learning outside the classroom to achieving the institution's educational purposes.

These characteristics work together in different combinations and toward different purposes — depending on the institutional context and mission, expectations for student and faculty behavior, and desired educational purposes and outcomes.

Mission and Philosophy
An institution's mission defines what a college or university is and aspires to be. The mission of a college is not necessarily what the institution says about itself (e.g., in the catalog, in public statements by the president), however. More important, as far as student involvement is concerned, is the "living mission" of a college — how students, faculty, administrators, graduates, and others describe what the college is and is trying to accomplish. When supported by complementary policies and practices, a clear, coherent mission provides direction to an institution in turbulent times and creates a distinctive image of the institution in the minds of its constituents and others knowledgeable about higher education.

An institution's philosophy is the means (policies, practices, standard operating procedures) by which it enacts its mission. Although many colleges do not explicitly articulate their philosophy (e.g., describe "how things are done here" in the catalog or mission statement), the assumptions and beliefs about human potential, teaching, and learning in which the college's philosophy is based can be discovered.

Although the missions and philosophies of involving colleges are diverse, they have four characteristics in common:
- clarity, coherence and complementarity of mission and philosophy
- high expectations for student performance
- the presence or absence of status or other distinctions among people consistent with the institution's educational purposes and students' backgrounds
- an unwavering commitment to multiculturalism.

Clear, Well Understood Mission
At involving colleges, current and former students, faculty members, and administrators understand and can describe — in their own words — what the institution is trying to accomplish. For example, anyone connected with Berea College in Berea, Kentucky, knows that the college is committed to serving students from Appalachia. Berea College's well-known Labor Program and the Seven Great Commitments (principles that give direction to all aspects of college life including the curriculum) ensure that students whose educational backgrounds and financial resources would otherwise

preclude college attendance have access to a Christian, interracial educational experience. The mission of Miami University, a state-assisted institution in Oxford, Ohio, is to emphasize the liberal arts in undergraduate teaching. One of the legacies of Robert Bishop Hamilton, the first president of Miami University, was the value he placed on learning outside the classroom. An agricultural heritage continues to influence the missions of Iowa State University and the University of California, Davis. And, as will become evident in Chapter Five, metropolitan involving colleges couple their resources with those available in the urban area to attain their missions and promote student learning.

Great Expectations

Involving colleges have high, but reasonable, expectations for student performance. How an institution holds students accountable for academic achievement and the types of support it provides vary depending on the characteristics of students and the institution's mission. For example, the vast majority of students at Earlham College, Grinnell College, Miami University, Mount Holyoke College, Stanford University, and the University of California, Davis, matriculate with well-developed academic skills. Other involving colleges, particularly the metropolitan universities, attract many students whose academic skills need to be sharpened.

At the same time, involving colleges communicate caring and belonging to students. Among other things, this ethic of care means that students are appreciated for what they bring to the institution; they are not seen as a drain on institutional resources or as an unwelcome diversion of faculty attention from research and scholarly activity. Involving colleges also expect newcomers to behave as full members of the community with all attendant rights and responsibilities. Moreover, this ethic of membership sends a clear message to students at involving colleges: "You are here because we believe you can succeed."

Interpersonal Distinctions

Distinctions among individuals and groups are deliberately accentuated or minimized to attain an involving college's educational purposes. To enhance students' chances for academic success and satisfaction, Earlham College, Grinnell College, Stanford University, and Evergreen State College aspire to be democratic, egalitarian learning communities unencumbered by political, social, and economic differences.

Berea's admission requirements and Labor Program illustrate how institutional levelers (programs, policies, and practices that establish equality among students) can create a level playing field. Students whose families can contribute more than $2,300 to the cost of attending college are ineligible for admission to Berea College. In lieu of paying tuition, every student is assigned to a labor position — from general custodial service to skilled crafts to faculty teaching assistant — all of which contribute directly to the various programs and industries of the college. The net effect is that everyone at Berea College starts from the same point: everyone labors; no one has any money.

Another example of a leveler can be found in the omnipresent bicycles at the University of California, Davis. Students, faculty, and administrators share a common means of transportation, riding together to class or offices and parking their bikes side by side.

Other involving colleges operate as meritocracies where hierarchical structures and processes regulate status attainment and academic achievement. For example, competition at Miami University is particularly intense for membership and leadership positions in most prestigious groups. Most organizations have hierarchies of involvement, from follower to senior advisor to the leader, a position achieved after long and significant service to the organization. Students must participate in highly competitive interview processes for appointments to many of the more prestigious student and university committees.

Commitment to Multiculturalism

An involving college aspiring to become a multicultural learning community is symbolized through strong statements about the value of individual and group differences; moreover, resources are devoted to establishing and supporting multiple subcommunities. Subcommunities may be formal such as living units organized according to cultural or ethnic background, or by academic interest such as the theme houses at Earlham College, Stanford University, and University of California, Davis, or student organizations based on gender, race, ethnicity, or sexual orientation. Through involvement in a subcommunity such as Earlham's Lesbian-Bisexual-Gay Persons Union, gay, lesbian, or bisexual students feel part of a smaller supportive community and are more confident about their ability to actively participate in the larger college community.

Subcommunities can also be informal such as older adult students at Wichita State University, international students at Iowa State University, and students of color at any of the predominantly white institutions. For example, an Asian student at the University of California, Davis, learns about her Asian-American heritage by being part of the Asian student community, about her identity as a woman by being part of a women's organization, and about leadership by being treasurer of her sorority. It is important to note that these institutions have become multicultural learning communities to a greater or lesser extent. That is, the multiculturalism theme in these institutions' missions represents an aspiration rather than something they have attained. The key is that an involving college aspires to multiculturalism and manifests this commitment by enabling the development of supportive structures.

Campus Environments

Two aspects of involving colleges' environments warrant attention: (a) how they use their location to educational advantage and (b) how they have created "human-scale" settings.

Location

An involving college campus is attractive and well maintained, and complements the institution's educational purposes. For example, the combination of Georgian architecture and assiduous attention by building and grounds personnel results in the Miami campus being "what a college should look like." The "Miami way to do things" is conventional, deferent to authority and tradition; hence it is no surprise that the campus is laid out in a geometrically proportioned grid. Residence hall dining tables have tablecloths, walls are wallpapered.

More important, no matter where they are located (a rural area, a large city), involving colleges assume their location is "a good place for a college." In a geographically isolated small town of 8,500 people, Grinnell students — most of whom are from more than 500 miles away — are forced to create interesting activities through which they learn more about themselves and others. Isolation also means that distractions from the external environment are limited, thus enabling intense learning opportunities. The former Grinnell College president, George Drake, observed that "one of the things that sets us apart from our peer institutions is the quality of our residential experience. We do not put the residential program above the academic program but because the residential program is so strong, it makes the Grinnell experience special." Grinnell College uses its isolation to immerse students in the development of individual responsibility and social consciousness.

But students at isolated involving colleges are not detached from or unconcerned about social, economic, and political issues. Through off-campus learning opportunities (e.g., internships, work-study opportunities, travel programs, speakers, public service opportunities), students are connected to the issues, problems, and challenges of the outside world. For example, more than 40 percent of Grinnell students study overseas; about 70 percent of Earlham's students participate in off-campus study programs.

Iowa State University and the University of California, Davis, seem isolated to many students, a perception shaped somewhat by the agricultural roots of these institutions that continue to influence the curriculum, campus climate, and traditions. At the same time, both universities are within a short drive of their state capital where various learning opportunities in government agencies and business and industry have been developed for students.

Metropolitan involving colleges use the resources of their city to enrich students' learning. Proximity to a city, however, does not guarantee that students will take advantage of cultural, academic-, and employment-related learning opportunities. Considerable effort is required by faculty and administrators to establish cooperative arrangements with the arts community, business, government, and industry to match work and cultural opportunities with students' interests, educational objectives, and career goals.

Human-Scale Settings

Involving colleges make good use of the properties of their natural environment by developing a human-scale physical plant — places where students feel a sense of mastery. The "feel" of the place is appropriate, comfortable, and manageable (e.g., small colleges seem larger and large universities seem smaller). Anonymity is discouraged. Features of indoor and outdoor spaces (e.g., nooks and crannies) encourage informal, spontaneous interaction. Moreover, opportunities for meaningful involvement are in ample supply (e.g., leadership positions in organizations). For example, at the University of California, Davis, 30 administrative advisory committees (ranging from Animal Use and Care to Regents Professor and Lecturer) allow students to influence the affairs of the campus.

Student residences have no more than 200 to 300 residents or small subcommunities in larger residences. The buildings at the University of California, Davis, for example, are no more than two or three stories high, arranged so that at no point can one see the entire physical plant. The effect is much like walking from one room to another in a large house, visually reinforcing the impression of intimacy and smallness at each point. Few classrooms hold more than 100 students. Facilities are readily accessible to anyone and available at times convenient for students and faculty.

A physical plant can encourage interaction if it is arranged in such a way that one or more physical features bring students together or serve as a central meeting point of the campus. At such colleges as Berea, Earlham, Stanford, and Grinnell, information is exchanged via posters and notes on bulletin boards at the centrally located campus post office. To encourage informal interaction among students and between students and faculty members, Wichita State University has created small eating spaces in the union and in lounges in academic departments.

Located near the center of the Grinnell campus, the Forum (the college union) attracts a large number of students. "Open Forums" are presented frequently (note the symbolic symmetry between the name of the building and what goes on there), an opportunity for students to exchange views on such matters of importance to the Grinnell community and beyond as race, gender, ecology, and peace. To encourage students and faculty members to use the facility between classes, a cup of coffee is priced at 16 cents with unlimited refills.

An involving college also acknowledges basic human needs for social and psychological comfort. It is difficult, perhaps impossible, for a student to be anonymous. This is not to say that tragedies do not occur or that debilitating personal behaviors are checked immediately by peer pressure, or that no one ever feels lonely. However, students who live on an involving college campus tend not to get lost. Indeed, the small involving colleges (Earlham, Berea, Grinnell, Mount Holyoke, Xavier) must involve students in meaningful ways to get the business of the institution accomplished. At large institutions, student participation has been intentionally stimulated. For example, at Iowa State University — where the undergraduate enrollment exceeds 20,000 — about 5,000 leadership positions have been created. In addition, faculty and staff encourage students to actively participate in one or more of the 133 departmental clubs that link the students' majors with a variety of in- and out-of-class activities and leadership opportunities. Similarly, Miami University has more than 300 student organizations. In the School of Business alone, there are 18 student organizations, one of which has about 600 members.

Operated by Wichita State University students, Informed Sources provides both information about campus programs and services (e.g., parking) as well as opportunities for students to become involved in the university. By sharing information and facilitating student access to needed programs and services, Informed Sources also reduces the psychological size of the university.

Whether geographically isolated, a short distance from a city, or surrounded by a metropolitan area, an involving college uses its location to educational advantage. It has created human-scale settings from natural surroundings and, through the careful design of physical structures, created living and learning spaces in which students do not feel anonymous.

Campus Culture

A college's culture is shaped by the assumptions that make up the institution's philosophy and determine what people think about, what they perceive to be important, how they feel about things, and how they spend their time. For example, metropolitan involving colleges assume that with hard work, anyone can succeed; hence, every student should have the opportunity to pursue a college degree. At Xavier University, a basic assumption is that anyone, if given the opportunity, can overcome overwhelming odds and be successful in college.

An institution's values can be discovered by examining what faculty, students, staff, and others assert to be important, such as egalitarianism, activism, community, and (of course) active participation in the life of the institution. For example, the ethic of membership discussed earlier indicates that everyone belongs and is expected to take part in community affairs. These values may be spoken ("we're a teaching institution") or unspoken, manifested in actions (teaching is rewarded more than other faculty activities). Values may be espoused but not enacted, as in the case of an institution that claims teaching as a primary value but gives the most rewards to faculty who publish. Valued behavior — such as teaching and research — may also conflict and create tension and uncertainty as community members try to determine which behavior is valued over others.

At an involving college, the institutional culture and dominant subcultures promote involvement and a sense of ownership among institutional participants. Some of the more visible cultural influences on student involvement include institutional history, traditions, language, heroines and heroes, and symbols and symbolic actions.

History

The circumstances leading to an institution's founding and the ways in which the institution has dealt with crises and change send messages about the importance of student involvement. The story of the founding of Xavier University by Mother Katharine Drexel and the Sisters of the Blessed Sacrament in 1915 is known by all members of the university community (see Chapter Six). The founder of Berea College, John Fee, established several educational institutions to serve persons of all races and poor backgrounds from Appalachia. Although African-American students were prohibited from attending Berea for a time because of the Kentucky Day Law (passed in the early 1900s), they were warmly received by the Berea College community as soon as the law was repealed in the early 1950s. Vestiges of the University of California, Davis' early years as the farm of the University of California can be found in students' active participation in institutional governance, recreational activities, and residence life — behavior that is consistent with the high degree of participation that characterizes life in small towns.

Wichita State University has undergone changes in mission and form of control. Founded as Fairmont College, a Congregational liberal arts college, Wichita State University became the University of Wichita in the 1920s, a municipal university with a strong liberal arts mission. In 1964, the institution became a member of the Kansas Regents Institutions and acquired its current name. The municipal history of Wichita State University continues to significantly influence its mission in that it is still very much the "city's university"; hence, participation by students and faculty in civic affairs is the norm.

Traditions

Involving colleges are rich in traditions that communicate important institutional values and affirm the importance of student learning and development through out-of-class experiences. At Berea College, for example, traditions include Scholarship Day (acknowledgement of outstanding academic performance), Mountain Day (an outdoor activity to celebrate Appalachian culture), and Labor Day (an affirmation of the intrinsic value of work).

Some traditions socialize students to how the institution expects people to behave. Homecoming at Miami University, for example, is a family affair (many students are sons and daughters of graduates) and provides an opportunity for youngsters to learn early about life at Miami. Another message is that Miami students must be actively involved in planning and implementing community-wide events (i.e., being a member of the Homecoming Committee is a prestigious, highly sought appointment).

Some traditions affirm members of different groups as full participants in the life of the community. For example, in April 1988, 60,000 people attended Picnic Day at the University of California, Davis — an open house for departments during which groups sponsor such activities as sports events, dachshund races, and information booths. The Whole Earth Festival, hosted early in May by the Experimental College, underscores the campus community's interest in ecology. People come from all over the western states to partake of the natural and ethnic foods, dancers, performers, speakers, and crafts offered by student and community volunteers. Cultural Days are celebrations that correspond to each of the largest racial and ethnic groups represented on campus: African-American Family Week, Asian/Pacific Heritage Week, La Raza Cultural Days, Native American Culture Days.

Because of changes in mission and the absence of a large undergraduate "collegiate corps" (full-time students 18-23 years of age), metropolitan involving colleges do not have as many distinctive traditions. The few traditions that exist often celebrate ties between the institution and the city in which it is located. For example, several events during Wichita's Black Arts Festival are held on the Wichita State University campus, another example of the seamlessness between the campus and the community. As we shall see in Chapter Five, the University of Louisville also has traditions that serve purposes similar to those at other types of involving colleges.

Language

Members of an involving college community use terms of endearment (institution-specific language) to signify full membership in the institution. For example, some phrases at Miami University ("Mother Miami," "cradle of coaches," "mother of fraternities") underscore a strong sense of family. The "Miami bubble" implies that the university is a safe place. "Miami mergers" are marriages between Miami students. The message of "Miami memos" (calendars students use to organize their time) is that students must live by precise schedules to get everything done.

Some terms of endearment place limits on student learning. For example, to some students the "Miami bubble" implies that campus life is, and should be, detached from the concerns of the real world. Miami students can, if they choose, avoid encounters with people whose backgrounds, views, lifestyles, and problems are very different from their own and so may become complacent about issues such as poverty, political oppression, hunger, and racism. Other illustrations of this point are found in several of the cases presented later (e.g., Earlham College, Mount Holyoke College).

Heroines and Heroes

Stories told about heroines and heroes (e.g., presidents, senior faculty, student leaders) affirm the institution's commitment to student learning and development. Chancellor Emil Mrak, the University of California, Davis' second chancellor, was instrumental in molding the "hands-on," involving heritage of the university. His philosophy, "helping students to help themselves," established a participatory tone for the campus that persists today. Although many current administrators and faculty never met Mrak, they know what he stood for; his legacy of commitment to students is affectionately passed on from one University of California, Davis, generation to the next.

The quality of out-of-class life was a high priority to former Miami president Phillip Shriver, who was described by several faculty as "the best dean of students Miami University ever had." He is still very student-oriented, appears in the residence halls at least once a week, and continues to be one of the most popular professors on campus.

James Rhatigan, the chief student affairs officer at Wichita State University for more than 25 years, intentionally emphasizes the pastoral (a spiritual concern for students' welfare) rather than the executive functions of his role. He is viewed as available, helpful, wise, nonjudgmental, and a "beloved buffer" between the students and the university. Examples of the influence of heroines such as Mary Lyon and Mother Katharine Drexel are presented in the Mount Holyoke and Xavier cases, respectively.

Symbols and Symbolic Action

Institutional symbols often reflect important values and elicit feelings of pride and identification with the institution. Symbolic action is an effort on the part of groups and individuals (often leaders) to bring institutional symbols into focus for community members, reminding them of the ideals for which they exist. For example, at Iowa State's university and college orientation sessions, the deans of academic units urge new students to participate in out-of-class activities. The message to students is clear: It is important to become fully involved in all aspects of campus life.

The themes of environmental preservation and egalitarianism are symbolized at the University of California, Davis, by the aforementioned ever-present bicycle. A network of bike paths and roads form the principal conduits by which students, faculty, and staff move about; the campus is virtually free of automobile traffic. Bicycles are both an expression of a California "thing to do" and a symbol of the belief that "we're all in this together"; even the chancellor rides a bike.

Cultural properties of involving colleges remind community members of values they hold in common: student initiative, ties with the past, equality, individual responsibility and respect, academic achievement, positive relationships with the surrounding community, the need to recreate, respect for differences, religious ideals, work, and communal bonding. Not all cultural aspects of these colleges and universities, however, serve positive purposes, an issue to which we will return in several of the following chapters.

Policies and Practices

Six clusters of policies and practices more or less characterize involving colleges:

- recruitment and socialization practices that clearly and consistently articulate the institution's educational purposes, values, and expectations
- orientation activities that welcome students and teach them how to act
- policies that make students responsible for learning and maintaining community standards
- blurred boundaries between in-class and out-of-class learning opportunities
- resource allocation processes driven by educational purposes and priorities
- policies that enable and support multiple subcommunities.

Because policies and practices are influenced by the institution's mission, philosophy, size, and culture, they take different forms in different institutional contexts.

Socialization through Recruitment

Concerted efforts are made to articulate expectations and help newcomers feel welcome. Between the time a prospective student first expresses interest in attending the college and matriculation, the institution describes on various occasions (e.g., college preview nights in high schools, campus tours, admission interview) what it values and how students are expected to perform. Examples of how involving colleges use the time prior to matriculation to begin the socialization process can be found in the Earlham and Stanford chapters.

Orientation Activities

A combination of formal and informal orientation activities also communicate standards and expectations for academic and social behavior. These activities, different at each college or university, bond students to the institution and students to students. The University of Alabama-Birmingham uses a simulation that compresses an academic year into 45 minutes to alert students to the diversions that can detract from academic performance. The simulation is run by the Blazer Crew, paraprofessionals trained in the usual matters related to institutional life.

At Berea College, orientation activities affirm the college's purposes and clarify the institutional mission. In the words of one student:

President Stephenson talks about the Seven Great Commitments [during orientation]. Also, other administrators and the head resident mention them. Really, that whole week, you hear them over and over and over again . . . You sometimes also hear the Commitments mentioned by students and the director of student activities sometimes brings them up when we talk about certain kinds of programs.

Grinnell College's Freshman Tutorial, the college's only required course, serves as both an academic and a social induction experience. While the content of the tutorial is important to the dozen students in each tutorial, learning how to learn is also emphasized. In addition to honing writing and oral presentation skills, students become familiar with the library and campus computing networks. Hence, the tutorial encourages establishing close relationships between students and faculty as well as among students, and often serves as a bridge to interaction beyond the classroom.

Structures to Promote Responsible Behavior

Involving colleges provide varying amounts of structure for their students to encourage development of autonomy and responsibility. The amount of structure imposed on students at involving colleges depends on the mission, philosophy, and student characteristics. For example, students at Berea, Xavier, Miami, and Iowa State are given considerably more structure than their counterparts at Earlham, Grinnell, Mount Holyoke, and Stanford. Most Berea students come from economically and educationally disadvantaged backgrounds; some Berea students require considerable assistance in developing study skills and the confidence necessary to succeed. Xavier University has established a "ladder" or set of programs and activities with steps, or rungs, to help students get involved, feel supported, and become academically successful (see Chapter Six). At Grinnell College, however, students are held responsible for the success of their educational experience; hence, students must make intelligent choices about what to do with their time out of class. The key to determining how much structure is needed is knowing and understanding students and their needs and capabilities.

Safety Nets. Involving colleges have attempted to remove institutional obstacles to students' pursuit of their academic and personal goals. Informal networks of faculty, staff, and students have developed over time and work together in times of crisis to assist students in need. Many senior Wichita State faculty members are part of an "invisible safety net" (a network of helpers) and refer students with problems to student affairs staff. Faculty members seem to be aware of students in trouble and know what to do when problems arise, in part because a senior staff person from the student affairs division meets with every new faculty member during the faculty member's first few weeks on the campus. Examples of safety nets at other involving colleges include The

House at the University of California, Davis, a student-run drop-in center where students can get help in dealing with problems, and First Resort, a student-run referral agency.

Structures have been developed by the metropolitan institutions to guide and, in some instances, "hold" students in place until they are capable of navigating the collegiate experience on their own. To assist new students — many of whom have been away from studies for several years or more — in meeting the university's academic standards, Wichita State University developed the transition semester. If a student's first semester grade point average is below 2.0, he or she may request that all grades be changed to credit/no credit. All grades of A, B, and C are translated to credit and lower grades are entered as no credit. In the following semester, the student may not enroll for more than 12 hours and must earn a grade point average of at least 2.0.

Blurred Boundaries

At Berea College, the convocation series (students must attend a minimum of 10 convocations each semester) is an intentional effort to blur the lines between in-class and out-of-class learning and underscores the relationship between how students spend their time out of class and desirable outcomes of college. Outside speakers focus faculty, staff, and students on broad social, cultural, and artistic themes and issues. Cooperative education programs at Wichita State University allow students to use off-campus resources and expertise through placements in business, government, industry, and health and social agencies. Programs are individually designed, enabling students to work directly with professionals in their field while applying knowledge gained in the classroom. Service-learning internships at the University of North Carolina-Charlotte provide learning opportunities for students (e.g., community centers, environmental action groups, the city of Charlotte, Mecklenburg County offices, social service organizations, United Way, the court system) while meeting the needs of the community.

Laws, Hall and Associates is a student-run advertising firm at Miami University that contracts with a major company each term to produce an advertising campaign. The 160 student participants are divided into three competing interdisciplinary "agencies," or teams, led by student account executives and charged with producing advertising campaigns to meet the promotional needs of a paying client. The campaigns include market analysis, strategies and tactics, budget and media plans, electronic media productions, and artwork and layouts for print media and direct mail. At the end of each semester, completed campaigns are judged by the client (e.g., Procter & Gamble, NCR Corporation, Marshall Field, BF Goodrich, Avon, J.M. Smucker Company, Stroh Brewery Company, and Ford Motor Company).

Resources

Involving colleges allocate resources according to expressed priorities consistent with the institution's educational purposes. Because every college has a seemingly infinite appetite (including involving colleges), there is never enough money to honor all requests; hence students, administrators, and faculty members must make conscious, deliberate, often difficult decisions about what is valued and necessary. In general, involving colleges adhere to five principles when allocating resources:

- resources are directed to new students
- students control and are responsible for allocating a substantial amount of resources
- students have relatively easy access to funds
- specific groups are targeted for resources
- resources are committed to support out-of-class learning.

New Students Are a Priority. By devoting resources to new students, the institution prepares them to be productive, academically successful, socially confident, and removes obstacles to attaining their learning and personal development goals. For example, at Miami University all freshmen, except those who live with their parents, must live on campus. The student-resident assistant ratio is 20:1. Academic advisers also live in the freshman halls. Hence, upperclass students and academic advisers are available to teach newcomers what is valued and how to navigate the system.

Finite resources mean that some programs must be terminated if new initiatives are added. Thus, hard decisions must be made not only about proposed programs that warrant support, but also whether currently funded programs should be continued. Many of these decisions involve discussions and debates and can be teachable moments as students are forced to choose among attractive, worthwhile options — an exercise that approximates life after college.

Multiple Subcommunities

For students to be successful and feel valued, they must have their interests and heritages acknowledged, legitimized, understood, and appreciated. Hence involving colleges enable the establishment of numerous subcommunities — groups of persons with similar academic interests and, very often, similar racial, ethnic, and cultural backgrounds. By recognizing the existence of multiple subcommunities, involving colleges more accurately reflect the larger society and make a strong statement about the nature of American higher education in the future and the importance of multiculturalism.

The University of California, Davis, supports various theme-oriented and alternative residences. Half of the 60 residents of the Multi-Ethnic Program (MEP) House are students of color. MEP-sponsored activities often emphasize such issues as "chilly" classroom climates for people of color and the contributions of African-Americans typically ignored in traditional history texts. Of the 65 students who live in Casa Cuauhtemoc, about three-quarters are from a Spanish-speaking background. A steering committee of faculty, staff, students, and graduates provides guidance for house activities which emphasize Chicano, Chicana, and Mexican-American culture. Baggin's End Domes are 14 fiberglass domes built in 1971. The domes house 28 students and feature gardens, fruit trees, and chickens. Pierce Co-op is a frame house that provides space for 11 students who share concerns about the environment. The residents of the Agrarian Effort, another co-op, share interests in home economics and agriculture and maintain a large garden.

At Miami University, the Honors Program subcommunity is an incubator for social change. The 900 participants share a commitment to enhancing the intellectual vibrancy of life outside the classroom and also have a strong public service orientation. Honors Program members perform 10 or 12 service projects each year. The Honors House at the University of Alabama-Birmingham, an old church located in the center of the campus, is a community of students and faculty who participate in the Honors Program and serves a purpose similar to that of the Miami Honors Program.

Institutional Agents
People are the heart and soul of any enterprise, including an involving college. It is no surprise, therefore, that administrators, faculty, and other institutional agents are key to engendering a campus climate with plentiful positive out-of-class learning opportunities.

Administrators
Presidents communicate the importance of student involvement in campus life by pointing to events in the institution's history that demanded students assume responsibility for their own learning and personal development. They acknowledge the importance of, and assiduously maintain, relationships with students and student affairs staff — relationships characterized by trust, loyalty, and mutual respect. Last, but certainly not least, they encourage faculty to spend time with students outside of class

and model this behavior by, for example, participating in orientation events and taking occasional meals with students.

The president's role in encouraging learning outside of class is shaped by the incumbent's previous experiences, length of tenure at the institution, personal interests, and personality. The impact of the president in setting the tone for out-of-class life is mediated by institutional features such as size. Small college presidents tend to be more knowledgeable about student life than their counterparts at large universities. For example, George Drake, the former president of Grinnell College (as well as a graduate of the college), believes that an important expectation is that he know and understand students. He often eats with students. According to students, "Anyone can see him. All you have to do is try."

Analysis of speeches and other public statements reveal much about the importance a president attaches to student involvement in out-of-class experiences. In his 1988 State of the University address, Paul Pearson, Miami University president, argued that learning was not confined to the classroom or laboratory:

> We need to stimulate . . . linkages between students and external publics (e.g., businesses, schools, and governmental agencies) through community service projects, internships, and collaborative research projects; student participation in off-campus professional and career-related activities; employment programs that allow students to serve the University and assist their peers in academic support, career guidance, job searches, and educational activities . . .

Recall also the influence of Chancellor Mrak in establishing a participatory tone for the Davis campus described earlier.

At most involving colleges included in the College Experiences Study, the chief academic officer (CAO) acknowledged the importance of a mutually-enhancing relationship between out-of-class life and the curricular goals of the institution. Some CAOs were more articulate about out-of-class experiences than others. Some were actively involved in and sensitive to the symbolic power of their role in this regard, particularly those at residential institutions. Encouraging student-faculty interaction was high on the agenda of Carol Cartwright, the vice chancellor for academic affairs at the University of California, Davis (now the president of Kent State University). Because of the shortfall of faculty expected around the turn of the next century, Cartwright urged, "We simply must do more to introduce undergraduates to the academic lifestyle. Only through developing personal relationships between faculty and students are students likely to view a faculty role as more attractive."

The remaining chapters address in detail the role and contributions of student affairs staff at involving colleges. Suffice it to say for the time being that student affairs staff at these institutions work long and odd hours to develop educationally purposeful activities consistent with the institutional mission. As faculty members spend less time with students outside of class talking about nonacademic areas of concern, student affairs staff increasingly are expected to bridge the academic program and out-of-class life. And, as with their colleagues elsewhere, they are the infrastructure of the invisible safety nets that "catch" students in academic, social, emotional, and physical difficulty.

Faculty

Although more faculty-student interaction may take place at involving colleges than at many other institutions, contacts between faculty and students are usually student initiated. Student-faculty interaction — when it occurs — is often related to academic issues such as discussions immediately following class to pursue points raised during class, or in departmental clubs. Even at involving colleges, changes in expectations and reward systems have altered faculty roles and priorities. As a result, two faculty cultures now exist as far as out-of-class life is concerned: student-centered faculty members—those who are committed to involvement with undergraduates (they tend to be older, tenured faculty) — and those who are not involved with undergraduates (often younger faculty or cosmopolitan scholars). However, those institutions with salient images as teaching colleges (Berea, Earlham, Grinnell, Evergreen, Xavier) continue to attract faculty who are willing to invest considerable time with students and participate fully in community governance and other activities.

Other Institutional Agents

Librarians, trustees, secretaries, custodial staff, buildings and grounds workers, and others welcome students and challenge them to do their best. At Miami University, for example, several powerful vehicles for learning outside the classroom (e.g., Laws, Hall and Associates, the Honors Program) rely on financial and personal support from the library. The contributions of Evan Farber, the Earlham College librarian, to encouraging learning across the curriculum and outside of class are described in Chapter Eight.

The whole of the contributions of institutional agents is greater than the sum of their individual parts. The complementarity among the priorities of faculty and student affairs staff, the blending of academic and student life objectives, and the compatibility of both with the institutional mission help to create a campus with rich out-of-class learning opportunities. Thus, institutional agents work in combination with the other factors and conditions to contribute to student learning and personal development.

Conclusion

An involving college has a clear, coherent mission and philosophy that communicate high but reasonable challenges for students buttressed by ethics of care and membership. Interpersonal distinctions are deliberately accentuated, or minimized, to attain the institution's educational purposes and a clear, unwavering commitment has been made to become a multicultural campus community. The physical setting (rural, near a city, surrounded by a metropolitan area) is used to educational advantage by creating human-scale settings that discourage anonymity and provide numerous opportunities for participation in the life of the institution. A complicated web of cultural artifacts (history, myths, sagas, heroes/heroines, traditions, rites and rituals, subcultures, institution-specific language) underscores the importance of involvement and communicates to students "how the institution works." Policies and practices hold students responsible for their own behavior and learning, blur the artificial boundaries between in-class and out-of-class learning opportunities, distribute resources consistent with the institution's educational purposes, and enable subcommunities of students to flourish, such as ethnic or academic theme houses. In some subtle and some not-so-subtle ways, faculty and staff promote student participation in educationally purposeful out-of-class learning activities.

Partitioning a college or university into what appear to be separate factors and conditions does violence to the holistic nature of an institution of higher education as a learning enterprise. The elements of an involving college are mutually shaping and inextricably intertwined; mission, institutional cultures, campus environments, policies and practices, and people work together to promote student involvement. To isolate one for emphasis is to overlook the symbiotic relationship among the parts of the whole as will become evident in the following chapters.

Chapter Three

Making a Large University Feel Small
The Iowa State University Story

John H. Schuh

Iowa State University is in Ames, Iowa, approximately 30 miles north of Des Moines. The easiest way to travel from the Des Moines airport to Ames is by auto. Perhaps my most vivid impression of approaching the campus is that as the high-rise residence halls came into view, I saw names written in bold colors on the outside of each building at what appeared to be every floor level. On my first trip to Iowa State University, I asked the driver about the names on the outside of the residence halls and she explained that those were the names of each of the houses. She told me the students were very proud of their houses, that they identified strongly with them, and that while Iowa State University has a very strict code which regulates hanging banners and displaying signs on the campus, the names of the residence hall houses are displayed proudly. I have never seen anything quite like the Iowa State house names before or since, and my impression of the names of the residence hall houses displayed on the outside of the buildings is a lasting memory of Iowa State University for me.

History

Iowa State University's chartering in 1858 by the Iowa General Assembly antedates the Morrill Act of 1862 but the university's development clearly was influenced in a profound way by the land-grant legislation. Iowa was the first state to accept the terms of the Morrill Act and in 1864 Iowa State University was chartered as Iowa's land-grant institution with the title of Iowa Agricultural College. With the expansion of various programs, the name of the institution was changed to Iowa State College of Agriculture and Mechanical Arts in 1898. Since 1959 the official title of the university has been Iowa State University of Science and Technology.

One of the key elements of Iowa State's history has been its role in providing service to the citizens of the state of Iowa. I will return to this point frequently in this discussion, but the person studying Iowa State University should never lose sight of the sense of service that is pervasive on the Ames campus. The land-grant philosophy holds that all citizens ought to have access to the ideas and knowledge of the university. As early as 1870, Iowa State University was holding educational institutes in Iowa towns and in 1903 the university set a pattern of county cooperative extension services which now can be found throughout the United States.

Role of Student Affairs

The College Experiences Study revealed that as institutions grow larger, the role of student affairs staff becomes more critical in planning and developing out-of-class learning experiences for students. Iowa State's student affairs staff understands the heritage and mission of the university and they have developed learning experiences, activities, and programs that build upon the rich heritage of the university. Student involvement in campus life is encouraged and supported throughout the student affairs division, from admissions and orientation to the residence halls, greek letter organizations, student activities, and recreation. Publications which describe the university to prospective students stress how important involvement in out-of-class learning opportunities is for students. Students are expected and taught to give of themselves through service to each other and the university. Every moment a student is enrolled in the university is perceived as a learning opportunity. The viewbook describes student experiences this way:

> Whether you are listening to a nationally acclaimed scholar in the classroom, working on an independent project with your professor's guidance, meeting professional colleagues at a chapter meeting, or planning the logistics of your sorority's or fraternity's next rush party, Iowa State teaches.

A healthy mutual respect characterizes the relationship between faculty and student affairs staff at Iowa State University. Faculty and student affairs staff collaborate on programs of common interest. An example of this collaboration is the work done by the orientation committee for the university. This committee consists of representatives from the academic colleges and student affairs staff and is chaired by a faculty member. Faculty, administrators, and student affairs staff deliver the orientation program to incoming students, which results in an excellent socialization experience for them.

Mission and Philosophy

The mission of Iowa State University, as articulated in the viewbook which is provided to prospective students, states:

> Iowa State is focusing and strengthening its mission of top-notch undergraduate teaching, research to lead the nation and the world, and a sharing of knowledge and developments that people can use to improve their lives.

The part of the mission which speaks to service is manifested in several ways. Iowa State University has a presence in the small towns and farming communities throughout Iowa and the university is proud of the ways it affects the lives of the citizens of the state. Many Iowa State students come from small Iowa towns and often they were preceded at Iowa State University by their parents or siblings. Service is something the university expects them to perform for the citizens of Iowa, and the students who attend the university seem to have caught a spirit of "pitch in and help" which extends to their involvement on campus.

Iowa State University is an institution where various constituent groups can describe what the institution is about. Students understand the land-grant heritage of the university and they have little trouble describing the institution's mission of service to the state.

Personal attention to students undergirds the philosophy the university has adopted toward student experiences. The viewbook underscores this philosophy when it points out that

> ...Iowa State is committed to nurturing the small pockets of interaction and sharing that lead students to know the warmth of human interest and contact as well as the most advanced technologies of the times.

The viewbook also indicates that "For many students, it is the out-of-class experiences and opportunities that make Iowa State special. Iowa State is the kind of university that enables students to set their own lifestyle pace, to build their niches, and to create their own environment for learning." In this discussion we will see how that philosophy is realized in a variety of aspects of student life.

32

Campus Environment

As was mentioned earlier, Iowa State University is in Ames, 30 miles north of Des Moines, the state capital. Ames is a small community, with a total population of approximately 45,000. Approximately 78 percent of Iowa State's 21,500 undergraduates come from within the state. A high proportion of the students come from within a 100-mile radius of the university. Over two-thirds of Iowa State's undergraduate students come from high schools with fewer than 200 students. It is very common for Iowa State students to have been involved in high school athletics; to have performed in high school musical and dramatic activities; and to have been a member of 4-H, Future Farmers of America, or a similar youth group. These students feel very comfortable at Iowa State University because it has an atmosphere which strongly encourages out-of-class involvement of its students.

Over 80 percent of Iowa State's first-year students, according to fall 1989 CIRP data, indicated that Iowa State University was their first choice for college attendance. The percentage of Iowa State students who indicated that their probable career occupation would be in either architecture or engineering exceeded the national norms by a considerable margin. Interestingly enough, while Iowa State University has agricultural roots, just 2 percent of the fall 1989 class reported their probable career in either farming or ranching. Over 15 percent of the entering students, however, reported their father's occupation was in agriculture.

Involving colleges take advantage of their setting and Iowa State University is no exception. Because the state capital and center of commerce (Des Moines) is a short drive from the university, Iowa State University has developed many collaborative relationships which enhance student learning. Iowa State students participate in internships and other work experiences in Des Moines that relate to their curriculum or career plans. For example, students work with the state legislature, television and radio stations, and other forms of media in Des Moines.

Campus Physical Properties

Iowa State University has made several conscious efforts to make this large university feel small. Perhaps the most successful effort in this regard is the residence hall house system which was alluded to earlier in this case.

The house system was started in 1948 at Iowa State University under the leadership of J.C. Schilletter, the director of residence, and his assistant Robert Hughes. Previous attempts at structuring the men's residence hall (Friley Hall) so that it would feel smaller to the residents had been unsuccessful. These efforts focused on dividing the building into several wings, but the affiliational unit was still too large to have the desired effect. After two years Hughes left and James G. Allen came to Iowa State University to continue work on the program. Allen was familiar with the house system that had been implemented in the residence halls at the University of Wisconsin-Madison and he came to Iowa State University at Schilletter's request to develop the house system.

What motivated Schilletter and his colleagues was a concern about the psychological size of the residence hall. Their thesis was that a smaller unit would provide for a better sense of identification on the part of students with the place they lived and that several benefits, such as greater participation in activities and house events, would result.

Each house consists of 50 to 60 students who live together on a floor or similar type of unit. As was mentioned in the introduction to this case, the name of the house often appears on the outside of the building in bold colored letters. These names clearly indicate that the entire building is comprised of a number of self-governing units. From 1948 until 1964, the house system was implemented only in men's housing. In 1964 Charles Frederiksen, a Department of Residence staff member who later replaced Schilletter as director of residence in 1967, brought men's and women's housing together and extended the house program to women's residence halls.

All of the houses, except one, are named for deceased Iowa State faculty, staff, or regents. The one exception is a house named for a former student residence hall officer who was killed in a car accident. When one walks through the house, one of the first things that is encountered is the house crest which also appears on tee-shirts, sweat shirts, stationery, and so on. Each of the houses has its own crest. At times the family crest for whom the unit is named is utilized but in other situations the students have designed their own.

During 1989-90, the Department of Residence at Iowa State University conducted a study of community in the residence halls using focus groups as the primary means for collecting information. This study indicated that new students especially appreciated receiving a letter of welcome from their resident assistants and house government officers the summer before moving into the house. Returning house members play a crucial role in developing a sense of community within the house because they are the students who remember the events of previous years and carry on the traditions of the house. Students emphasized that the development of community in the house depends not just on events and activities but rather on the process by which many house members are involved in the planning and development of the major events of the house each semester.

Two stories illustrate the strength of the house system. In a meeting I had with students and residence hall staff, I asked about the extent to which students identify with their houses. Staff and students told me that in the case of a disagreement between roommates, if these roommates were given the option of separating and moving to another house or staying together and working out their problems, the students invariably prefer to stay together in the same house and resolve their problems. Students do not want to leave their houses.

The other story was told by many people who reported that upon returning to Iowa State University for homecoming, many graduates return to their houses to meet with the current students and see how things are going.

Attempts at creating a house system have been made at many campuses across the country with varying degrees of success. At Iowa State University, the house system is a part of the fabric of student life. The house provides a source of identification for students, many of whom have grown up in communities smaller than Iowa State University. It is the locus around which activities, intramural teams, leadership opportunities, and other sources of student involvement are centered. Iowa State University has done about as good a job as can be found at making its large residence hall system feel small to students. This is a textbook example of an intentional effort to compensate for the physical expansiveness of the campus and to create human-scale residences, which is consistent with the philosophy of the university.

Involvement

Many, perhaps far in excess of the majority, of Iowa State's students have been actively involved in school and community affairs before enrolling at the university. Remember that many Iowa State students come from small towns and have graduated from small high schools. As a result, they are used to participating in a variety of activities while growing up and they have seen Iowa State University extend its services to their communities. And, many Iowa State students' parents and siblings have attended the university, so they have a sense of the university's expectations for their involvement in out-of-class learning experiences.

Involvement is emphasized almost from the moment students set foot on the campus in Ames. At their initial orientation session, Iowa State students meet with the dean of the college in which they intend to enroll and learn from the dean that involvement in clubs and other departmental activities is something that is expected of them.

To aid students' involvement, Iowa State student affairs staff have encouraged the development of a substantial number of leadership positions for its students.

Approximately 5,000 leadership positions exist for its students, so the potential exists for roughly one out of every four or five students to hold a leadership position at any given time. Faculty and administrators encourage students to be involved in one or more of the 140 or so departmental clubs on campus. There are also over 400 special interest clubs and other organizations which provide opportunities for students to learn outside the classroom.

Not all Iowa State students, however, have been leaders in high school so there is a program to help them develop their leadership skills. Kenneth Stoner, currently director of student housing at the University of Kansas and former president of ACUHO-I, developed TULIP (The Undergraduate Leadership Intern Program) to assist these students specifically but anyone who is interested can participate. Approximately 75 to 100 students enroll in the TULIP program to acquire and sharpen their leadership, time management, and organizational skills so that they can fully benefit from their out-of-class experiences.

Recreation is an important avenue for student involvement at Iowa State University. Over 13,000 students participate as members of 5,000 teams in 60 intramural sports. Thirty-three club sports, ranging from archery to weight lifting, are listed in the student handbook. Employment is provided for 400 students by the recreation program; students hold jobs as officials, lifeguards, building supervisors, and outdoor recreation supervisors.

Fraternities and sororities provide another avenue of involvement for Iowa State students. Approximately 3,600 students participate in 54 greek letter organizations, 45 of which have chapter houses in which students reside. As with many avenues for involvement at Iowa State University, the greek system has a long history. Fraternities and sororities have been a part of campus life since 1875.

At various large universities around the country, it is common to find either a strong greek letter organization system or an excellent residence hall system. To find both, as is the case at Iowa State University, is somewhat rare. That there is strength in both is not serendipity. Rather, there has been a conscious effort on the part of student affairs administrators to strike a balance between the greek organizations and the residence halls. Resources and attention are given to each. The result, of course, is that students have excellent potential for a wonderful experience regardless of whether they choose to live in a residence hall or a chapter house.

Given the nature of the curriculum, it is not surprising that Iowa State University has a large number (approximately 2,400) of international students. A variety of programs and services have been developed so that these students, too, can participate actively in campus life. The International Student Council is a representative body for all international students. This organization sends a representative to the Government of the Student Body (GSB) and also has a member serve on the Council of Student Affairs, which advises the vice president for student affairs. This representation symbolizes an effort to get international students into the mainstream of university life and to make sure that special attention is focused on their unique needs. The Office of International Educational Services reports to both the provost and the vice president for student affairs, which represents another link between academic life and student affairs. In this way, a unified focus is developed to meet the needs of international students.

Specific programs which address the needs of international students and celebrate their heritage include the weekly Ports of Call programs held in the fall. Each week a specific country is featured, including its food, artifacts, and customs. An International Week is held each fall and an International Fair occurs in the spring. Each of these events also describes and celebrates the cultures and people of the various countries of students who attend the university.

One other avenue of involvement for students at Iowa State University is worthy of note. The university makes a variety of opportunities available for students who are interested in writing and publishing. Publications that are student edited cover such subjects as design and visual arts, forestry, creative writing, engineering, and agriculture, in addition to the student newspaper and yearbook. The university claims it has the largest number of student-edited publications in the country.

People at Iowa State University suggest a variety of reasons why involvement is encouraged so strongly at the university. One reason offered is that campus involvement has been a student tradition at Iowa State University. Each generation of students encourages its successors to be involved and so it goes from one group to another.

Another reason student involvement is encouraged is that employers have told Iowa State faculty and student affairs staff that they prefer to hire students who have been involved. Involved students show more depth, are better managers of their time, and are stronger prospective employees than those who are not involved. Faculty stressed that students who were involved in activities that provided them with hands-on experience were better prepared for their careers than those who have only a theoretical orientation to their discipline. The chair of one department explained that students who participate in out-of-class learning experiences are more rounded and better able to deal with issues related to developing a career and family life.

Still another reason that is probably as valid as any other has to do with the background of the Iowa State students. At the risk of being redundant, these are young men and women who have led "involved" lives during their formative years. When they enroll at Iowa State University they continue their involvement, although this time their focus is on learning experiences outside the classroom. Undoubtedly, students could provide a variety of reasons why they are involved in out-of-class learning experiences, but for many of them their involvement at Iowa State University is a continuation of what, ultimately, will be a way of living for them.

Policies and Practices

Iowa State University has several policies and practices that support the quality of out-of-class education on campus. All student organizations are required to have a faculty adviser. On some campuses this would be seen as a burden, and obviously not all Iowa State faculty hunger for this experience. But many faculty seem eager to work with students outside the classroom; serving as an organization adviser provides an excellent avenue to do so. In our meetings with faculty they were quick to identify a wide variety of learnings which resulted from their students' out-of-class involvement.

Iowa State University has begun a program for freshman honors students which has excellent potential. In this program, students, without regard to their academic discipline, are assigned to faculty members as junior research assistants. They provide support to faculty who are conducting research projects in whatever way appears to be mutually beneficial. This program has been so successful from a faculty point of view that, according to the director of the program, no faculty member has ever withdrawn from the program.

Students also are given substantial authority and control over resources. More will be said about this later in the case, but as a matter of practice Iowa State University trusts its students to make good decisions about expending substantial amounts of money.

Anticipatory Socialization

Some prospective students hear about Iowa State University from their local county extension office. University-sponsored extension programs touch approximately 500,000 Iowans annually and communicate the value of service to those who consider attending Iowa State University. Many Iowa State students first visit the campus as participants in a summer engineering program or leadership development workshop. Iowa State admissions staff encourage prospective students to visit with others from their town who have attended Iowa State University to get a personal, firsthand evaluation of the Iowa State student experience.

Personal attention continues for Iowa State students when they participate in the summer orientation program. In many ways the orientation program is typical for a large university, although the encouragement that the deans offer to students about their involvement in out-of-class experiences is important. What is particularly noteworthy about summer orientation at Iowa State University is that each student has an individual appointment with an adviser during which the student's academic program is planned for the fall term. This kind of personal attention is another deliberate attempt by Iowa State University to personalize the institution and make it feel small to students.

Resources

At involving colleges, students have substantial control over their resources and Iowa State student affairs staff are proud of the work that students do in this regard. The undergirding philosophy is one of confidence in students' ability to exercise judgment in managing their fiscal affairs. The residence hall student government prepares and allocates its budget without the involvement of administrators. The director of residence at Iowa State University pointed out that he could not recall one instance when he had overruled a student government budget decision in his 23-year tenure.

The Government of the Student Body (GSB) also plays a significant role in the allocation of mandatory student fees at Iowa State University. GSB disperses nearly $750,000 annually to student organizations and activities on campus. Along with the United Way and city and county government, GSB provides funding to city and county social services — another example of the students' commitment to the "pitch in and help" ethic that permeates campus life.

Stipends are available to many students to help them defray their costs of attending Iowa State University and provide them with an opportunity to focus on their involvement as student government leaders. GSB officers and cabinet officials earn stipends as do approximately 24 residence hall student leaders. The financial remuneration to these officers underscores the seriousness with which student leaders are taken. The stipends allow them to devote whatever time is necessary to do their important work.

The university makes deliberate attempts to hire students to help them defray the cost of their education. Approximately 5,000 students work for pay at the university and another 1,000 or so receive payment in-kind for their work. It was estimated that nearly half of Iowa State's students work on or off campus.

Traditions

Iowa State University has crafted a campus environment where involvement is a tradition. Students are encouraged to be involved from the moment they make contact with the university. The first five pages of the Student Information Handbook are devoted to describing how students can get involved at the university. This is another clear attempt on the part of student affairs staff to make sure that students know that there is a plethora of involvement opportunities at Iowa State University and that it is easy to get involved in campus life.

Iowa State University's spring festival, VEISHEA, is an example of student involvement as a tradition. VEISHEA is a four-day festival which combines some of the best elements of Iowa State's heritage with avenues for student involvement.

It began in 1922 when a student, Wallace McKee, suggested that several colleges combine their spring open houses for high school students into one celebration that would include athletic events, honor ceremonies, and musical entertainment for the campus community. A parade was added to the festival in 1925.

VEISHEA is an acronym for each of the colleges in existence at the time the festival was founded. V stands for veterinary medicine, E for engineering, IS for industrial science, HE for home economics, and A for agriculture. The current VEISHEA festival attracts as many as 250,000 people to the campus from all over Iowa and the Midwest.

Open houses are still held for prospective students during VEISHEA. Displays and demonstrations are sponsored by the colleges, including their clubs and various subdivisions. An example of an open house was the display of the Hotel, Restaurant and Institution Management Club which demonstrated the modernization of food preparation equipment and the history of cherry pie, which has been sold at every VEISHEA since 1922.

The parade has had as many as 100 units, including floats built by residence halls and greek houses, marching bands from high schools and colleges, and novelty units such as a residence hall floor which performs tricks and drills with lawn chairs. VEISHEA athletic competition includes such activities as college boat races; 5k and 10k runs; bicycle and canoe races; tennis, golf, and softball tournaments; volleyball; a 1,400 mat Twister game sponsored by residence hall student government; and an exhibition football game played by the Iowa State varsity team.

Entertainment has become a big part of the festival and includes activities such as a carnival, a rib cook-off, a battle of the bands, a beach party, an art fair, and the "Stars Over VEISHEA" production which has included musicals such as "Hello Dolly" and "Grease."

VEISHEA is coordinated by a central committee of students that is advised by two former student committee chairs and two faculty or staff members. Iowa State students chair the various VEISHEA committees and over 200 students are involved in the actual planning and production of the event.

VEISHEA festivities culminate in three days of the university's being an "open house" to the state of Iowa, reflecting Iowa State's land-grant heritage with its mission of service to the state through a variety of activities that extend through the festival, including college exhibits, programs for high school students, and involvement of state and local organizations and people in all of its activities.

A Final Word

Iowa State University is not perfect. Not every student who attends the university has a splendid learning experience. To claim otherwise would be unrealistic. But the student affairs staff, in addition to the faculty and others associated with the university, has done a thorough job of studying and understanding itself, its heritage and its students, and has developed learning opportunities for students that are superb. In many ways, Iowa State University serves as a powerful example of what a large, residential institution can do when it determines that superior out-of-class learning opportunities are important for its students.

Commentary

The Iowa State University Story
Arthur Sandeen

It is a bit difficult to review this university in an objective manner — I served as associate dean of students from 1967-69, and as dean of students from 1969-73 there during one of its most volatile periods. Moreover, my affection for and attachment to the institution remain strong. With those biases clearly stated, I will proceed to comment on the university's continuing efforts to improve the quality of its campus and community life.

The experiences students gain at Iowa State University are very positive, and are a tremendous asset for the institution. They are the result of efforts made by faculty, student affairs staff, alumni, administration, and community members over a period of many years. The ethos of the institution is well known throughout the state, and is greatly enhanced by an extensive network of local clubs, organizations, and other activities all directed at youth. Iowa State University has both capitalized on this arrangement and been dependent upon it for decades. The university has a well-deserved reputation for genuineness, hard work, and caring. It goes out of its way to enhance this reputation, and there is a spirit of cooperation and good will on the campus which is unusual at large, land-grant universities.

At the same time Iowa State University has enhanced its popularity with students, parents, and the general public, it has perhaps become too conforming and inclusive as a campus community. Many folks at Iowa State University are conscious of this, and understand that this academic provincialism is at once their greatest asset and their greatest liability. For those students who are from small towns in Iowa, are white, are of traditional age, and are oriented toward group activities and campus involvement, the system works very well. For students who do not fit neatly into this pattern, the match is sometimes not a good one. Iowa State University does not want to become a cultural island for white, middle class, traditional-age students; it desires to become a more diverse university and community. Herein lies its most exciting challenges in the years ahead — to retain the best parts of its involving and caring culture, while also extending itself to a broader base of students and faculty whom it is not now serving very well.

There is much to be learned from Iowa State University, although it certainly is dangerous to try to transfer programs and policies from one campus to another without careful thought and planning. The house system works quite well for many students in the residence halls, but not for all, of course. It clearly would not work on another campus if there were not an excellent and committed staff, good facilities, and a caring faculty. With a more diverse student body, especially one with students from different backgrounds (e.g., urban settings), the house system might seem like a stifling conformity to a strange set of values. This might also be true at a more competitive institution which places less value on cooperation and sharing than Iowa State University does, and distances itself more obviously from undergraduates.

The house system works reasonably well at Iowa State University largely because students come from background experiences and families that are very consistent with it. It seems natural for most of these freshmen to live in a residence hall, and to work and live cooperatively with other students. In fact, this is their expectation before they arrive, and certainly one of the major reasons they select the institution. Before another university adopts a similar approach, it should examine the nature of its students very carefully, and decide if they might be receptive to the house system. Most likely, they may find that certain groups of students may be inclined to this option, but many others may not be. Thus, a sensitive student affairs leader would assess the various student cultures and the amount and quality of faculty and staff support before transferring a program from Iowa State University, such as the house system.

In a student body which is remarkably homogeneous for a large, land-grant institution, Iowa State University has reasonable success with the house system, but even there, it is not for all students. The best student affairs leaders will not force a single model on all undergraduates, no matter how attractive it might appear. They will experiment with several approaches and options for students, and remain very sensitive to the special needs of their campus.

Among the most attractive of the many assets Iowa State University has is its cordial relationships between faculty and student affairs. This is not an accident, and has been nourished for many years by leaders in both areas. There are, of course, many pockets of faculty on the campus who are not involved in undergraduate student life, but there remains a substantial number who are. This aspect of Iowa State's community life cannot be overstated in its importance to quality undergraduate experience. Student affairs leaders on other campuses can initiate efforts to involve more faculty in student life, with the support of their presidents, provosts, and deans. They can also create many ways for faculty to participate, through committees, study groups, seminars, joint grant projects, and community service. But all of this, of course, cannot be done in one year, and the process is never complete.

On large campuses, it is the responsibility of student affairs leaders to enhance the amount and the quality of faculty participation in student life, and to improve this each year. Iowa State University has a long tradition of this type of involvement (largely because of its 4-H and extension activities throughout the state), and still, the student affairs staff works very hard at getting faculty involved every year. The process must begin somewhere, and despite the considerable obstacles to getting faculty more involved with student life, student affairs leaders must become active in this area.

It is also important to have a talented and dedicated student affairs staff, which Iowa State University has enjoyed for years. It is not a good idea to invite faculty to be active participants in student life programs if the student affairs staff cannot command the professional respect of the faculty, or are not able to deliver good quality programs. Thus, the student affairs leader must again assess the distinct nature of his/her campus, and initiate actions which are consistent with the resources, traditions, and personnel available.

One of the major problems (some might say it is an asset!) at large, land-grant universities is that there really isn't a core experience for undergraduates. What there is at most large universities now is a collection of loosely related smaller communities, sometimes organized around a particular curriculum; a residential area; a cultural, ethnic, or racial group; or a set of personal interests. At Iowa State University, despite its relatively large size, there still is a distinctive spirit and "common experience" shared by most undergraduates. This is unusual for large universities and, from my perspective, a very valuable asset to retain. However, it would be a very bad mistake for a chief student affairs officer to assume that such a common experience for undergraduates might be possible (or desirable) at another campus. Indeed, failure to recognize the special communities that comprise the "student body" at most large campuses is an error made by several student affairs leaders. It is a considerable challenge to find ways to support and enhance the quality of life in these distinct and largely separate student communities (no less to try to bring them together!), but if the student affairs staff does not do this, then it is missing real opportunities to educate students.

Iowa State University also has smaller communities within the institution, of course, but there is still a common experience and shared sense of mission on the part of most people associated with the university. To try to duplicate this on another large, diverse campus would be extremely difficult.

Iowa State University has achieved enviable success as an institution. Its most valuable assets are the enthusiastic graduates who naturally sell the university to others. Its reputation is earned and deserved, and cannot be bought. It has continued to flourish because it knows who it is, and knows its clientele, and what their values and expectations are. A high quality of student life does not occur because of a new president, a particularly dynamic student affairs leader, a highly selective student body, a beautiful residence hall, or a nationally renowned research facility. It is the result of years of hard work on the part of the entire university community, and cooperation and support from throughout the campus. New policies and programs can be put in place by student affairs leaders, but if they are done in isolation from the kinds of support Iowa State University has enjoyed for so long, they will be largely ineffective.

Iowa State University may be a unique island in the family of large, land-grant universities in America. Its genuine (and non-self congratulating!) caring for students, its strong traditions, its excellent staff, its warm relations between faculty and student affairs staff, and its ability to direct its efforts to students it understands should be understood by others as the essential elements that have brought it success. Many of these principles can be developed by other colleges and universities, but they must be pursued with a very careful sensitivity to the distinct nature of each campus community. It must also be realized that each principle will require hard work on the part of the entire campus community, and will not take place overnight.

Chapter Four

Caretakers of the
Collegiate Culture
Student Affairs at Stanford University

George D. Kuh

Stanford University is one of the premiere research universities in the world. One factor that sets Stanford University apart from other universities with similar student profiles and excellent faculty, however, is that — by and large — Stanford undergraduates take advantage of many of the opportunities the institution has assiduously cultivated to enrich out-of-class learning.

As Schuh pointed out in Chapter One, involvement is not only a function of institutional resources (e.g., people, facilities) but also of how people use resources. Considerable effort is expended by staff in the student affairs division, faculty, and others to encourage undergraduates to use Stanford's academic, social, physical, and human resources. It is in this regard that Stanford University excels and warrants closer examination to determine how student affairs contributes to the collegiate experience. In this chapter, the term *collegiate experience* refers to the sum of rich out-of-class learning experiences that challenge students' previous response patterns and demand that they acquire new ways of thinking and behaving — socially and intellectually — to be successful (Sanford, 1962).

Overview

In this chapter, the contributions of student affairs to student learning outside the classroom at Stanford University are described. First, how Stanford University mirrors many of the qualities of an involving college (Kuh et al., 1991) is summarized. Then the role of student affairs in supporting the institution's academic mission and promoting student participation in out-of-class learning opportunities is discussed.

Caveat

The information reported in this chapter was collected during the 1988-89 academic year. In 1989, Stanford University initiated a planning process designed to reduce expenditures. As with most other units, student affairs has taken its share of cuts. Hence, what was true then may not necessarily be the case now. Nevertheless, most of the principles and assumptions about student life and learning outside the classroom discussed in this chapter almost certainly will persist in some form because they are inextricably intertwined with the institution's philosophy and culture. In addition, many of the properties that make out-of-class life at Stanford University special are products of capital investments (e.g., small residences) that are unlikely to change significantly.

Selected Characteristics of Involving Colleges
Common to Stanford

In this section, Stanford's mission and philosophy, campus environment, culture, and the role of selected institutional agents are described to establish a context within which the contributions of student affairs can be understood and appreciated.

Mission and Philosophy

At the time Stanford University was founded, higher education in the United States was being redefined. Faculty returning from study in German universities brought with them an increased interest in research and graduate training, activities that provided a sharp contrast to the English college liberal arts tradition that characterized undergraduate curricula and college life. Out of this confluence of circumstances, including the expectation that knowledge should be used to address practical problems, emerged the research university.

As with other major universities, research is the dominant orientation of Stanford faculty and exerts considerable influence on the undergraduate academic program. But since its formative years, Stanford University has been committed to balancing research, graduate study, and undergraduate education. Baccalaureate programs usually reflect a blend of practical and humanistic learning. More than 6,000 courses, from arts to engineering, are offered annually in more than 60 major fields of study. Distribution requirements expose students to different points of view. Engineering majors, for example, take more humanities courses than their counterparts at other schools with engineering programs. Similarly, liberal arts majors must take one course each in mathematics, natural science, and technology. Undergraduates also must demonstrate competency in foreign language and mathematics.

It is no surprise that such academic values as breadth of understanding and developing critical thinking skills are emphasized in Stanford's mission. Also underscored is the importance of a sound body (as well as a sound mind) and learning outside the classroom. Consider the following excerpt from Stanford's mission statement (May 1, 1983):

> To bring knowledge and understanding to each new generation of young people; to instill in them an appreciation of scholarship, and of health and physical vitality; and to provide the basis for ethical and responsible lives, productive careers, and contributions to the public welfare. To attain these purposes, Stanford provides instruction in analysis, reasoning, and expression; in human and self-understanding; in their own and other cultures; in the fundamental skills and methods needed in a rapidly changing world; and in preparation for professional life and studies. Stanford's purposes are also pursued by providing a campus environment and activities through which students develop attitudes and values in the midst of a diverse population.

Indeed, as we shall see, Stanford University has gone to great lengths to create formal and informal links between the undergraduate academic program and students' lives outside the classroom. Some of these links, such as residential education, will be discussed later. And while Stanford's mission is not as distinctive as that of such colleges as Earlham or Mount Holyoke, the collegiate experience — particularly the residential component — leaves a distinctive imprint on Stanford graduates.

Philosophy

Shaping Stanford's policies and practices is a deeply rooted and long-held belief in the desire and ability of students to exercise independent judgment and to take responsibility for their own lives and intellectual and social-emotional development. The cornerstone of Stanford's philosophy is the Fundamental Standard: "Students are expected to show both within and without the University such respect for order, morality, personal honor, and the rights of others as is demanded of good citizens. Failure to observe this will be sufficient cause for removal from the University."

The Honor Code (which applies to both students and faculty) was initiated by students in the 1920s and is an indication that the institution trusts students and expects them to act with integrity, take responsibility for their own actions, and respect the rights of others. Among other things, the Honor Code means that there are few proctored exams. University administrators, faculty, and staff state, in various policies and in public forums, that they trust students. Tuition bills and grade reports are sent to students, not their parents or guardians. Students are expected to actively participate in the governance of their organizations and residences and — to a lesser extent — in the governance of the institution. Students also have considerable autonomy in selecting courses. For example, there are virtually no restrictions on what courses undergraduate students may take or any mechanisms to regulate the number of people who may choose a particular major (e.g., differential grade point averages for admission to such popular majors as human biology or economics).

In communications between the institution and newcomers, the university consistently sends the message that "Because you have chosen Stanford, and Stanford has chosen you, we will do everything we can to help you succeed." Although the "ethic of membership" is not a formal policy nor is it often discussed, its influence can be seen in many practices. For example, consistent with the ethic of membership, Stanford University believes that a student's transcript should be a record of success (although faculty are not of one mind on this point); hence, no failing grades are given (during Stanford's first four or five decades, grades were not used, only Pass or No Pass). Students in academic difficulty in one or more courses simply drop the courses and repeat them later. Also, students are encouraged to stop out for a time to work, travel, or provide community service. Students can resume their studies at the beginning of any academic term provided they were in good academic standing when they left. Students not in good academic standing can also resume their studies through an appeal to the Academic Standing Office.

Campus Environments

Adjacent to Palo Alto, California, the attractive, 8,000-acre Stanford campus is, in a sense, a community unto itself. About 88 percent of the undergraduates live on campus. Many faculty live in residential neighborhoods (on land leased from the university) contiguous to student row housing near the academic core of the campus.

The academic heart of the university includes classroom buildings, athletic facilities, a medical center, and student residences. Additional campus lands are occupied by the Stanford Shopping Center (which leases space to such stores as Macy's, Saks Fifth Avenue, Neiman-Marcus, and Nordstrom), a very large industrial research park (the heart of Silicon Valley), and many inviting vistas of the vast open spaces in the nearby foothills being preserved for future generations. Stanford's entrepreneurial spirit also is manifested by the approximately one dozen lunch places distributed throughout the campus, many of which are privately owned and operated.

From its inception, Stanford University has assiduously cultivated a human-scale environment. The Stanford physical plant attempts "to make every place work for people" without resorting to stifling, overly formal architecture. To capitalize on the special qualities of the location, the original architect had to convince Leland Stanford (the founder) that the bricks and ivy common to eastern universities would not be appropriate in northern California.

Most buildings are only three or four stories above ground level. Almost every student residence has green space in view from most windows, an intentional effort on the part of planners to allow the open feel of the campus to drift into the relatively small dorm rooms, making the rooms seem larger than they actually are. Community groupings are not dense; small gathering places have been established around the campus that engender a sense of closeness, of community. Informality marks the little courtyards or "eddies," small "congregating places" out of the main flow of traffic to encourage spontaneous interaction among students, faculty, and others. Each is unique; people gravitate to those they find appealing and comfortable.

The Quadrangle is homogeneous in purpose and design (e.g., Romanesque), suggesting a sense of institutional stability compatible with the climate and topography. Constructed of user-friendly components (e.g., hearts, balls, and whimsical swirls on the columns; small pieces of stone; earth-tone colors), the Quad is not mammoth but rather human scale; one can actually put an arm around one of the "homey, friendly, huggable little columns." Arcades connect all the academic buildings and architecturally symbolize connections between different elements of the physical environment. In this sense, the arcades reflect a unity of physical structures in which diverse activities occur (e.g., the academic buildings, residences, and playing fields work together).

As a result of renovations, most academic buildings now offer spaces where individuals and small groups can communicate informally or congregate spontaneously. Bulletin boards are strategically located in residences and elsewhere so that students can relay information easily. Wide hallways and stairwells and benches enable students to stop and visit without obstructing movement of others. To encourage spontaneous interactions, such spaces are being designed into new buildings.

Tresidder Union faces the White Plaza in the center of campus. To take advantage of the pleasant climate, many union rooms can be entered from outside the building as well as from an inside hallway. Other architectural features of Tresidder create "crossroads" and "magnets" which draw people into the facility. The plaza itself creates a sort of interdependency of buildings and functions. The Music Department is an example of "structuring the environment in anticipation of social difficulties." Located near White Plaza, a high traffic area, the Music Building has extra sound proofing and an arcade so that bicycle traffic from the residence halls can move through it onto White Plaza.

Campus Culture

Several themes permeate the Stanford culture: responsibility, integrity, entrepreneurialism, egalitarianism, and a touch of whimsy. Entrepreneurial behavior is fueled by the expectation that students should take the initiative in getting to know faculty members, creating organizations that meet their intellectual and social interests and needs, and seeking out or creating other meaningful ways to participate in the life of the community. Within Stanford University, however, there are strong egalitarian forces at work that ameliorate differences within and among groups. For example, for the first 30 years, Stanford University did not charge tuition. Also, exchanges between students, faculty, and administrators are typically unencumbered by such trappings as rank, title, family name, or socioeconomic status. More often than not, people address each other by first names. Intercampus memos usually begin with such salutations as "Dear Don" rather than "Dear President Kennedy" or "Dear Evan" rather than "Professor Porteus."

The thread of whimsy interwoven into the Stanford culture is symbolized by the Leland Stanford, Jr., University Marching Band. The band is open to any student who can play a musical instrument, and, occasionally, some who cannot. They do not wear traditional marching band uniforms and do not typically perform in formation. However, on rare occasions (about once a decade), they have been known to square up, form lines, and march well. Students (and more than a few faculty and graduates) find the band's parody of "real" marching bands to be hilarious, and a reminder not to take themselves too seriously.

History

Stanford University was built on farm land and additional extensive acreage donated by Leland and Jane Stanford to memorialize their son who died in his teens. Hence, the name of the university is the Leland Stanford, Jr., University, something the Stanford band makes clear at every opportunity. Construction began in 1887 and classes began in 1891.

Many distinctive elements of Stanford's culture were introduced by David Starr Jordan, Stanford's first president. Jordan's vision was to build a world-class university, and he immediately began to recruit high-quality faculty members. Because California was still perceived as "the Wild West" at that time, attracting people from such eastern institutions as Cornell, Harvard, and Yale universities took considerable persuasion. Jordan also formulated the Fundamental Standard mentioned earlier. However, one of Jordan's legacies is that he invited fraternities and sororities to colonize to provide housing for students. As we shall see later, this initiative has presented obstacles to achieving some of the institution's aspirations (e.g., egalitarianism).

Traditions

The traditions that persist over time seem to be as much a function of administrative interest as student culture. Such social traditions as the Mark Twain Dance hosted by the Twain House and the Oxford and Viennese Balls have links to personalities and themes from Western culture. Other traditions reinforce the institution's commitment to multiculturalism (e.g., EAST FEST, a celebration of Asian culture and arts, and "Club Ujamaa," dancing, food, and casino-like games hosted by the African-American theme house). As with other universities, Stanford has a complement of traditions that reflect some behaviors associated with psychosocial phases traditional-age students experience (e.g., "Full Moon on the Quad" — a kiss from a senior under a full moon at midnight in the Quad makes one a Stanford man or woman; some students even check IDs to verify senior status!)

Other traditions instill institutional loyalty. Gaieties is a spoof of faculty, administrators, and students. The Big Game (University of California, Berkeley, versus Stanford in football) tradition is alive and well. Happily (as far as most undergraduates are concerned), the bonfire and "bear-ial" (disposing of the University of California, Berkeley, mascot) persist. On occasion, this tradition has been modified in ways more consistent with Stanford's educational values and purposes. For example, a senior resident assistant encouraged her floor to celebrate the game by hosting a Chinese dinner to honor the memory of the Chinese laborers who built the railroads that helped Leland Stanford amass his fortune.

Language

Many students, faculty, and administrators refer to Stanford University as "the Farm" (recall the campus was originally farm land). Using a homey term for a world-class research university seems, at first glance, to be inappropriate. In fact, the Farm is a term of endearment and, like the Leland Stanford, Jr., University Band, is another reminder that Stanford people should not take themselves too seriously. Recall that by using first names, rather than titles, the Stanford language emphasizes the similarities among people rather than superficial differences. Similarly, the gender-neutral term *frosh* is promoted by student affairs staff and others to counter indiscriminate use of the masculine freshmen.

Another term of endearment at Stanford University — indeed across involving colleges — is *dorm* (many Stanford students also refer to their residences as houses). *Dorm* is almost always used with affection; certainly students do not consider the word pejorative. Moreover, the dorms and houses at Stanford University are rich living-learning environments (as will become evident later) where students often take responsibility for themselves and the welfare of members of their living unit. The implications of this point for student affairs are discussed more fully in Kuh et al. (1991).

Institutional Agents

People from many different groups (e.g., graduates, academic administrators) encourage student involvement at Stanford University. In this section a few observations are offered about the president, faculty, and students themselves. The role of student affairs staff will be discussed later.

President

The Stanford president is expected to be the president not only of the faculty and staff, but of students as well. Donald Kennedy meets that expectation very well. He makes about two dozen appearances in the dorms and houses annually! While recognizing the many challenges associated with serving as the president of a research university (e.g., attracting and retaining the best and the brightest faculty, which may or may not include people who have a keen interest in the lives of undergraduate students), Kennedy is sensitive to the quality of student life.

The institution's egalitarian aspirations are modeled by the president. As alluded to earlier, Donald Kennedy is "Don" to faculty and administrators. Occasionally student leaders greet him as Don, although many (perhaps most) other students see him as "D.K." or "the President." Although he is informed and eloquent about the importance of the residential experience to Stanford's educational purposes, Kennedy identified the student affairs staff as the principal architects of the high-quality, out-of-class experiences that characterize Stanford University. Nevertheless, his behavior significantly influences how others on campus view the relationship between out-of-class life and the quality of the collegiate experience.

Faculty

As with other colleges and universities, the character of out-of-class relationships between faculty and students can be described as "some do and some don't." While many faculty may not volunteer their time to attend social events or advise student groups, a significant number of students establish relationships with one or more faculty members. In addition, there are numerous mechanisms (e.g., resident fellows, Public Service Center, Undergraduate Scholars Program, senior theses, undergraduate advising, dinners in the residences, individual faculty-student research projects) that bring students into contact with faculty, perhaps more than at comparable institutions. The faculty with whom we talked recounted numerous benefits from their interactions with undergraduates (e.g., modifying expectations for courses, how to more effectively present material in class).

Students

As with other large universities, it is difficult to accurately characterize the Stanford student body. Students are diverse in geographical, racial, and ethnic origins. Almost a third are students of color (African-American, Asian-American, American Indian and Native Alaskan, and Mexican-American and Chicano and Chicana). In other ways, however, Stanford students are very homogeneous. For example, almost all are within the top 1 or 2 percent of college-bound students (based upon traditional academic indicators). Most had significant leadership, athletic, artistic, or other accomplishments in high school. Also the achievement orientation and the "entrepreneurial individualism" that characterize Stanford's culture are manifested in student behavior. Hence the character of the student body is best understood as the sum of its parts, an organic total community.

Certainly the quality of out-of-class learning is due in no small measure to the quality of students. They are friendly, uncommonly so for a prestigious research university. Although this open, welcoming attitude is influenced to some degree by the climate, many programs and practices described later (e.g., Frosh Information Project, orientation) also reinforce that newcomers are immediately full members of the Stanford community — with all attendant rights and responsibilities.

Voluntarism

As with many other institutions, public service has been popular among students. The Public Service Center was established in 1982 at the urging of President Kennedy. Students tutor children in East Palo Alto, teach English to Spanish-speaking Stanford employees, and perform physical labor on the Zuni reservation in New Mexico during spring break. Other public service projects are supported by fraternities, sororities, residents of houses and dorms, and ethnic community centers. Students also collaborate with the co-op residences and other campus food services to donate leftover food to a local hunger project.

Fraternities

In the eyes of many faculty and administrators, the fraternity system has been a major disappointment over the past 15 years. Because of the ethic of membership, it is expected that all students should have equal access to all educational resources. In the case of fraternal organizations, the decision about whether a student can belong is the prerogative of the group, not the individual student. Hence, there has been no expansion of housed fraternal organizations; the ten residential fraternities are essentially "grandfathered" in the residential system. Indeed, at one time there were 27 national residential fraternities at Stanford University; now there are ten and most take in boarders to remain financially solvent. One former fraternity house, Theta Chi, is now a coed co-op; Alpha Sigma is a coed fraternity, which generated considerable consternation among its former members.

As with fraternities, sororities were formed when classes began in 1891. However, decades later women students themselves suggested that sororities should be discontinued because they no longer housed significant numbers of students and had become "too exclusive," thereby conflicting with the institution's egalitarian ethos. In 1976, the ban was lifted and sororities were once again allowed but only as nonresidential organizations with membership and governance policies and practices free from the control of national organizations. Today, Stanford sororities are, in general, strong and vibrant.

Academics

Students usually do not talk about their grades. When friends ask "How is it going?" the typical response is "Okay" or "Fairly well," or "I'm not doing too well"; they tend not to mention specific grades. The absence of discussion about grades may be misleading. Although students take their studies very seriously, they refrain from talking about them with peers; they are more likely to take up such matters with advisors and counselors.

James Rosse, the Stanford provost, provided some insight into this observation with an analogy. He compared Stanford undergraduates with ducks on a serene pond. On the surface, the ducks seem to be gliding effortlessly across the water, moving at their own pace, doing what they prefer to do against a scenic backdrop. Yet, under the water's surface, the webbed feet are paddling at a rapid rate! This is an apt characterization of collegiate life at Stanford University; students appear to be enjoying themselves, taking advantage of the numerous opportunities to socialize and learn from each other. But make no mistake, Stanford students work hard; considerable stress is associated with academics, a point to which we will return.

The Contribution of Student Affairs to Stanford

Research universities expect high levels of scholarly productivity from their faculty. As a result, faculty at such institutions as Stanford University spend less time with students than do their counterparts at liberal arts colleges (Carnegie Foundation for the Advancement of Teaching, 1990). It should not be surprising, therefore, that peers, student affairs personnel, and other staff (e.g., advising associates, resident assistants — undergraduates selected and trained by student affairs staff to assist with residential education) have become more important in fostering a campus climate conducive to learning. Indeed, at Stanford University student affairs staff are the de facto caretakers of the collegiate experience, attempting to preserve and protect the values, policies and practices that encourage students to take advantage of the rich learning opportunities outside the classroom. To understand the contributions of student affairs in this regard, it is necessary to describe the characteristics of people who work in the Department of Student Affairs and how its policies and practices complement the institution's mission and philosophy.

Personnel

The student affairs staff is a hard-working team, characterized by *esprit de corps* and mutual respect. All those with whom we met were bright, intellectually inquisitive professionals. Many staff are "overheated"; that is, they invest considerable time and energy in their jobs and, on occasion, exhibit symptoms of burnout. Some are disgruntled that they are not eligible for sabbaticals. Nevertheless, they appear highly productive, energetic, enthusiastic, positive, and dedicated to their work.

How student affairs personnel approach their work has been influenced to a considerable degree by the former chief student affairs officer, James Lyons. There may not be a better match between an institution's mission and ethos and the beliefs and values of a dean of students. Stanford's expectations for self-reliance, responsible behavior, and trust were personified by Lyons (who had been at Stanford for 17 years at the time this study was conducted). Several student affairs staff predate the dean. For example, the senior associate dean came to Stanford University in 1967 as a graduate student in counseling psychology and has since served in a variety of capacities. Other key staff have been students at Stanford University. Many student affairs staff have performed different roles at the university at various times. While many have advanced or professional degrees, few have graduate preparation in student affairs, higher education, or counseling. In fact, a "grow your own" staff mentality has been operating for some years. For example, at least three of the current professional student life staff began their employment at Stanford University as secretaries.

In the context of Stanford University, the continuity of student affairs staff must be considered a strength, primarily because of the quality of the people. At some institutions, staff who have been around a long time all too often become jaded and tired, and lack innovative ideas. However, this does not seem to be the case at Stanford University.

The front line staff mirrored the diversity to which Stanford University aspires. At the time of this study, the six residence deans included an Asian-American, an African-American, an American Indian, and a Mexican-American. The other two residence deans were white women. Residence deans are, in effect, "trouble shooters" and comprise one of the "invisible safety nets" by mobilizing institutional resources (faculty, medical and counseling resources, relatives, and others) to respond to students who are in trouble academically, socially, emotionally, and physically. Staff of the four ethnic community centers (Black Community Services Center, El Centro Chicano, Native American Cultural Center, Asian-American Activities Center) serve as (among other things) internal consultants, advisors, and mentors on issues related to intra- and intergroup relations and individual student concerns.

Resident assistants (RAs) actively participate as members of resource teams coordinated by the residence deans. They also involve students in planning activities in residences that are meaningful and challenging to previous ways of thinking and behaving. These expectations do not differ appreciably from those of their counterparts at some other institutions. What distinguishes Stanford RAs is that they are not expected to serve a disciplinary function. Violations of the Fundamental Standard are dealt with by a judiciary. The residence deans and others deal with routine disciplinary matters. Thus, the confusion about the RA's role that students sometimes experience ("Is the RA my friend, advisor, or a police officer?") is ameliorated to a considerable degree, allowing the RA to focus on educational and cultural programming as well as helping students in times of trouble. Thus, RAs are educators and counselors in the best sense of the terms. Finally, the RA position is considered by students to be one of the most prestigious positions to which a Stanford undergraduate can aspire.

Student Life Policies and Practices

As with other involving colleges, student life policies and practices at Stanford University are consistent with the mission and philosophy of the institution. For the most part, these policies and practices are simple and straightforward; they are not confounded or complicated by many stipulations or a great deal of specificity. This is consistent with the Stanford expectation that students act responsibly and take care of themselves. Student affairs staff, in response to student inquiries and the perennial behavioral issues, continually review policies. Indeed, no policy is sacrosanct; anything is open to challenge.

Admission

Equity is the watchword in the admission process. Every application is read, but not by regional admissions representatives who may have a bias favoring the region of the country from which applicants come. An effort is made to evaluate candidates in the context of their individual backgrounds. Deadlines are strictly observed; no one gets special treatment in spite of, for example, calls made to file an application after the deadline. Also, there is no early admission pool; everyone is considered and offered admission at the same time. However, there are preferential categories (i.e., all things being equal, an applicant who is the child of a graduate or a person of color from the affirmative action categories may be given preference).

The need-blind admission policy (i.e., students' applications are evaluated without consideration of ability to pay) is a powerful institutional commitment. Even so, socioeconomic stratification does exist among students. As a result, some students do not have the resources to take advantage of certain activities that money makes available to other students (e.g., weekend ski trips).

Resource Allocation

Stanford University is a good example of how an institution can "front load" resources to promote involvement. Prematriculation contacts with the institution (e.g., literature from the admissions office, orientation activities) encourage new students to take advantage of every resource the university offers. Members of the Frosh Information Project (now New Undergraduate Student Information Project, NUSIF), which is similar in function to the freshman dean's office common to many eastern colleges, coordinate what were at one time disparate mailings from a variety of offices. New students receive about 15 mailings (e.g., letters from the president, dean of students, RAs) during the summer prior to matriculation describing what they can expect and how they can take advantage of the university's resources.

Orientation lasts for almost a week and is a blend of academic and social activities. Students are welcomed by RAs and orientation volunteers (OVs) wearing bright Cardinal tee-shirts. A picture book identifying newcomers helps RAs and orientation staff greet students by name when they arrive. Graduates from earlier decades can still recall in vivid detail the events staged during Orientation Week and their wonderment at how so many people with impressive accomplishments (e.g., valedictorian, salutorian, National Merit Scholar, captains of the tennis, track and volleyball teams) were living in their residence. Moreover, graduates recount with fondness and appreciation the warm welcome and bonding experiences that make them feel at home and an integral member of the Stanford community.

Advising

All Stanford frosh have an academic advisor with whom they meet during orientation; the advising relationship continues until the student chooses a major. About 150 of the 240 frosh advisors are faculty. Advising associates are undergraduates who work in teams with faculty and staff advisors in the dorms and houses. Some important aspects of the Stanford ethos are introduced in these early contacts between newcomers and upperclass students, faculty, and staff.

Housing

Almost every student wants to live on campus. About 88 percent of the undergrads and about half of the graduate students live on campus. All frosh live on campus; about 60 percent reside in all-frosh houses and, with the exception of a small number in married student housing, the rest live in four-class houses. Except for one all-female house and ten (as of 1989-90) all-male fraternities, housing is coeducational. Although campus housing is guaranteed only three years, about 70 percent of the undergraduates live on campus for four years.

There are more than 70 residences; none has more than 280 students, some have as few as 30 residents. Within this array are many living arrangements: co-ops, student-managed residences, apartments, academic and ethnic theme dorms, and many different traditions of lifestyles and dining arrangements (e.g., eating clubs). In some housing units, students purchase the food, plan menus, and cook their own meals. The dorm or house is a student's "family unit," a place where they will be supported and to which they will establish a strong identification and attachment. Some houses even have reunions (e.g., the annual Thanksgiving dinner at Hammarskjold House, the international co-op).

About 37 of the Stanford houses or dorms have resident fellows, most of whom are faculty or senior staff. The resident fellow lives rent free with his or her family, spouse, or significant other and takes his or her meals in the dorm. While resident fellows do not receive a stipend, they save a significant amount of money on housing and food costs. The tenure record for faculty members who are, or have been, resident fellows is comparable to that of faculty who have not served in this role. The resident fellow program has been so successful that applications for appointments exceed the number of vacancies in any given year.

Because of the small size of residences, it is almost impossible for a student living on campus to be anonymous. Resident fellows, RAs, and peers sense when things are not going well for a student. When a roommate or friend is away for a day or two without informing anyone of their whereabouts, students often alert an RA or resident fellow. Thus, an intricate but, for the most part, natural set of safety nets is in place for most students. This does not mean, however, that tragedies do not occur similar to those on other campuses.

Residential Education

Two goals provide the vision for education in the residences: (a) to develop inclusive communities and (b) to stimulate the intellectual life of the residence and the campus. By integrating curricular experiences with students' lives outside the classroom, the residential education program is integral to the high-quality, out-of-class learning that characterizes Stanford University. For example, Structured Liberal Education is a residence-based program, similar to a freshman honors program, in which some senior faculty teach. In all residences, theme sessions, discussions about current issues, and trips (e.g., to plays, to the beach, to other public events) are commonplace. In general, students are responsible for planning and coordinating these efforts. While the academic experience is obviously very important, virtually every student with whom we spoke mentioned the powerful learning distilled from the residential experience — from living with, getting to know, comparing oneself to, and learning from others who are different.

Stanford's commitment to multiculturalism, individuality, and egalitarianism is reflected in student residences. For example, four of Stanford's residences are cross-cultural: Casa Zapata (the Chicano/Chicana and Mexican-American theme house), Okada (the Asian-American theme house); Muwekma-tah-ruk (the American Indian theme house) and Ujamaa (the African-American theme house). These houses not only provide supportive communities for students from different backgrounds but also enable students who are not members of those groups to expand their cultural awareness by learning about people who are different from themselves.

Students are expected to take ownership of their living units and have considerable leeway in determining the organizational and governance arrangements in their residences and for the acculturation of new residents. For example, each house can determine for itself, on an annual basis (or more frequently perhaps), appropriate behavior standards and how house members will respond when those standards are abridged. They determine how much they will contribute individually to house dues and how those funds will be spent. Students also assist resident fellows or RAs plan and implement educational and social programming.

Alcohol

As with other universities, encouraging responsible use of alcohol continues to be a major challenge. Alcohol and substance abuse programs are available through the Health Promotion Program. The Department of Student Affairs' alcohol policy is as follows: Because students are expected to behave as adults, the only rule — enforced by civil authorities — is the state law regulating alcohol use. Many Stanford students use alcohol openly and freely. Resident fellows, RAs, and others are free to use alcohol if they choose in the presence of students. In this sense, responsible alcohol use is modeled by responsible adults.

This is not to say that alcohol does not become a problem. When tragic events or irresponsible behavior occur, alcohol is often involved. Furthermore, there are many incidents each year when the police (who are under the command of the county sheriff) cite underage students for public drinking or driving under the influence. The police do not enter student residences without adequate cause; in most cases, however, the possibility that minors are drinking does not constitute adequate cause. The point is, the legal age of drinking is a public law, enforced by the police, not by the institution. As one residence dean put it, "We are concerned about the hazardous use of alcohol — not age. A drunken and out-of-control student is no less drunk and out of control just because he is 25 years old!"

Discussion

Stanford University is rich in learning opportunities for its undergraduate students. Its many strengths include a human-scale physical plant located in an almost ideal climate, a philosophy based on themes of equity and egalitarianism, and intellectually inquisitive faculty, staff, and students. But Stanford University also faces many challenges on the eve of the 21st century.

The Egalitarian Dream

Egalitarian aspirations are deeply rooted in the institution's history. For example, tuition was free until sometime in the 1920s. Yet there is evidence that the egalitarian aspiration that Stanford University holds dear is far from being fully realized. In some ways the institution is built on a foundation of elitism. From the beginning, Stanford University recruited the best and the brightest, the cream of the crop. Vestiges of a "culture of affluence" can be found in the student body (even though many students come from very depressed socioeconomic backgrounds). Recruiting highly able students, whether they can pay or not, does not necessarily cull out insensitive bigots. Thus, Stanford University has an interesting challenge ahead in realizing its egalitarian aspiration, given its history and mission as a research university.

Stress Among Students

Another challenge is determining how to respond appropriately to the high level of student stress often associated with self-imposed high expectations for academic performance — expectations which are not unrealistic in students' eyes, given their achievements during high school. Moreover, it is not acceptable to be just "adequate" in any endeavor at Stanford University, which is one of the disadvantages of the academic elitism and entrepreneurial spirit that pervade the campus. Socioeconomic status also is a confounding factor. That is, students who perceive themselves as privileged are reluctant to show they are experiencing academic or social difficulties.

At times, many students feel a sense of inadequacy, particularly during their first year. The "imposter syndrome" (i.e., "Stanford people are of such high ability and talent, how did I get here?"; "Maybe I am the Dean of Admissions' mistake") exacerbates the "normal" amount of stress associated with a rigorous academic program and is particularly debilitating for students of color and some athletes. This feeling among many African-American students often is intensified by the "ultimate doom" syndrome (Saufley, Cowan & Blake, 1983). That is, because of the perception that they do not belong (at a predominantly white, highly selective institution), it does not matter what they do or how hard they work, failure is just ahead: "The [minority] student views each academic success not as proof that he or she can make it but that the ultimate failure is near" (Saufley et al., 1983, p. 10). Even those students who successfully negotiate the pervasive Euro-American culture of Stanford University may have passed the point of no return to their own culture, neighborhood, friends, and family. In other words, they can never "go home" again because their ideas, aspirations, and expectations of themselves and others have changed so much (H. Blake, personal communication, May 30, 1990).

Part of the problem may be that for students of color, Stanford's safety nets are not only invisible — but they do not always work. On occasion, cultural mismatches occur. For example, "the Stanford way" is not to involve parents in students' decision making or problems. Yet between student needs and available support systems, this becomes problematic for Asian-American and many Mexican-American students for whom connections to the family are expected and especially powerful influences on student behavior. On the one hand, student affairs staff are sensitive to the possibility that the safety nets may be literally invisible for some students. On the other hand, they do not want to appear to be worrying too much about how students handle such matters. After all, the Stanford way is self-reliance and autonomy.

The Multiculturalism Agenda
Perhaps the most critical issues facing the Stanford community are learning how to live together, helping students work through emotional issues related to differences among people from various ethnic and racial backgrounds, and discussing and celebrating those differences in the context of a lack of knowledge on the part of many students, faculty, and staff about such differences (e.g., 80 percent of Stanford undergraduates come from nonintegrated community experiences). A related challenge is finding a constructive balance between community and diversity — between celebrating commonalities and celebrating differences. For example, the presence of ethnic theme houses is sometimes interpreted by white students as "an accommodation" to the special needs of students of color. Some observers predicted that such houses may not persist and that what is perceived by some as separatism will not always be necessary. Yet, there have always been distinctive groups at Stanford University and it is likely that special themes or considerations will be reflected in the future as they have been in the past.

Individual students — of any color — may ask themselves why they seem to be excluded from certain groups or why other groups seem to separate themselves. Why must groups or individuals be confrontational about matters related to race and ethnicity? Stanford University is one of the first universities in the United States to openly deal with (in some cases, embrace) tensions generated by students simultaneously using the community and their (ethnic, racial, other) group as a basis for identity.

One seemingly inevitable phase in Stanford's transformation into a multicultural learning community is grappling with what Steele (1989) called the "politics of difference, a troubling, volatile politics in which each group justifies itself, its sense of worth and its pursuit of power through difference alone" (p. 49).

[O]n campuses, the use of racial power by one group makes racial or ethnic or gender differences a currency of power for all groups . . . Very quickly a kind of politics of difference emerges in which racial, ethnic, and gender groups are forced to assert their entitlement and vie for power based on the single quality that makes them different from one another (Steele, 1989, p. 52).

In an environment in which differences become a source of power, groups will devote considerable effort to maintain their distinctiveness, thereby heightening intergroup tensions, inhibiting efforts to identify and pursue common interests and purposes, and sustaining historic inequities (Finn, 1990; Steele, 1989; Will, 1990).

Donald Kennedy (1989) knows what the politics of difference can do to a campus:

Time and again we have seen the promotion of racial understanding linked to a more focused — and less broadly understood and accepted — political agenda. That kind of load is probably too heavy for a delicate structure to bear all at once . . . Nothing, to be sure, can be entirely free of politics; but too much is too much. Nor is it readily understandable to many students why racial incidents are so frequently followed by demands that bear little relation to the circumstances or the environments in which the incidents took place. Freeing our goal of racial understanding from this heavy political weight would, I think, make it easier to achieve — and also reduce the possibility of backlash (p. 3).

At the core of this dilemma is the clash between the historically dominant campus culture — described by some with whom we spoke as "elitist," "patriarchal," "western," or "white" — with the diverse cultures of people of color and women. These dynamics led the University Committee on Minority Issues (1989) to acknowledge two compelling ironies:

First, racial problems have been increasing at a time when the University has achieved unprecedented racial diversity. Second, racial tensions have been more openly expressed during a time when university leaders are stating vigorously to students the importance of . . . "diversity," "pluralism," and "appreciation of differences" . . . (p. 1).

Even something as precious to the Stanford community as the Fundamental Standard may be perceived as a mechanism by which the powerful class (white males) establishes psychological and moral foundations for others (Burrell & Morgan, 1979; Giroux, 1983). Is it possible that the Fundamental Standard, in the context of an institution where more than a third of the undergraduates are people of color, demands conformity to the dominant culture? Simply put, whose sense of order and morality does the Fundamental Standard endorse? Critical observers suggest that such guiding "golden rules" as the Fundamental Standard can be "pluralism traps" (Giroux, 1983) that maintain the social, political, and economic order preferred by the administration, faculty, and external constituents and thereby co-opt political action and fundamental institutional change.

To Stanford's credit, substantial energy and resources are being devoted to examining the experience of people of color with an eye toward modifying institutional policies and practices. A University Committee on Minority Issues has been at work since 1988. The chair of this committee concluded:

> We can't assume any longer that students, faculty, and staff have the skills to interact effectively across racial and ethnic lines . . . If we are going to be able to work, teach, learn, and live together, then we'd better learn how to start to understand one another (Walsh, 1989, p. 9).

Stanford University has established an Annual Review Panel of faculty, trustees, students, graduates, and educational leaders from other schools and organizations to monitor the institution's progress toward implementing the recommendations made by the University Committee on Minority Issues. The Annual Review Panel, which functions much like an accrediting team, expects to meet annually.

Stanford University is engaged in a struggle to redefine itself and to realize more fully its goal of becoming a multicultural learning community. The final report of the University Committee on Minority Issues (1989) is an account of what Stanford University must do to realize this aspiration. Yet the students, faculty, and staff at Stanford University would be the first to say their institution is not (yet) a model for the rest of American higher education. Nevertheless, Stanford's experience is instructive because it, like other colleges and universities committed to multiculturalism, has embarked on an uncharted expedition; the route to the destination — which itself cannot be clearly specified — is risky and arduous, forcing the institution to examine the way it conducts its business, both formally and informally. Stanford University merits our attention because it has elected to deal openly with these complicated, wrenching matters. In this sense, Stanford University is a model.

Conclusion

The Stanford collegiate experience — a rich feast of learning both in and out of the classroom — is sustained by some student-centered faculty, a core group of resident fellows, a dedicated student affairs staff assembled by a visionary dean, and the students themselves. Stanford University works as well as it does because of the plentiful opportunities to take part in the life of the campus community, the variety of settings (e.g., residences) that have been developed to provide challenging intellectual and social-emotional interactions, and the excellent people Stanford University attracts. The few rules that are in place seem to empower rather than constrain.

Stanford University is truly a special place. In many ways it cannot help but be "involving," given the quality of the people who are there and the environment in which it is located. Whether Stanford University will be a lighthouse for similar institutions will depend on the degree to which it realizes its vision of a multicultural community committed to learning in all forms and forums.

Commentary

Student Affairs at Stanford University
William D. Gurowitz

This commentary offers suggestions to medium-size research universities interested in increasing student involvement in the life of the campus community, thereby providing them with a better and more complete education. In doing so, I will indicate what works toward improving involvement and what works against it. In addition, I will raise some issues about student life at Stanford University.

Alexander Astin, on a visit to Cornell University in 1990, cautioned us to look not at what institutions say but at what they do. Kuh (Chapter Two), in looking at involving colleges — specifically Stanford — recommends the same. I have had the good fortune to visit Stanford University on several occasions, including a stay of several days when I served on a visiting committee some years ago. These visits, when coupled with the case by Kuh, lead me to conclude that Stanford University does an excellent job of involving students. Stanford University implements its mission statement.

Some credit for Stanford's success must be given to the former dean of student affairs who built a staff around a philosophy of inclusion and participation. The statement in Chapter One captures the dean's philosophy — ''A learning opportunity is missed every time a teacher . . . does something for students that students could do for themselves.'' As Kuh stated in the Stanford case, "There may not be a better match between an institution's mission and ethos and the beliefs and values of a dean of students." My first recommendation is, therefore, that colleges and universities make sure there is a congruence between the chief student affairs officer's philosophy and the institution's mission.

Stanford's Residence System

In my view, the key to Stanford's success at involving students is the residential system, which encompasses residential education, resident fellows, a wide variety of living and governance (organizational) options, and the residence hall environment. Residential education is based on programming in the halls, most of it planned and executed by students with staff acting as facilitators. The resident fellows have a role in residence hall programs and in classes which are held in the halls. While observing these classes I noted that professors and students appreciated the relaxed setting because there was no pressure to leave to go to the next class. They often lingered to discuss points raised in class. Even after faculty members left, students continued the discussion. Indeed, I was so impressed with the program and its beneficial effect on the overall education of students that I started a similar program at Cornell. (I was also influenced by residence education at Brown University.)

Another benefit of the resident fellow program is that participating faculty improve their teaching after seeing at close hand how the course material is processed by students and receiving immediate feedback from them. The resident fellow program represents a sizable commitment by the institution, in terms of funds allocated to support the program as well as the rental income lost from the assignment of student rooms to fellows. Nonetheless, Stanford University has determined that the cost of the program is worthwhile given its benefits.

Schuh (Chapter One) aptly described the Stanford environment as "being of human scale." Throughout the campus there are small areas devoted to quiet contemplation and intimate encounters. Nowhere is this more evident than in the residence halls, where one finds an abundance of space of different sizes and functions. This, too, reflects a considerable financial commitment by the institution. Indeed, the space devoted to development activities in some of Stanford's newer facilities is almost extravagant and reflects an understanding by the administration of the contribution of that space to the education of students.

The wide variety of living options and the responsibility for governance given to students permits each individual to choose the most suitable residence and then be involved in deciding how the residence community will function. Stanford University has made a further commitment to students by providing sufficient housing so that virtually all students who desire to live on campus can do so and benefit from the residential program.

The Stanford residence system is a good one and can be used as a model for institutions that wish to implement a residential education program. First, however, the leadership of the institution must be educated about the benefits of such a system and start-up funding must be identified. Then a beginning — a model program — however modest must be implemented. If the model program proves successful, funds necessary for its continuance and expansion must be found. This is a commitment that the president should make even before the model program is undertaken.

Beyond the Residence Halls

Creating a human-scale environment away from the residence halls also requires an institutional commitment as well as the involvement of campus planners and others outside of the student life staff. Landscaping, benches, and other modifications of the physical environment can be accomplished without a great expenditure of funds. Renovations and new construction should be planned with an understanding that small spaces create a human-scale environment.

The interpersonal environment of an institution may be more difficult to alter. For example, fostering a climate of trust on a campus where it currently does not exist is a formidable challenge. The challenge may be more manageable, however, if we can learn from the Stanford experience. An initial step toward building may be the development of an honor code. What if a university community was challenged by the president to develop the equivalent of Stanford's Fundamental Statement and Honor Code? If, after thorough consideration, these recommendations were adopted by the community, the foundation may be laid for creating an environment in which students feel trusted and trustworthy. Having a statement about honesty to which all members of the campus community subscribe is an example of how institutional values can come alive for students to the extent that they feel involved in maintaining those values.

Another key to involving students is to communicate frequently and consistently that the institution values involvement and urge students to find ways of getting involved that are appropriate to the individual students and the educational purposes of the institution. Stanford University communicates these messages when students first inquire about admission, sustains them through graduation, and continues in the university's communications to graduates.

Other Issues Related to Student Life at Stanford

As is the case with any higher education institution, Stanford University is not perfect. The topics included in this section represent other issues related to student life at Stanford University that are addressed briefly.

Greek Life

Among the areas at Stanford University that struck me as potentially working against involving students is the fraternity/sorority system. The greek system has been a problem for Stanford University and appears to be on its way out. My view is that it will not disappear but, instead, will take another form. Perhaps there may be a way for the greek system to exist within the educational framework of the university.

Developing a greek system within Stanford's value system could be a teachable moment for the university and its students.

Academic Advising

I was disappointed by what others see as a strength of the Stanford environment — 150 out of 240 frosh advisers are faculty. Because the first days of a student's college experience are so important and may determine how the remainder of his or her college experience will go, I recommend that all frosh advisers be faculty members.

Intercollegiate Athletics

Athletes were not mentioned in the Stanford study, yet athletes clearly are highly involved students. Much has been written about athletes in big time sports not being involved in the life of a campus, and concerns have been expressed that this limits their education and development. A recent study (Adelman, 1990), however, raises questions about the accuracy of this commonly held belief. Special attention should be paid to intercollegiate athletes in developing plans for involving students. Stanford University may provide guidance on this issue since several of the university's top athletes have gained international recognition in their sports while maintaining excellent academic records.

Multicultural Initiatives

Stanford University has made a commitment to multiculturalism but it is unclear how that commitment affects students of color. I worry that Stanford, along with other colleges and universities, is simply modifying a white perspective to accommodate the views of people of color. The continuing unease among people of color at Stanford University supports that possibility. Is the nub of the problem a lack of acceptance of all people and their perspectives? Are people of color separated from the mainstream of campus life? Is Stanford (along with other institutions) prepared to start from scratch to develop a new and inclusive Fundamental Standard and Honor Code? Even if the resulting code proved to be the same or quite similar to its predecessor, it would be viewed not as a vestige of a Caucasian, Eurocentric system, but as a product of true multiculturalism. Think of the message that would be communicated to all members of the community!

Stanford University has led the way in pursuing multiculturalism — an important and difficult effort — and I do not raise these issues as criticism. Stanford University involves students and the rest of the community in exploring multicultural issues.

Students are participating in this exploration and their development as maturing young adults is enhanced as a result. Nevertheless, other institutions should not stand by and wait to see the results of Stanford's efforts before initiating an effort of their own. They should monitor Stanford's programs and learn from it, but at the same time they must launch programs of their own to create truly multicultural learning communities.

Financial Issues

Stanford University is not unique in having undergone severe budget cuts in the past year or two. Virtually all of higher education is suffering from such woes. These are financial times that test our resolve. What will be telling is how programs that involve students fare. That will be a test of the institution's understanding of and commitment to the value of involving students. At Stanford University, eight months after the retirement of the dean of student affairs, there was an acting dean, substantial budget reductions occurred, and there was potential for the loss of direction and momentum of student life programs. Whether these are temporary or permanent dislocations will be determined by the events of the next months and years.

Are there alternative organizational structures that could meet budget reduction targets and still involve students in a meaningful way? Probably, although none is identified easily. While no organizational structure should develop into a cult dependent on one person, there must be someone at the helm with a strong sense of direction and an ability to navigate the ship through often troubled waters while maintaining direction.

One solution explored by some institutions is not promising. Student affairs at such places, including Cornell University, has been moved to the academic side of the institution. To the best of my knowledge, none of these shifts has proven successful.

Stanford's recent financial problems associated with the indirect costs of doing government-sponsored research raise fears that Stanford University may be tempted to take an expedient, lower cost reimbursement arrangement with the student affairs budget absorbing more reductions. If that occurs, the momentum achieved in involving students may be lost.

Chapter Five

Emergence of a Metroversity
The University of Louisville Case

C. Carney Strange

The University of Louisville was chartered as a municipal institution in 1798, when the city was only 20 years old and the Commonwealth of Kentucky just six years old. The history of the university reflects the history of the city of Louisville itself. In the 1830s the city fathers promoted several civic improvements, including the establishment of the Louisville Medical Institute (1837) and the Louisville Collegiate Institute (1838). In 1846 these two institutions merged to form the University of Louisville, which also added a law school.

By 1900, the University of Louisville had seven medical schools and one of the largest medical school populations in the United States. While the city was able to support several medical schools, the university's liberal arts division struggled and was more or less moribund until 1907. Rising standards in medical and legal education, the revival of the College of Arts and Sciences, and regular municipal funding dramatically altered the university by the early 20th century. In 1910, the university began to receive regular appropriations from the city. Despite the economic depression of the 1930s, the period was marked by academic expansion and dedication to high educational ideals. The Louisville Municipal College opened in 1931; the School of Music in 1932; the Graduate Division of Social Administration in 1936, which later became the Kent School of Social Work. In the 1950s and 1960s, the university added schools of business, education, and justice administration.

By the early 1960s, the university faced serious financial problems. According to some observers, the University of Louisville has always been somewhat of a "stepchild" to the city. The city of Louisville could not and did not support the university to the extent it should have. As a semiprivate, semimunicipal institution, income from the city became smaller and smaller while tuition skyrocketed. The city was unwilling (perhaps unable) to provide the needed additional support. After several years of difficult negotiations, the university was brought into the state system of higher education in 1970. In 1977, the Kentucky Council on Higher Education made the University of Louisville the state's "urban university," which affirmed its municipal heritage and long-standing educational and cultural traditions in Louisville and Jefferson County, Kentucky's largest urban area. By 1980, tuition and fee revenues had declined as a proportion of the university's income while state support became more prominent.

The student population doubled from 1970 to 1980, while at the same time the university administration was learning how to adjust to the university's role as a public institution. Major accomplishments during the period included a Health Sciences Center (1970), addition to the School of Nursing (1979), and the opening of a new university hospital (1982). In 1981, Donald Swain became the 15th president of the University of Louisville and in 1983 the College of Urban and Public Affairs consolidated several existing schools and programs to add coherence to and further emphasize the emerging urban mission of the institution.

Today the University of Louisville supports 11 schools and colleges and offers 43 degrees in 146 fields of study across three campuses and a downtown center, spanning the Louisville metropolitan area. The 140-acre Belknap campus, adjacent to the Old Louisville neighborhood, hosts arts and sciences, business, engineering, education, law, and many other programs. The Health Sciences Center, near the downtown business district, is a modern medical complex with its own library and teaching hospital. It houses one of the oldest and most respected medical programs in the nation (founded in 1837). And the Shelby campus, named for Kentucky's first governor, Isaac Shelby, is located on a 238-acre site in eastern Jefferson County and hosts the National Crime Prevention Institute, Weekend University, and many continuing programs.

The University of Louisville has the reputation of being the most liberal public institution in Kentucky and is expected to be so by the rest of the state. It almost always is the first institution in the state to try something different. Part of its institutional culture has always been to track social progress and to be willing to confront controversial issues on campus (e.g., the university was integrated in 1954 and was the first institution in the state to have black athletes).

The campus community and culture historically have exhibited a concern about individual and human rights, a tradition supported over the years by institutional presidents noted for their social consciousness and local benefactors noted for their investment in social causes. Perhaps the most striking symbol of the campus' tradition is that it is the burial site of the noted American jurist, Louis D. Brandeis (1856-1941). The first Jewish justice on the Supreme Court (1916-39), Brandeis is best remembered as a liberal dissenter and was frequently at odds with the court's conservative majority. He often stressed the importance of social and economic justice in his opinions and favored most of Franklin D. Roosevelt's New Deal legislation.

Student Characteristics, Subgroups, and Cultures

Over half (55 percent) of the 21,000 students are enrolled full time, 76 percent (about 14,000) are undergraduates, 77 percent come from Jefferson County, 7 percent from other states or countries, 52 percent are female, 12 percent represent various ethnicities, and the average age is 26 years (50 percent of the students are classified as adult learners). Only 7 percent of the students live in university housing and less than 50 percent of the students receive some form of financial aid.

CIRP data indicate that University of Louisville students exhibit a relatively low self-concept compared with students at other kinds of institutions. According to national norms, only 61 percent of University of Louisville students say they will do well in college compared with 72 percent of students at other institutions. Twenty-five percent of the new students go directly into the preparatory division because of their test scores, indicating a need for remedial preparation in reading, writing, and mathematics.

Almost half of the 56,000 alumni reside in the Louisville area, reflecting the unique fact that the city has more people who were born and have stayed in Louisville all their lives than any other urban area in the United States. About 42 percent of Kentucky's physicians, 81 percent of Kentucky's dentists, 34 percent of the Kentucky Bar Association's members, and 48 percent of Kentucky's engineers are graduates of the University of Louisville.

The student body contains at least five noted subgroups:

- collegiates, which include traditional-age college students who live on or near the campus, such as members of various greek organizations
- students of color, comprised mostly of African-Americans
- adult learners, those students 25 years of age or over
- traditional-age, part-time, and commuting students
- students reflecting a variety of background characteristics, but who are enrolled in the downtown Health Sciences Center programs.

Additional groups are found within each of these categories as well.

Student subgroups are further complicated by what seems to be three different collections of students which influence the campus climate. From about 8 a.m. to 3 p.m., the University of Louisville looks very much like any other public university, in terms of class schedules and types of faculty and students; from about mid-afternoon to about 8 p.m., the university resembles more closely a community college, with a steady stream of traffic and a potpourri of courses. From 8 p.m. to midnight, however, the university is perhaps more like a residential college, with a small core of students living nearby and in the residence halls who actively participate in various campus-sponsored activities.

For the majority of students (71 percent), the University of Louisville is their first choice, although for a sizable portion (i.e., the remaining 29 percent) the institution represents a selection compromise of sorts. Of course, for many students (e.g., part-time students and adult learners with family and job commitments), the university is, for all practical purposes, the only choice although several other institutions in the metropolitan area (Bellarmine College, Indiana University Southeast, Jefferson Community College, Louisville Presbyterian and Baptist Theological Seminaries, and Spalding University) offer cross-registration privileges through the Metroversity consortium. In any case, area residents hold the University of Louisville, its resources and opportunities, in high esteem.

Campus Involvement Factors

The distinction of the University of Louisville as an involving metropolitan institution is supported by its mission and philosophy, features of its multicampus environment, elements of institutional culture, its policies and practices, and various institutional agents. The student affairs division brings a strength of tradition and professionalism to the campus as a key partner in shaping the institution's effectiveness and presence in the Louisville metropolitan area.

The University of Louisville's professed mission and philosophy has rallied and solidified, in recent decades, within the tradition of the great urban universities dating back to medieval Europe, where cities fostered intellectual growth. It is clear that the University of Louisville aspires to be "one of the best metropolitan institutions in the United States," where the city becomes part of each student's education, presenting numerous opportunities and resources for students and faculty to test theoretical knowledge, where research generates new knowledge to benefit the public and private sectors, and where a response to private industries and public agencies fosters a spirit of partnership and problem solving that addresses the demands of a complex society. The embracing of a metropolitan mission and philosophy has all but liberated the institution from a second place, and often unproductive, competitive relationship with the flagship campus of the University of Kentucky. Its mission and philosophy, policies, practices, and resources now chart a distinctive course within the statewide system of higher education.

The University of Louisville's Belknap campus, the center of most of the institution's schools and colleges, is ensconced in the Old Louisville neighborhood (the first suburb of the now metropolitan area of over 800,000 people) offering some of the finest 19th-century Victorian residential architecture in the country. The campus itself, 148 acres of tree-lined walkways and lawns, combines the clean, modern lines of new facilities in music, education, law, chemistry, business, and library with the charm of historical buildings dating from the last century, offering an attractive oasis of reflection for those seeking alternatives to the often crowded conditions and hectic pace of urban life.

Much like the typical modern shopping center showcased in most urban areas today, the campus offers a place of convenience and opportunity for a variety of needs and interests of area residents. Two features are perhaps most striking to the first-time visitor (or student) to campus, both of which convey the intent and purpose of this institution. The first is the recently completed $24 million, five and one-half acre Student Activities Center which offers a host of facilities and resources to the campus community. The second feature strikes a familiar pose in the form of Rodin's famous sculpture "The Thinker" (first displayed at the St. Louis World's Fair in 1904), inspiring University of Louisville students, and now overseeing the spring commencement ceremonies, since its installation in 1949 on the steps in front of the administration building. Together they convey that the University of Louisville is both a contemplative respite from, as well as an active and exciting reflection of, the dynamic urban community that surrounds it.

Elements of institutional culture at the University of Louisville, not unlike those at other metropolitan institutions, are somewhat diffuse and perhaps more a product of formally planned mechanisms rather than of long-held traditions. The usual cloned residential models like homecoming parades and dances meet with modest success, undoubtedly reflecting the difficulties of maintaining traditional forms of involvement more apparent on campuses with a significant number of undergraduate, traditional-age, resident students.

The role and tradition of sports, intercollegiate as well as intramural, has been obvious at the university. During the 1940s the university's basketball team, the Cardinals, began to build a tradition culminating in several national championships (one as recently as 1986), a feat that has been matched by the cheerleaders, mascot (Redbird), and precision dance team (Ladybirds) as well. Perhaps the growing recent successes of the institution's intercollegiate football program, under the leadership of Howard Schnellenberg (himself an architect of national championships), signal the development of yet another dynasty in that tradition. In addition, active programs such as the NBA (Noon Basketball Association) assure a short supply of court space each day as faculty, staff, and students gather for pick-up basketball games over the lunch hour. To the credit of individuals like Ellis Meldelsohn, a nationally reputed "intramural guru" and an inductee in the Intramural Hall of Fame, the University of Louisville has been quite successful in engaging campus constituents in common pursuits of leisure and recreation.

The preeminence of the metropolitan mission and philosophy also drives a host of institutional policies, programs, and practices designed to meet the needs of a varied student population and to encourage the joint learning opportunities of campus and community. By institutional policy, faculty members are urged to hold office hours at least once a week, underscoring the importance of faculty-student interaction. An extensive Cooperative Education Program dates back to the 1920s and serves to connect, for students from 36 different majors, academic study and professional work experiences in the Louisville area, thereby affording students an opportunity to explore the demands of a chosen career field, to earn money to defray college expenses, and to make themselves more marketable upon graduation. The benefits to the community are obvious in a recent estimate that during one academic year more than 7,800 University of Louisville co-op students earned $15.6 million working for approximately 3,100 employers in Kentucky. The institution also sponsors a range of programs, including the Center for Academic Achievement, the Faculty Mentoring Program, the Directed Academic Study Hours (DASH) Program, and an Adult/Commuter Evening Student Services (ACCESS) Center, to directly serve the learning and involvement needs of a diverse student body. Throughout the administrative structures of the campus is a clear emphasis on service and support, conveying an attitude that the institution cares and that students matter.

Finally, the role of institutional agents at the University of Louisville (e.g., trustees, administrators, faculty, and students) is apparent in shaping the involving characteristics of this institution. President Donald Swain, a self-described "action-oriented chief executive officer," has brought a vision and energy to the institution that has virtually transformed the campus in recent years. Flowers now adorn many areas of the campus; trash is regularly picked up; the campus looks and feels cleaner. New signs and campus maps, visitors' centers, and other inviting markings not only make the campus attractive, but also permit visitors and those less familiar with campus facilities find their way around.

President Swain underscores the university's long-standing commitment to the city of Louisville and understands the honorable, venerable tradition of cultural, economic, and educational integration with the city (he himself serving a term as president of the Louisville Chamber of Commerce). It is Swain's intention, noting the adaptive quality of the institution throughout its history, to make the University of Louisville the most responsive, boldest, and most innovative university in the Kentucky system. Swain and his colleagues are committed to strategic planning and to the inevitable risk-taking posture that often accompanies the goal of being responsive to changing needs.

One illustration of this commitment by Swain is the public/private partnership established between the university and Humana Hospitals. Humana essentially took over the university's teaching hospital which treats many indigent patients. Since the partnership was consummated, an annual loss of $4 to $5 million has blossomed into a revenue-sharing arrangement, with the university's portion reaching about $1.5 million per year. President Swain acknowledges the difficulty of getting students involved in the campus, many of whom are part time and have other pressing commitments, but he also acknowledges the importance of out-of-class experiences to realizing the metropolitan mission of the institution. Swain is committed to a responsive service-oriented future for the institution. He often asks his staff to put on their "university hats" when making decisions, emphasizing the need to overcome petty insecurities and turf protection in order to plan with the best interest of the university and its constituents in mind.

Other significant institutional agents, in the context of the University of Louisville, include: trustees who, through moral and financial support, have committed themselves to improving the quality of campus life (including a $5,000 annual award to a faculty member who contributes the most to campus life); exceptional student affairs staff members who remain professionally involved and who enjoy the respect of faculty and other administrators; faculty who are open and supportive of the diverse types of students on campus, do considerable advising, and are viewed as approachable and accessible by most students; and students who are willing to assume the responsibilities of an elected position to the Board of Trustees and to spend inordinate amounts of time (especially for a commuter campus) organizing a variety of programs and opportunities for fellow campus participants.

The Role of Student Affairs

The role of the Division of Student Affairs has been an integral one, over the past 20 years, in transforming the University of Louisville into the premier metropolitan institution it is today. Primarily through strong creative leadership at the highest levels of the division, a clear emphasis on responsive and caring service and provision of numerous organizational opportunities and roles, student affairs has contributed significantly to creating a challenging and hospitable learning environment on the University of Louisville campus, both in and outside the classroom.

Vision and Leadership

With the inclusion of the University of Louisville in the Kentucky statewide system of higher education, and in response to recommendations of the Southern Regional Education Board, the institution increased its commitment to the student affairs division. Prior to 1970 only a handful of student affairs staff were working on campus; thus the division itself is relatively young compared to counterpart units on many residential campuses. In general, the University of Louisville student affairs professionals enjoy the respect of faculty and other administrators. A good number of the staff are natives of the city and/or graduates of the institution. Loyalty to and pride in the institution are quite apparent among them, as are satisfaction with and dedication to their work. In addition, the university's metropolitan mission is fully understood and embraced by the staff, a posture that is also reflected (and recently endorsed by faculty and administration) in their student affairs graduate preparation program at the institution.

Leadership in the student affairs division has been exceptional. Both the current vice president, Dennis Golden, and his predecessor, Edward Hammond, have enjoyed national visibility among their peers and both have a knack for attracting and motivating exceptional staff. Hammond served as the first vice president of the Division of Student Affairs, employing an entrepreneurial style to accumulate resources and additional staff for the division. Under his leadership, student affairs emerged as a robust, responsive unit with many dedicated, talented staff.

Under the current vice president's leadership, emphasis is being placed on increased coordination and collaboration between student affairs and academic affairs and on enhancing the minority student experience at the university. Symbolic of the caring, supportive attitude of the student affairs staff under Golden's direction is the phrase,

"Take 'em to raise." In that phrase is a Kentuckian's commitment to take someone in and treat them as their own — offering support, encouragement, and respect so they can attain their potential. Such a notion seems to appropriately describe the vision of the student affairs staff at the University of Louisville.

Welcoming Students to Campus

One of the principal mechanisms an involving college uses to teach new students about the institution and to create a welcoming, human-scale experience is the frontloading of resources. The University of Louisville has established several key programs employing this strategy, including the TLC Program and the Freshman Orientation Course. The TLC (Tender Loving Care) Program was initiated several years ago in response to a perceived retention crisis on campus. The program was the brainchild of the chair of the Board of Trustees at that time, George Fischer. The TLC Program creates a welcoming, friendly atmosphere and enhances student-faculty interaction outside the classroom. It recognizes that a responsive attitude on the part of faculty and staff, which says "we care" and "you matter," is important to an overall retention effort. In addition, an important goal of the TLC program included increased communication with new students throughout the first year. Thus various interventions were instituted such as Welcome Stations and Welcome Houses (information centers located around the campus that are staffed by student volunteers and administrative staff members and designed to offer friendly assistance to newcomers in the beginning of the year to quickly acclimate them to the campus), Cardinal Feet (cardinal footprints with the TLC logo painted on the sidewalks directing students to various important destinations around campus), and Cardinalgrams (a TLC newsletter delivered to each student at various times each semester, welcoming them to campus and providing information as well as support and encouragement — especially during finals week).

Other TLC initiatives include institutional courtesies like exam posts during the year where coffee and cookies are available to students as they move from one location to another, and various special events for first-year students, such as Freshman Night at the homecoming football game and pizza parties at the Red Barn. Faculty can also obtain funds (up to $200) from the TLC resources to support interaction with students outside the classroom. For example, one faculty member invited students to her home for piano juries, allowing students to practice in front of peers and to get to know each other — representing a different approach in the program where, by nature, much of the instruction is individualized rather than group-oriented. Another faculty member had a "bring your own rock party" wherein students from the physical sciences were asked to identify their rock. The Biology Department often uses TLC funds to go to the zoo. In all, the estimated $146,000 spent in various activities related to these initiatives in one recent year has had a positive impact on the retention rate.

The Freshman Orientation Course, an ungraded one-credit hour course, required since the fall of 1989 of all students prior to completion of their 18th hour of credit, is another way in which the University of Louisville frontloads resources to acclimate students to the college experience and campus life. Faculty and staff are matched as co-instructors with upper division students and meet for two 50-minute periods a week with 25 to 30 new undergraduates or transfer students to consider various topics related to career planning, time management, campus life, and opportunities for involvement. Through the use of formal reading materials (e.g., *Becoming a Master Student*) and journal entries in response to a variety of prompter phrases (e.g., "I enjoy coming to this class because..." or "It's frightening to me when..."), students are encouraged to actively reflect upon their experience at the institution and to seek resources to meet their needs.

This semester-long course functions in addition to seven two-day orientation programs offered during the summer for traditional-age, first-year students and a series of post-admission newsletters and postcards. Through all of these frontloading initiatives the University of Louisville is very successful in communicating its mission and philosophy, as well as its many resources, that it aims to be an inviting and friendly place to learn, and that it is sincerely interested in the goals, aspirations, and lives of the students it serves. All of this stands in perhaps sharp contrast to the typical conditions of modern, complex urban life where impersonal confrontation is more often the rule and response to individual differences usually unexpected. In many ways the university is successful in suspending the rules of urban life to create an attractive and personable institutional environment.

Getting Students Involved

With the majority of students living off campus (about 90 percent), getting students involved in many activities is a challenge for the University of Louisville staff. Yet, a tradition of organizational involvement has clearly emerged over the past 20 years at the institution, primarily through the efforts of students and staff associated with the Red Barn and the Student Activities Center (SAC).

Perhaps in defiance of the cycles of decay and renaissance of most cities the size of Louisville, the large, concrete-floored, brick warehouse structure, known simply as the "Red Barn" (the former Caldwell Tank Factory) has given rise to a relatively brief (about 20 years) but powerful history of involvement that is exemplary among institutions of this type. Located on the edge of the Belknap campus, the Red Barn was saved from demolition, after standing vacant for a year, by several industrious students and the late Woodrow Stickler, then president of the institution. It was thought to be a great place for parties since it was already "so run down and it couldn't be messed-up any further" (claims the *Belknap Campus Walking Tour Handbook*). Supported by a $500,000 bond issue, the facility was renovated in 1979 to conform to various safety codes and remains intact, adjacent to the new SAC building.

The Red Barn recently celebrated its 20th anniversary with a full range of special activities. The hallmark of its successes over these past two decades has been its encouragement of student participation in the decision-making process. Students are encouraged to take responsibility, with minimal supervision, to design programs and activities which are, on occasion, quite innovative. Staff members demonstrate an obvious caring attitude and communicate to students that they are trusted to try new things. Students themselves do a lot of recruitment for various activities and for additional staff and programs, and such involvement is not limited to traditional-age students. Thus, in 20 years, over 10,000 Red Barn programs and activities, under the auspices of the Student Activities Board, have recorded a total attendance in excess of one million admissions, have generated more than $2 million revenue, and through hundreds of charitable benefits with other student organizations and interested parties, have contributed over $30,000 to various causes.

The Red Barn attracts students of various backgrounds and ages and is one of the more distinctive and well-known facilities on the campus due to the high-quality activities promoted there and communicated to the campus community through the Red Barn calendar each semester. Many young people (high school age and older) come from around town to congregate and meet on the campus during the evening. The university is becoming known as a fun place to be, largely because of Red Barn programming. The level of energy and commitment on the part of the students and staff associated with the Red Barn is impressive, particularly with regard to the quality of leadership in social and recreational opportunities this small staff provides for the University of Louisville community. Perhaps no better testament to the efficacy of this program over the years can be found in the fact that, in 1985, the Red Barn Alumni Association was established to raise scholarship funds, purchase equipment for the Red Barn, and to encourage and foster the interaction of alumni who have been associated with the Red Barn. This association now has a member on the University of Louisville Alumni Board and thus far has raised over $10,000.

The traditions of information sharing and decision-making responsibility nurtured through the Student Activities Board were carried forward with the completion of the new Student Activities Center in 1990. With the participation and input of the Student Activities Center Advisory Board (SACAB), whose membership includes five students, five staff and/or administrators, two faculty, one alumnus, and the director of the Student Activities Center, the center offers to the University of Louisville community a 253,000 square-foot, state-of-the-art facility for a wide range of involvement opportunities, including: an art gallery, information center, ticket services, rathskeller, student lounge, automatic teller machines, 216-seat theater, bookstore, cafeteria, intramural and recreational sports facilities — eight racquetball courts and four basketball courts, athletic training and coaching offices and areas, a 1,053-seat varsity gymnasium and locker facilities, leisure services, 10 student organization offices and storage areas, 3 meeting rooms, and a multipurpose area which can be divided or used as one large room. The center also houses offices for Student Activities Center administration (i.e., the director and two associate directors, one for operations and facilities and the other for programs), Student Activities Board, and student government, all of which share a common reception area and conference room, an architectural feature purposely designed to continue the tradition of interaction and participatory decision making established during the emergence of the Red Barn program.

In addition, this building provides offices for the student development area, including the associate vice president for student development, athletic academic services, career planning, special student services, resource library, and the student life area, including the assistant vice president for student life, greek affairs, legal services, and student life programs. Financing of the $24 million facility will come from a $15 per student/per semester building fee, assessed for 25 years; a contribution of $3.1 million from the Athletic Association; and the balance from the Commonwealth of Kentucky through the sale of bonds.

Responding to Individual Differences

Typical of most metropolitan institutions, the University of Louisville serves a student body with a variety of needs. From traditional-age commuter and residential students, returning adult learners, and students from diverse cultural/ethnic backgrounds to those who are less prepared for the demands of college academics and those who excel at the challenges of graduate and professional preparation, the university is accustomed to responding to various groups and to engaging their participation in a rich array of program, traditions, and services. The presence of multiple subcommunities on campus is acknowledged and supported through such programs and services as the Center for Academic Achievement, Office of Minority Services (OMS), Adults on Campus (AOC), and Adult/Commuter Evening Student Services Center.

The Center for Academic Achievement was established in 1984 to assist students in developing basic skills and problem-solving techniques. Originally called a "retention center," students suggested the name be changed to more accurately reflect the aspirations and abilities of students. Through the center, students also are encouraged to consider different academic fields and take part in career awareness activities as they become more comfortable in the university environment. Although the center originally emphasized the minority student experience, its programs and services are gradually being opened to all students. Three tracks of programs are supported through the center: financial, tutorial, and faculty mentoring. Tuition remission scholarships are available to qualified students who earn a 3.0 grade point average, as are supplemental aid and work-incentive funds. Tutorial aspects of the program are two-pronged.

Supplemental instruction meets the needs of students enrolled in specific high-risk courses (where 30 percent of students regularly earn a D, F, or withdraw) by providing instructional assistance (e.g., review sessions, discussions about class material, notes, assignments, and exams) before encountering academic difficulty. Supplemental instruction is now available for over 30 different courses. The second tutorial component is the Directed Academic Study Hours (DASH) program where supervised academic study, group and individual tutorials are arranged for individual students. Finally, a faculty mentoring program has been implemented where students are to meet with a faculty mentor ideally four times a semester to get assistance in academic planning, study skills, course selection, and exam preparation. Faculty receive $1,000 per semester for their contribution. In addition, a group of peer advising leaders (PALS), students who have had a faculty mentor and have been successful in the program before, are available to work with the faculty mentoring program. PALS receive an hourly stipend and work about six hours per week. These various programs serve both as a transitional bridge for students by providing them with the academic skills necessary for college-level work and as an early warning system to identify students who are encountering difficulty with academic demands.

The Office of Minority Services (OMS) was organized in July 1986 to actively help students of color adjust to college life. Its purposes include: promoting a welcoming and supportive environment for students; facilitating communication and assisting the efforts of various other student service offices on campus; assisting students in resolving problems, in learning how to participate more fully in university life, and in utilizing available university programs and services; developing and coordinating cultural programs and activities for students, faculty, and staff of color; and providing a minority perspective in policy decisions. A number of enrichment programs sponsored by the OMS reach out to the Louisville community to promote values of education among low-income and first generation college-going youth. Among these are Upward Bound, My Future is Now, the Collegiate Cadet Program, and the Youth Towards Excellence Program. Other programs bear titles indicative of what they attempt to accomplish: INSPIRE (Increasing Student Preparedness and Interest in the Requisites for Engineering), BUILD (Business United in Leadership Development), and INCREASE (Increasing Career Recognition and Enriching Academic Skills for Engineering). In addition, the office coordinates and implements programming on campus as it relates to the African-American experience (e.g., African-American History Month, Martin Luther King, Jr., Lecture, art exhibits, and concerts), publishes *Minority Voices Magazine*, and encourages students to participate in many campus organizations that focus their attention on minority issues, experiences, and concerns (e.g., Black Diamond Choir, Harambee — a black Christian organization, Minority Project Fund of the Student Government Association, Black American Law Student Association, Black Engineers and Technicians Association, Student National Medical Association, Black Science Student Organization, and the Association of Black Students).

The university is attentive to the needs of returning adult learners, as well, through a variety of organizational and program responses. For example, students 60 years of age and older may enroll in degree-granting programs or take courses for other reasons without paying tuition. Over 800 students took advantage of this program during the 1988-89 academic year. Other components of the institution's response are the Adult/Commuter Evening Student Services (ACCESS) Center and the Adults on Campus (AOC) organization, committed to making the college experience for these students more meaningful, to give them a sense of unity and the opportunity to meet and associate with other nontraditional students who share common concerns and problems. Various events are planned on a semester basis, including dining opportunities and participating in other larger campus community events with a built-in peer group of adult learners.

Transitions is another program specifically oriented toward nontraditional students, providing an opportunity for older and commuting students to talk about who they are, what they want from college, and to recommend services and courses that might benefit others. A staff and student childcare service is also available on campus for up to 100 children of ages six weeks to kindergarten, with priority given to students.

The student government also endorses the institution's sensitivity to various student needs through support of the Peer Assistance Center. On a walk-in basis students can get information about various resources on campus or even receive peer advice about academic choices and concerns. In addition, the student senate assumes an advocacy role in lobbying for various campuswide issues such as campus safety and security and the need for better lighting.

Maintaining a Collegiate Core

An important ingredient for involvement at the University of Louisville is found in a small core of students (''collegiates'') who live on the campus, or nearby, who essentially compose the nucleus of the traditional undergraduate student experience there. These are the students who attend football games, take part in active leadership roles in campus activities such as homecoming, and participate regularly in Red Barn activities and Student Activity Center programs. The university is committed to increasing this core and recently added a new six-story, suite arrangement, residence hall (Louisville Hall) to further accommodate the 2,000 students who now call the campus their home. The residence life program thrives in a very supportive professional atmosphere resulting from a recent reorganization, creation of an active Residence Hall Association (RHA) and Student Judicial Board system, and an administrative commitment to upgrading and improving the physical facilities. Area coordinators with master's degrees in student affairs now supervise graduate assistant resident directors, 50 percent of the vending revenues are allocated in support of RHA activities, and "room remission" arrangements have been established for the top four RHA offices — 100 percent for president, 80 percent for vice president, and 60 percent each for secretary/treasurer and publicity chair.

An important feature of the residence hall system is its 35 percent minority composition (in comparison to about 7 percent of the general student population). With the institution's increased emphasis on recruiting students from the outlying areas of Kentucky as well as out of state, a real opportunity is afforded through the residence system to explore various models of the dynamics and politics of human differences in a way that is unique to the larger urban community where, for the most part, housing remains fairly well segregated by history and access.

Campus Events and Traditions

Perhaps one of the more difficult tasks facing student affairs administrators on urban commuter campuses, especially those involved in the areas of student activities and organizations, is the maintenance of traditions and events. These are aspects of the campus culture that serve to bind students quickly to the institution and that form the basis of a common participatory experience. Yet without the supportive and ready presence of a significant residential population, consistency and continuity is often difficult. Nevertheless, the University of Louisville is modestly successful in supporting several major events that qualify as campus traditions. In addition to many of the Red Barn and Student Activity Center events scheduled from year to year, Town and Gown Week, which underscores the connection with the city of Louisville, and homecoming are perhaps the two most prominent campuswide traditional events. Although homecoming has had its ups and downs in the past few years, and the traditional parade was just recently replaced by a very successful banner contest, the future may bode better times for this event with the growing successes of the intercollegiate football program. The rejuvenation and "feel" of campus pride that has accompanied the opening of the new Student Activities Center may also emerge as an important factor in revitalizing some of these traditional symbols of collegiate culture.

The university hosts 18 national fraternities and 9 national sororities in houses adjacent to the campus and the core of students associated with these groups continue to support several campus traditions. The most prominent of these is the annual Frieburger Sing, in memory of Agnes Moore Frieburger who served on the music faculty from 1932 to 1939 and who established a significant reputation for her enthusiastic instruction in music. In response to the new understanding and deeper appreciation of music gained in the tradition of her classroom, students return the gift to the campus in the form of their voices. Although sustained primarily by the greek organization students on campus, other groups are now getting involved in this event in recent years. The alumni are particularly interested in continuing to revitalize this tradition.

Other events of campus culture and tradition have been organized over the years around the university's various professional schools and programs. Some of them are designed to introduce prospective high school students in the metropolitan area to the challenges and programs of a particular profession or field, such as the annual Engineers Day when the Speed Scientific School invites local students to tour the campus over a Saturday-Sunday weekend and challenges them to build the best bridge out of balsa wood or to construct a protective egg cage that must stand the test of a freefall from a predetermined height. Other events sponsored by several other professional schools and organizations on campus simply fulfill the need for students to gather together to enjoy themselves and to celebrate the completion of another year. These traditions include the Law School Ball, the Cadaver Ball (the Medical School), the Dental School Gong Show, and the ROTC Ball.

The University of Louisville understands the importance of the traditions and events that engender a cohesive bonding to the institution and among student groups, and the administration has taken steps recently to enhance and to strengthen some of these events. The vice president for alumni and development is now in charge of homecoming planning and expects to increase the visibility of this tradition through the use of certain mechanisms to involve greater numbers of students and alumni. Among these is the recent formation of SOAR (Student Organization for Alumni Relations), an organization which has become involved in sponsoring a homecoming picnic and pep rally (complete with a Howard Schnellenberg "Look-Alike" contest), and delivers birthday cakes to students upon subscription of a parent or friend.

Observations and Conclusions

The University of Louisville has made considerable strides in its desire to become "one of the best metropolitan institutions in the United States" and a substantial number of mechanisms are in place to involve students in meaningful ways that complement the institution's educational mission. Indeed, metropolitan campuses such as this must have many mechanisms if students are to become aware of, and take advantage of, the variety of out-of-class learning opportunities available both on campus and in the city itself. The student affairs division contributes to those mechanisms principally through sensitizing the institution to the diverse needs that are present, responding to those needs with an array of opportunity-rich programs and structures, and creating a campus climate that offers an attractive and personalized experience for individuals who are perhaps accustomed to, or have come to expect, a much harsher reality of urban life.

The symbiotic, town-gown relationship between the university and the city of Louisville has not been without its costs, though, both to the institution and to the metropolitan community. As one city alderman noted, "When the university makes a decision, it makes its mark on the city, good or bad." For example, the recent NCAA national championship in basketball brought a good deal of positive visibility to the Louisville community; it was a windfall public relations event that jelled a reinvigorated sense of spirit and pride among residents of this Ohio River community. On the other hand, the university's recent decision to accept an invitation to the 1991 Fiesta Bowl in Tempe, Arizona, where voters recently rejected a statewide referendum to observe a

88

Martin Luther King, Jr., holiday, has raised considerable controversy and has resulted in much political posturing both on the campus and in the city. There are even some concerns that this decision may have cost the community dollars, in terms of lost convention revenues from several black organizations which the city has been working very hard to attract.

Embracing the Louisville community as both the source and the recipient of the institution's mission has left the university vulnerable to the agenda of the community. In fact, the nature of such institutions often lends them as convenient forums or highly visible and powerful stages upon which players in a variety of social and community controversies can deliver their lines. Nevertheless, the university is clearly a better educational institution because of the rich array of resources available in the Louisville community; and the city of Louisville is clearly a better community because of the presence of the university.

In conclusion, this is an institution that has not hesitated to accept the challenges of its metropolitan mission and with it the responsibility to attend to an incredibly diverse set of needs. Unlike other involving colleges presented in this volume, the University of Louisville thrives on being "all things to all people" and responds well to meeting the complex needs of an emerging urban center. The student affairs staff is a significant partner in accomplishing that mission. For example, several strategic thrusts identified by the institution for the next few years, in that respect, include managing the balance between graduate and undergraduate enrollments, serving a growing population of at-risk students, increasing racial and ethnic diversity, and enhancing the quality of campus life — all tasks that have engaged the student affairs division as a critical force in shaping the various institutional processes that will make it all happen.

Commentary

The University of Louisville Case
Carmen Witt

Student affairs professionals at metropolitan universities generally face challenges different in nature and intensity from those encountered at institutions that attract primarily traditional-age students. At most metropolitan schools, diversity abounds — in the expectations and needs of students, their cultural backgrounds, their preparation for learning, economic status, and age. Various enrollment patterns (e.g., more part-time students, more students stopping out for a term or more) coexist and produce discontinuity in the student body. Thus, it is probably more appropriate to derive the year label for a class of students from the date of entry rather than graduation. For many metropolitan students their time on campus is limited and, among life's endeavors, often their academic pursuits are not preeminent. The University of Louisville has recognized and tackled these challenges well and in many respects has been successful in implementing the principles that distinguish involving colleges.

Academic Links

A Perspective on Student Affairs (NASPA, 1987) asserts that the academic enterprise should be paramount. Metropolitan universities exemplify this belief to a high degree. Students on these campuses seek academic experiences primarily, if not exclusively. To include the greatest number of urban students, opportunities for involvement must be concentrated in academic settings or closely linked to academic activities. The University of Louisville's cooperative education program is an outstanding example of meaningful involvement that complements academic work. Involving nearly 8,000 students in 36 major fields, this program, through taking students beyond the campus, is an invaluable learning opportunity, one not available without concurrent enrollment in the university. As such, it is a model from which much can be learned by other metropolitan institutions. Further, it provides an excellent opportunity for collaboration between academic affairs and student affairs, enabling units such as career planning and financial aid to create partnerships with academic departments. Part-time employment, particularly when it is on campus, is a potent mechanism for involvement at metropolitan institutions. In fact, the time limitations and job necessity common to nontraditional students may make this the only realistic avenue for nonacademic college connections.

Involvement with faculty beyond the classroom is another key ingredient for learning enhancement. Perhaps because of low expectations, metropolitan school students are especially gratified when faculty know them personally. Students believe these contacts add significantly to the overall value of their education. Even with student initiative, however, widespread personal interaction may be more difficult to achieve on large urban campuses due to the self-selection of faculty at such institutions. Faculty seeking positions at metropolitan universities may prefer the privacy and role separation that large settings offer and be more reluctant to make their faculty role an all-encompassing one. The University of Louisville places a value on faculty-student interactions and mandates or facilitates them in a variety of ways. The policy calling for regular office hours, the $200 grants to fund social activities with students, the $5,000 annual award from the trustees for contributions to campus life, and the faculty mentoring program for which faculty are paid leave little doubt that the campus esteems faculty committed to student learning and personal development in as well as out of class. Fostering such exchanges is an important role for student affairs at other metropolitan universities as well, one ripe for joint ventures with academic units. While a $5,000 prize from the trustees may be out of reach for many campuses, other incentives and facilitating steps are possible. These can range from letters of thanks copied to deans and department chairs, to funding of assistants and professional travel as rewards for faculty involvement in student life. Faculty can relate as mentors and socially as is true at the University of Louisville and they can contribute in many other ways. Among the options is service as an organization advisor, dinner guest, or orientation presenter.

Facilities Promote Community

Without campus residences or nearby apartments to serve as home base, commuting students remain detached from the campus unless the institution takes steps to create an inviting atmosphere and facilities that promote the gathering of large and small groups. Too often at metropolitan institutions the "service station" model has dominated, leading to a focus on conveniences like parking, transportation, lockers, and fast food units. While important, these are insufficient for fostering student learning. In addition, facilities that give students a sense of belonging and promote meaningful interaction need emphasis. The University of Louisville has made such facilities a priority and has met with significant success as a result. The Red Barn, an enduring campus tradition in addition to being valuable program space, and the new Student Activities Center work together to increase the interaction of students with the campus and with one another. A large variety of events have drawn university and community participation and the new activity center broadens the scope of activities that can be scheduled.

Even though the Red Barn attracts many high school students to its activities, it appears serious problems have been avoided. Most metropolitan universities that have attempted such programs have had to curtail, if not discontinue, them. Too often high school students drawn to such events are not those whom the campus would like to enroll in the future, and their presence has caused university students to stay away. In some cases campus safety has been compromised. The University of Louisville's success with these programs is commendable but may be unique and not transferable to other metropolitan institutions.

It is not apparent from the description in this chapter whether the Student Activities Center includes smaller spaces for subgroups of students other than offices for a handful of student organizations. Just as students create dirt paths across lawns forcing diagonal sidewalks to follow, students appropriate spaces in buildings to congregate with those of mutual interest. Corners of lounges or dining areas, even corridors, become well-known meeting places for certain groups. Campuses need to acknowledge these needs for territoriality and allocate space for various subcommunities whether they are comprised of adults, commuters, international students, or students of color. While such spaces are necessary, locating them within a larger complex such as the Student Activities Center maintains a proper balance between integration and seclusion. Metropolitan universities would do well to provide headquarters for a significant number of student organizations either in the student center or an academic building if the group is so affiliated. Student-run clubs can be powerful instruments for connecting students if the groups are supported with facilities, funds, and programming assistance.

The University of Louisville's decision to locate lounges in academic buildings for socialization among students and with faculty is a strategy worthy of note and replication elsewhere. For those students who rarely venture beyond the locale of their classes and the library, expanded involvement can be enhanced through the availability of such spaces. Student affairs personnel on urban campuses should be persistent advocates for campus planning that encompasses such components.

Commitment to New Students

Most impressive among the array of excellent programs developed by student affairs at the University of Louisville is its extensive programming for new students. The companion TLC Program and freshman orientation course constitute a superb means of achieving social integration and facilitating academic success. The summer portion increases the comfort level of entering freshmen and provides an understanding of campus expectations and opportunities. The fall information component (booths and newsletters) provides quick access to information and assistance when needed. In the orientation course students learn survival skills and ways of using campus resources. Due to disproportionately large numbers of first generation students, "frontloading" as done by the University of Louisville is essential. The commitment of resources to both components of their program is sizable and may be beyond the reach of many campuses. Despite lesser resources elsewhere, the principles inherent in targeting resources to newcomers (Kuh et al., 1991) should guide the planning of programs for new students at other metropolitan institutions.

There is a tendency to view nontraditional students as disadvantaged when compared to students with more typical enrollment patterns. While the characteristics of many nontraditional students (e.g., first generation, low income, multiple commitments) represent hurdles to reaching their educational goals, such students are sometimes advantaged over their more traditional counterparts. For many metropolitan university students, college entry is not necessarily accompanied by social isolation and disruption of other connections which are supportive and satisfying. They are not cut off from family support, long-time friends, and jobs at which they excel, all of which can counterbalance rocky times in academe.

Students attending residential institutions may need involvement to compensate for some of the losses not suffered by students who stay at home and attend a metropolitan university. Yet to the degree involvement correlates with learning (the more involvement with the campus, the more learning takes place) (Pascarella & Terenzini, 1991), achieving involvement with nontraditional students remains important. Orientation programs for new students must recognize the differences in the types of involvement best suited for traditional and nontraditional students.

Communication is Key

The multiple strategies employed at the University of Louisville demonstrate that urban universities must work hard at communicating with students and commit considerable resources to the task. Lack of knowledge concerning opportunities is an explanation often given by students who are bystanders rather than participants. The methods common to most institutions (e.g., bulletin boards, campus newspapers, dining table notices, literature racks) fall short on campuses where students are not in residence and have limited exposure. The University of Louisville's use of periodic newsletter delivery for new students, "Welcome Stations" at the beginning of the year, and information tables rotated among classroom buildings during evening hours and staffed by the ACCESS Center are effective ways to transmit information and convey the desire to help solve problems. The university subscribes to the principle that "It's better to take the information to the students rather than make them search it out" — a maxim worth echoing elsewhere.

Multiculturalism and the Mainstream

The University of Louisville has resisted the temptation to treat its students as a homogeneous group with uniform, albeit unconventional, needs. Metropolitan universities enroll significant numbers of traditional students, often more than most institutions in their states. Responsiveness to emerging populations does not allow metropolitan universities to neglect their corps of traditional students. At the University of Louisville, a new residence hall, the variety of campus events taking place in the Red Barn and the Student Activities Center, and the maintenance of traditions sustained by fraternities and sororities reflect a strong commitment to the "collegiate core." Especially noteworthy in the residential life program is the housing of 700 minority students comprising 35 percent of the total residential population. The university obviously recognizes the positive relationship between living on campus and retention. Moreover, residential life at the university simulates life in the next century when a third of the nation will be people of color. All of the students with this campus experience will be better prepared to live and work in a pluralistic society. Multicultural programs which achieve interaction among diverse populations are essential on any urban campus.

With a goal of helping minority students "participate more fully in university life," the Office of Minority Services (OMS) is the linchpin of Louisville's efforts to serve the ethnic minorities who represent 12 percent of the student body. There are contrary views concerning merged minority centers versus units for individual ethnic groups as well as differences about the use of the term "minority," especially on campuses where minorities are the majority. Nonetheless, metropolitan universities must give priority to enrolling and retaining underrepresented groups, especially people of color. At the University of Louisville the campus commitment is clear and the high priority evident. Throughout the league of metropolitan universities student affairs must be a key player in initiatives to enhance diversity.

94

Serving Adults

The University of Louisville has recognized that helping adults achieve a successful transition into the university and facilitating peer support after entry are the most important ways that a university can serve adult learners. The ACCESS Center and the Adults On Campus (AOC) student group are the cornerstones of the Louisville adult learner support program. Located in a classroom building, the ACCESS Center is a warm hospitable environment and provides specialized counseling and orientation to entering adults. Outreach is accomplished through various publications and by rotating outstations in academic buildings. Regardless of resources, all metropolitan campuses can mimic the University of Louisville and serve adults by easing transitions and enabling peer contact.

Effective Leadership

It is always desirable for a president and student affairs chief to be committed to common goals and to achieve a professional rapport that is mutually reinforcing. The pivotal role of academics on urban campuses rules out a supplemental or ancillary role for student affairs and demands full partnership if extensive student involvement is to be achieved. Student affairs at the University of Louisville has attained an enviable level of faculty and administrative respect and support, and has had remarkable success in building a strong division on a solid base.

As was true for many metropolitan universities, Louisville's enrollment burgeoned 20 years ago at the time increased public funding for higher education began its initial slide. It is particularly noteworthy that the institution made its strong commitment to student affairs at a time when the competition for resources must have been extremely keen. The personnel put in place at that time lived up to and exceeded expectations thus maintaining the momentum of increased student development programming. Over time, institutional goals and student development goals have converged and the values embraced by student affairs parallel those of the campus.

The talented and dedicated student affairs staff, experts in their field, are able to extract the maximum educational benefit from each contact students have with the campus. The phrase *teachable moment* has been used in this volume as a way of expressing the notion that all the time students spend on campus is a learning opportunity. For student affairs professionals at metropolitan institutions, it is an apt metaphor, conveying the essence of their work as educators. For urban students, moments on campus are fewer in number and often unconnected. There can be no common set of beginning points, developmental programs, and outcome measures as many student development theories assume. Thus, each encounter with any segment of the campus needs to be exploited for its full learning potential. The student affairs professionals at the University of Louisville perform well as educators in this context. Metropolitan university professionals everywhere can follow this lead and remain especially alert to opportunities to teach and help students develop, however fleeting and short lived those opportunities may be.

Summary

Student affairs at the University of Louisville has developed numerous programs worthy of replication or adaptation at other metropolitan universities. Most exemplary are the orientation course and summer programs for new freshmen, superb facilities for campus interaction, the expertise and enthusiasm of professionals, and special initiatives for involving diverse populations.

Kudos to the University of Louisville for these fine examples of good practice.

Chapter Six

Where Achievement is the Rule
The Case of Xavier University of Louisiana

Rosalind E. Andreas

A recent visitor to Xavier University of Louisiana wrote that he had witnessed "a miracle in action . . . a miracle of doing what popular wisdom says cannot be done . . . [one] that bucks the national trend in higher education. However, most impressive is the fact that the miracle does not deal with objects, but with the transformation of human attitudes, self-perceptions and personal achievement" (Boschmann, 1990).

Xavier graduates have distinguished themselves in the sciences, education, and government service. Among them are the first black mayor of New Orleans, the first black to hold a seat on the New York Stock Exchange, the first woman president of the American Pharmaceutical Association, and educator George McKenna. Xavier graduates' accomplishments are all the more remarkable given that many students come from disadvantaged educational backgrounds and must overcome significant odds to succeed academically.

Characteristics of Involving Colleges Common to Xavier

Xavier University is the only black, Catholic university in the Western Hemisphere. As we shall see, this distinctive characteristic influences virtually all aspects of university life, including its mission and philosophy, campus environment, culture, policies and practices, and faculty, staff, and student behavior.

Mission and Philosophy

The story of Xavier's founding by Mother Katharine Drexel provides an excellent example of how an institution's mission fosters involvement in educationally purposeful out-of-class activities. The daughter of a banker whose family taught the values of stewardship, Mother Katharine was appalled at the oppression of American blacks and Indians, so much so that she considered entering a closed order. Instead, she founded the Sisters of the Blessed Sacrament and migrated to New Orleans at the request of the local Catholic archbishop. Upon her arrival in New Orleans, she discovered limited higher educational opportunities for black youth in the area because they were being denied admission to local colleges and universities. In an audience with the Pope, she beseeched him to send missionaries to these oppressed groups in the United States. According to the story, the Pope asked her why she did not do that herself.

Xavier University opened in 1915 with a college preparatory school and a normal school two years later. The College of Arts and Sciences was established in 1925. The College of Pharmacy, added in 1927, is the only one in the nation at a historically black institution and is often described as a centerpiece for major programs of the university.

Enrollment increased rapidly and in 1929 Mother Katharine obtained land near Washington and Carrollton avenues for the campus. In 1932 the college division moved into the Gothic administrative/academic building that has become a landmark for New Orleans. The graduate school, added a year later, currently awards degrees in educational administration, guidance and counseling, curriculum and instruction, and theology. Now sandwiched between an interstate and a canal, Xavier University serves as a beacon to the blighted urban neighborhood in which its faculty and students work to "bring others less fortunate along" and prepares black professionals in a tradition of excellence.

Xavier's educational purposes are firmly rooted in and reinforce its black and Catholic heritages. Xavier's catalog states that its mission is to provide each student with a "liberal and professional educational experience in a pluralistic environment for the ultimate purpose of helping to create a more just and humane society." The 1988 yearbook quotes Vice President for Development Clarence Jupiter: "Xavier is a no nonsense school. You take what you have, do the best with it, and don't make any excuses." This theme was repeated in senior interviews; one student related that no matter what obstacles he personally faced, no one at Xavier University would allow him to use such obstacles as an excuse for not achieving his academic goals.

Xavier University seeks students who rank in the top 50 percent of their class or who score 16 on the ACT or 700 on the SAT. Sister Rosemarie Kleinhaus, vice president for academic affairs, tells stories of individual students, admitted below admissions standards who work vigorously with untold support to correct poor study and learning habits. Equally important, Xavier faculty believe their students can achieve.

Particular emphasis is placed on service to the black community. The student body president told us that the purpose of knowledge is to help those less fortunate; he went on to tell of his plans to attend medical school and open a clinic in rural Mississippi. The director of volunteer programs stated that everyone, "from the President on down," emphasizes the service mission of the university. President Norman Francis talked about "administering in the Catholic way — what is right and just is what we should be doing . . . A society is judged by how it treats its young and its old. If we are true to our mission, then they (the students) will be motivated to be concerned."

Students are keenly aware of the institution's mission; they know Xavier's history and understand the obligation to serve. Trustee Randolph, a Xavier graduate, describes with pride how students awaken intellectually as a result of attending the university and about her own efforts to organize graduates to tutor in the middle schools and high schools to keep black youth in school and "bring them along." Xavier's distinctive mission and philosophy shape shared values and purposes that permeate campus environments, culture, policies and practice, and socialization of new students and faculty.

Campus Environments

Winston Churchill once said that we shape our buildings and afterwards our buildings shape us. Xavier University emphasizes academic achievement and excellence through "overcoming personal odds" and "bringing others along." Thus, it is probably not surprising that decisions about Xavier's facilities have been driven by the push for academic excellence. The major campus buildings are the pharmacy building and the Norman Francis Sciences Building. Moreover, those academic buildings are the sites for much of the interaction between students and faculty, be it around classroom, laboratory, research, or student organization matters.

The Xavier educational experience is linked economically and programmatically with the political, educational, and religious communities of New Orleans (the Pope appeared on campus during his visit to the United States). In part, this is because Xavier is, in some ways, a commuter institution. Two-thirds of the students commute to campus each day; the remainder live on campus. About half of the students become involved in out-of-class activities during the course of the day. As with other institutions with a large number of commuting students, it is a challenge to attract students to the campus at night. Hence Xavier University has developed ways to use the urban setting to educational advantage. In this sense, Xavier University is very much a part of New Orleans.

Xavier University is a member of Campus Compact and COOL (Campus Outreach Opportunity League). Under the auspices of campus ministry, students are engaged in a variety of service activities. As a part of class requirements, some students study problems in nearby neighborhoods, tutor black youth, join the community's battle against drugs, and conduct voter registration. Students reach out into the arts community with faculty to do exhibits or perform, participate in internships at City Hall, hold off-campus jobs located by the work-study coordinator, and present research findings with faculty at professional meetings. Several students served as reporters at the 1988 Republican National Convention.

While its mission and educational purposes connect the university to the urban neighborhood beyond the canal and the freeway, Xavier's Gothic architecture and Catholic symbols indicate that the campus is also "a place apart" from the rest of New Orleans.

Campus Culture

Stories about Xavier's founding by Mother Katharine Drexel permeate the institutional culture. New students, parents, faculty, and visitors are greeted by pictures of Mother Katharine in all campus buildings. Mother Katharine's saga is that persons who face overwhelming odds can excel if they are provided educational opportunity. Today, this saga is played out in many forms and forums. Celebration of religious holidays, the continuing presence of sisters (even though the order is waning), and an active campus ministry program keep the Catholic mission alive.

By retelling Mother Katharine's story and the circumstances surrounding the university's founding, the annual Founders Day Convocation affirms the institution's mission for all present — faculty, staff, students, trustees, and others. During this ceremony, outstanding teaching and student scholarship are recognized, new student and faculty leaders are commissioned to lead justly, first-year students are welcomed, seniors are challenged to prepare for their final year, and service awards are given to faculty and staff. The president relates the meaning of Mother Katharine's life to circumstances of the present day, and calls on all in the community to create a just and humane society. The tradition powerfully links the founding with mission which reaffirms the purpose of student and faculty effort and involvement.

Ann Harvey, dean of student services, described Xavier University as having a strong family atmosphere. The student newspaper, *Xavier Herald*, also referred to the university community as a "family." Indeed, the family analogy came up repeatedly in conversations with other division staff, students, the president, and the vice president for academic affairs.

Sister Rosemarie Kleinhaus spoke of the importance of using strict "standards with sympathy" and "understanding" to guide and motivate students. President Frances stated there was always someone willing to talk with you here. The ethic of care was repeated throughout the interviews. "Faculty care about us," the newspaper editor stated; "Professors take time for us" reported another student. Student affairs staff described the faculty as "dedicated caring professionals who push students." One of the trustees described "a sense of belonging to a caring community." One student even noted that when graduates return to the New Orleans area, "they leave their kids on campus," implying that "the Xavier family" cares for them too.

Students described several distinct subcultures: "The leaders, the immature, those only into academics, and those who have to work too much." Some of the students in the greek system tended to make that their primary affiliation and represent a distinct subculture. Yet students describe a sense of teamwork among themselves. Students are willing to help each other and — above all — are "not cut throat." During one of our visits, three students saw each other for the first time that semester outside the career placement office. They could not contain their exuberance, and actually were quite noisy. The appearance of a sister in attire approaching immediately had a quieting influence on the students' decorum!

As with other involving colleges, language plays an important role in shaping behavior. Last names and titles are used conscientiously. This practice affirms the value of historically black institutions to recognize those who have gone before and achieved despite the odds. The titles "Doctor," "President," and "Sister" acknowledge achievement and status which is accorded as a result of effort and accomplishment. The message is clear: Although everyone in the institution is deserving of respect, one earns respect through hard work.

Policies and Practices

Xavier's policies and practices are, by and large, consistent with its mission. Higher education institutions that engage their students tend to use effective anticipatory socialization practices and policies from the time a prospective student first indicates interest through matriculation. Examples abound of anticipatory socialization, a process by which newcomers become familiar with the values, attitudes, norms, knowledge, and skills needed to function acceptably in a new environment (Bragg, 1976). Consider University 1010, a year-long orientation class, during which students learn in more detail about Xavier's history and traditions and how to use the broad array of support services which will help them succeed there. At Xavier University, anticipatory socialization experiences even begin prior to matriculation.

One student stated that when you enter Xavier, you need "a crutch of study skills." Instead of lamenting that their students are not as well prepared as they might hope, Xavier faculty and staff members have developed structured sequential experiences that are "ladders for success." The faculty work as partners with middle school and high school teachers, as well as counselors in the predominantly black schools in New Orleans, designing structured, sequential programs to prepare students of all backgrounds to succeed. MathSTAR, ChemSTAR, BioSTAR, SOAR1, SOAR2, and Super Scholar are summer programs that have received national attention. These programs emphasize principles of analytic reasoning and problem solving. Other mission-driven practices are reflected in faculty working in the black community to keep students at risk of dropping out interested, engaged, intellectually alert, and aware of their ability and potential. In essence, faculty nurture their pool of prospective students by acquainting them with Xavier's expectations and preparing them to be successful academically and socially in college.

Other examples of intentionally created ladders for success — or, in President Francis' words, "leaving nothing to chance" — are found in the strict rules and regulations that govern use of student services and formulation of out-of class activities. Some of these will be discussed later.

Xavier University also attends to the socialization of parents. Even at orientation, the president begins talking with parents about life after college — graduate and professional training. He encourages parents to nurture, push, and encourage their sons and daughters to aim high, to excel; he knows that Xavier's policies and practices will build students' self-esteem and show them the way to achievement. Integral to Xavier's ladder of success is parent participation in, for example, the summer programs. Parents are recognized in opening ceremonies during which some receive certificates and commendations for providing opportunities for their sons and daughters to achieve by arranging carpools and making sacrifices to allow their children to participate (Boschmann, 1990).

Xavier University targets resources to new students buttressed by personal support and nurturance. New students are surrounded by faculty, staff, and students who build a positive atmosphere for success. Many of the best instructors are intentionally assigned to the early courses. Faculty routinely prepare course supplements and note-taking tips. A battery of assessment tests places students in appropriate classes; tutorial and drill sessions are arranged; skill building in vocabulary, interpersonal relationships, time management, and study habits is created to surround students with the means to excel.

Xavier University also systematically introduces new faculty to "the Xavier way." Those who come to Xavier University and stay, do so for the love of teaching and motivating students to learn and excel. Sister Rosemarie helps teach those values. She takes every new faculty member to lunch; she tells stories of Mother Katharine and of students who have excelled in spite of overwhelming odds. She also links new faculty in mentoring relationships with established faculty who help reinforce the "Xavier way" with the initiates.

Institutional Agents

In the final analysis, an institution's educational purposes come to life through people. Institutional mission and philosophy, campus environments, culture, and policies and practices reveal the values, aspirations, and visions of people. People — presidents, chief academic and student affairs officers, faculty, student affairs staff, and students — are at the heart of an involving college. As with other involving colleges, students are expected to take responsibility for their own learning; certainly faculty and student affairs staff at Xavier University make that expectation clear.

Students

About 94 percent of Xavier's 2,400 students are African-American. More than half of the student body now comes from outside Louisiana with 30 different states represented. The vast majority of students (90 percent) say they selected Xavier University because of its excellent academic reputation, particularly the strong undergraduate science programs. In fact, more than two-thirds major in the sciences. Sixty percent of the students graduate with 20 percent continuing to medical and dental schools.

President

What students choose to do in their out-of-class time is of great interest to Norman Francis, the president of Xavier University. In his 33 years with the university (first as a student, then later as dean of students), Francis has pushed everyone at Xavier University to help create black professionals and black faculty. He believes that white students, too, can learn much from black faculty, particularly their views of what is just and right.

President Francis plays a pivotal role not only in symbolic ways, but in translating the mission and philosophy of Xavier University into words and actions that have meaning in contemporary society. He knows that because students are not always certain about how to become involved, many need considerable structure and encouragement in order to take advantage of educationally purposeful out-of-class activities. He believes deeply in the need to educate the whole person and talks with students about the kinds of involvements which are consistent with Mother Katharine's vision. He spends time regularly with students in an advisory group, mentors individual students, is accessible to faculty and to the chief student affairs officer, and leaves "nothing to chance." He models what Xavier is about, a university that shows students how to be successful through commitment, hard work, self-respect, and bringing others along.

Administrators

Both the academic vice president and the dean of students play important roles in involving Xavier students. Their efforts will be described later. One example illustrates the chief academic affairs officer's (Sister Rosemarie) passion about faculty and student life at Xavier:

> I meet with the department chairs a day before the fall faculty institute and I try to inspire them to be leaders, not act as administrators, hand in course schedules and so forth. Then I meet with the new faculty once a month during the first year to tell stories about this place, about why Mother Katharine founded the institution, about our policy with respect to cheating, about advising students, about the athletic program and how it ties into the academic program. I also talk about the history of the University to the new students in all 16 sections of U1010, the required orientation course. As we grow, I don't want to lose the spirit that makes Xavier unique.

Suffice it to say that the chief academic affairs officer is not detached from the out-of-class life of students at Xavier University, and the dean of students is not detached from in-class life. The structures, practices, policies are woven together to support academic achievement and service to others as expressed in the mission.

Faculty

Rather than lament that their students are not well-prepared for college-level work, faculty work vigorously to nurture minds and self-esteem, and to motivate students to succeed. All energies are geared to building a positive atmosphere for students. Lecturing and time for research away from students are antithetical to "the Xavier way." The academic program is assembled for the students and created to respond to students' varying levels of learning. In the words of J.W. Carmichael, chemistry professor and pre-med adviser: "They say they can't do something and I give them every incentive or provocation to prove to them that they can" (Blum, 1991, p. A3).

Xavier faculty unabashedly proclaim teaching to be their priority and spend considerable time with students outside the classrooms and laboratories. Faculty typically seek out students who miss their class, do not perform well on tests, and have not sought tutoring. For example, within a matter of a few weeks, almost every new student will have heard the story of Sister Mary Grace who goes looking for students who were absent from her class! Tutoring announcements abound on bulletin boards; about 60 percent of students are involved in tutoring, either giving it or receiving it. Faculty guides, tutors, peer deans — all provide safety nets to help the student learn the culture and requirements of this achievement and service-oriented environment; one that accepts no effort short of one's best.

"The role of the contributions of institutional agents is greater than the sum of their individual parts" (Kuh et al., 1991). The match of people at Xavier University with the mission, culture, and traditions of this unique place has resulted in an experience that transforms students into achievers who understand their obligation to serve and to bring the black community along.

The Contributions of Student Affairs

Traditional distinctions between student and academic affairs simply do not apply at Xavier University. Student affairs at Xavier University is administered in a somewhat different manner than on other campuses in the study. Xavier University does not fall in the category of the campuses which could be described as "undermanned" (*sic*) where much in campus life is left to the students to create. Rather, the same intentionally structured approach to learning is followed in the student affairs out-of-class settings as is found in the academic programming.

The Student Services Division consists of the dean of student services, an assistant dean for student life who oversees the Student Government Association, the

Inter-Organizational Council, Pan-Hellenic Council and Student Activities; the counseling and career development area which includes the placement and counseling center, the latter of which works with a peer leader program; Housing; and Health Environment Services. Unlike many of her staff, Ann Harvey, dean of student services, is not a Xavier graduate but graduated from another historically black college. Prior to coming to Xavier University, she worked in the New Orleans city administration with a Xavier graduate. She joined the counseling center in 1978 and later directed it before becoming dean of student services in 1984.

Student Services Philosophy

According to Harvey, Xavier student affairs staff have a need "to touch everything our children are involved in." Yet she was quick to underscore the importance of students participating in decisions affecting the quality of their out-of-class lives. She spoke at orientation of students' responsibility to participate — to achieve, to serve. Any out-of-class experience where students have to take responsibility is deemed to be a good experience in her eyes.

As with the academic program, little is left to chance in student life. The practice of creating structures and sequences to reinforce success out of class as well as in class emanates from the student services leadership as well as from academic and other institutional leadership. The values can be traced directly to the founding and mission to provide educational opportunity to those who might not otherwise find it, as well as to support learners to overcome personal odds and excel in their fields.

Student life policies enumerated in the student handbook emphasize structure and discipline. Far more space is devoted to rules and regulations than to resources for students. Student services staff feel that expecting more of Xavier students is legitimate to "ensure a child's success." They clearly believe they have a responsibility to help students set limits on freedom and time to be successful. For example, in career placement, students must participate in a set of programs to receive full access to all services. Students who do not participate in resume-writing sessions cannot schedule interviews with prospective employers visiting the campus. This staff speaks of "being brought up in the Xavier way"; they teach responsibility and accountability for actions from the time students first arrive.

Many students seem to understand and appreciate the structure; some reported that those faculty and staff who influenced them most were those who demanded excellence from them. Not all students, however, respond favorably to the structure and the *in loco parentis* philosophy. Those who find the structure stifling tend to spend more time off campus in work and in off-campus social settings.

Student Organizations

During the 1988-89 academic year, the Student Services Office listed 71 student groups, including six social greek-affiliated organizations, class councils, a publications board, music and cheerleading groups, residence halls groups, and academic-related clubs and societies. The latter group constituted the overwhelming majority of the student clubs and organizations. All groups are advised by a faculty or staff member who aids in financial matters, advises in planning, and countersigns all official group documents (e.g., contracts). The role of advisers is "to steer," which appear consistent with the overall philosophy of structuring experiences. The 12 pages in the student handbook devoted to organizational regulations describe the role of the "adviser/chaperone" at club and organization activities.

The close tie of club and organization activity with the academic and professional life of students is highly visible in the list of organizations. Students frequently mentioned the honors banquets and awards ceremonies connected with the academic and professional groups. Officers must maintain a minimum 2.5 grade point average and "a clean conduct record" (only two or three students a year are removed from school for conduct violations). All clubs and organizations must be approved by the Inter-Organizational Council within the Student Government Association and the Student Services Office.

Organization recognition is given on a provisional basis for one year, giving a group an opportunity to "prove itself" through its activities. Groups must register activities and have them approved by the Student Services Office as well. The handbook also includes tips on conducting meetings and planning events. Security matters are also addressed, reflecting Xavier's location in the heart of New Orleans.

Consistent with the commitment to service embedded in the founding and in the culture, student organization leaders are installed and commissioned at the annual Founder's Day Convocation to lead in the spirit of the founder, Mother Katharine. At the October 11, 1988, Founder's Day celebration, President Francis called for all present to "do for others as she has done for us . . . to rededicate personal goals and the goals of society to serve." He went on to challenge students to "believe in themselves, develop their minds, and learn to sacrifice to achieve goals."

Students in the greek system tend to be fairly visible, gathering in "the yard" just outside the student center over the noon hour or in the early afternoons. About 175 students are members of fraternities and sororities. Several suggested that the system may lack substance and present problems for social and intellectual development. In his Founder's Day Convocation remarks, President Francis challenged members of greek-letter organizations to step back from their rituals and "think about what you stand for; develop the mind; talk to your younger brothers and sisters about the need to stay in school." Others suggested that the greeks' materialistic and consumer values were in conflict with the service orientation Xavier University espouses. One student stated that greeks were so highly social that the activity gets in the way of academic accomplishment and Xavier's mission. Hazing activity was also reported.

Concern that the presence of greek-letter organizations conflicts with the institution's mission is not a new issue; these groups were banned from 1958 to 1968. On the other hand, several students spoke of very meaningful learning experiences, particularly from black women in positions of community leadership, who spoke to and worked with undergraduate members.

Counseling and Career Placement

The counseling center staff was instrumental in getting the university to establish the University 1010 orientation course. As they worked with students on personal and academic adjustment, counselors determined that directing resources to new students would assist students in their adjustment to Xavier University. In like manner, staff work with faculty, campus ministers, and others who are in regular contact with students. Parents also are encouraged to alert the staff to student needs.

Career placement prepares programs at the request of faculty to help link students with professional opportunities in their fields. It is not unusual for career center staff to make presentations in classes, or for faculty to give released time for students to attend programs sponsored by the center. The center and academic departments have collaboratively created internship opportunities for students in many fields. Students discuss with great pride their summer opportunities and internships. One senior told us:

> I did two summer internships with an insurance company in New York City. They were fantastic! I learned that I loved auditing work, could leave home and find places that suited me, get involved in a new community, learn different things about different places outside of New Orleans. That was very important because I knew that to be successful in my career, a big part of my life would be traveling and living in different cities. In fact, I've accepted a job in Atlanta after I graduate.

Faculty, student services staff, and the president acknowledge that the time after interns return to the campus is a critical period to debrief, discover areas of new confidence, and identify other areas of development needed prior to leaving Xavier University for professional work or graduate study. Seniors exude a sense of confidence in their knowledge and skills and in their ability to adapt in almost any setting outside of Xavier. One recent graduate, who has returned as a counselor and adviser, reflected the belief that students who graduate from Xavier University "can succeed at whatever they choose to do."

Carolyn Thomas, the career placement director, estimated that about a third of the seniors use the services of the office. About half of the students who go on to graduate school work with the staff. The Student Career Placement Association was founded in the mid 1980s and is composed of 30-40 student volunteers from across the disciplines. They promote student awareness of the support systems in the office among students in their academic programs, sponsor career fairs, assist with resume workshops, and videotape interviews. I happened on a senior waiting to meet with an interviewer, one I had seen earlier, changing into her interview suit in the student center restroom after commuting to campus on the bus. One of the many students who commute, the student was a communications and political science major interviewing for marketing and sales work. As we spoke, she communicated high confidence built by the nurture of faculty and staff and her internship with *Black Collegian*. Xavier University had also helped her secure work in the public relations office of the New Orleans civil engineering department. She was gathering her thoughts about how she would communicate to the interviewer her confidence that she was ready for sales and marketing opportunities in New York City.

Residential Life

Residential education and facility expansion is an area that requires attention. The residential life program seemed least directly related to the academic programs of the campus. The system is overcrowded. Xavier University can house only those students coming from places other than New Orleans. Of the four residences, three are occupied by women. Two of the residence directors (one of whom was the former dean of women) view residential education as "finding activities the students like to do, that they can develop personally" such as aerobics, nutritional information, grooming, fashion, cooking, and crafts. Many of the activities provide entertainment, to give students a much needed break from academic pressures.

The university has submitted a second application to the Department of Housing and Urban Development (HUD) for support for residential facilities, and a review of residential education and resident assistant training and development had begun. This reflects the same targeted approach which previously enhanced the counseling center and career placement efforts.

Student Center

The student center is rather spartan, providing some meeting space for clubs and organizations, office space for student services, placement, the bookstore, a small gallery, a banquet room, and the commuter and residence cafeterias. Little space is available for students to socialize or for informal interaction among faculty and staff. An accreditation report from the late 1970s recommended expansion of space and program to meet recreational and cultural needs. The limitations in the center will have to be addressed at some point, but it is clear that the space and program as it is now constituted cannot compete with the academic program. The space available has been dedicated to functions that complement the educational mission.

Blurred Boundaries Between Academic and Student Affairs

Student affairs is integral to attaining Xavier's educational mission. Student affairs programs, services, and personnel clearly complement faculty and institutional efforts for academic excellence and achievement. In addition, the institutional philosophy of "bringing others along" permeates not only the campus practices, but also those of the student services division. All of these ties are reinforced by the campus culture as noted by one of the faculty, "I don't have to teach social values here. I can just teach engineering." Those values are part of the culture.

As mentioned earlier, faculty are intensely involved with students in reinforcing student success and achievement. They also draw upon the resources of student affairs to accomplish this end. The counseling center receives many referrals from faculty. Faculty refer to the center "the anxious ones, the dozing ones," those burdened with personal and family issues. The director of the counseling center came from the faculty herself, formerly in the social sciences. She retains her strong ties with faculty and staff colleagues. In addition to responding to students referred by faculty, the counseling center challenges students to be leaders and to adapt to the values of achievement and service.

The complementarity of academic and student affairs also can be seen in the role that the chief academic affairs officer takes in support of divisional goals. Recall that student affairs urged the introduction of University 1010, a course to orient the students to the history and traditions of the campus and to the services and support networks available to all students. The effort would not have succeeded without the interest and support of academic affairs. In fact, Sister Rosemarie serves as one of the five lecturers in 16 different sections. She tells stories about the history of the university, its founding, its purposes, its belief in the ability of students to overcome difficulty. She also teaches students the academic policies — the standards to which they will be held accountable. Student services staff teach the support systems to help students meet the standards. Sister Rosemarie imparts those standards "with sympathy" and illustrates by stories "strictness with understanding." Then, in her role, she signs all the letters to students in academic difficulty, and interacts with those students to determine constructive pathways. She makes the decisions on whether "students can or cannot make it." She also controls the scholarship programs so that "the desperate come to me."

Much interaction with faculty and student affairs staff follows to determine next steps for those students who make it. Sister Rosemarie also keeps in touch with students in their out-of-class lives, particularly in the arts. She made a point of commenting that she attends all concerts and performances as she finds the student effort so inspiring.

In speaking with faculty, the overriding commitment to student academic, personal, and professional success is a recurring theme. A faculty group composed of professors from engineering, music, art, history, and communications indicated that their out-of-class contacts with students contributed to "the humanization of our students." They used such phrases as "We make what they are learning come to life." Students from all across the curriculum participate in the university chorus. According to the chairman of the Music Department, Xavier was the first historically black university to offer full-length opera productions performed by the students themselves. That occurred in 1934. The science education faculty involve their students as group leaders, tutors, and guides in the summer high school and middle school programs. The art faculty engage their students in exhibits and shows in the greater New Orleans area. We also spoke with faculty who involve students in their own research. One of the seniors in pharmacy spoke of her research activity:

> I got involved with research in the pharmacy department . . . I did it as an elective
> because the professor kept asking me so I said "what the heck, I will do it." We applied
> for a big grant . . . and we got it. The research was pharmaceutical chemistry. It was
> pretty intense but very interesting. At times I was frustrated . . . He would say, "What
> will you do now?" I would say, "I don't know, you are the one with the Ph.D." And he
> would say, "I know, but tell me what you think." So that made me think and stretch.

Lines between faculty and student service out-of-class involvement with students blur just as in-class and out-of-class distinctions for student learning blur. Understanding the mission and purposes and sharing values among faculty, staff, and students forge unified goals and activities. One does not hear complaints about student services staff from faculty, nor about faculty from student services staff. Unity of purpose and shared goals — student achievement and accomplishment with the spirit of service — create the complementarity.

Discussion

The vast majority of Xavier students are actively involved in university governance and other community affairs and expressed a strong sense of "fit" with Xavier University, its striving for excellence, its desire to teach students to serve. It is not uncommon for a pre-med student to be a member of a fraternity and participate in student government, sing in the gospel choir, and be a SOAR leader or a peer dean. Even students who worked a great deal found time for one or more club activities, usually related to an area of academic interest.

Other students connect with a vibrant campus ministry subcommunity. Many of the students reported involvement in campus volunteer activities. The students expressed varying stages of belief in themselves. Some were clear about their direction. Most spoke of the strong sense of family, of the care of faculty for students, of how much they were learning and being pushed. Yet, as with other good institutions, Xavier University has some unmet challenges.

New commuting students who have not yet formed strong connections in their academic departments or found an affinity group tend to be less well connected. They tend to congregate in the commuter dining area, usually with friends from their high schools in the New Orleans area.

Business and computer science students feel that science is emphasized to their detriment. White students are in the minority here and are concentrated in the College of Pharmacy, where, incidently, student leadership can just as easily be white as black. Some tensions are reported in social settings from members in the pharmacy honors group. Another tension surfaced in the senior interview process: how light or dark one might be could have an impact on one's status and influence. A white student reported how uncomfortable she felt to learn that light skin appeared to be more valued than dark, which to her expressed denial of the goodness and strength of blackness. Student forums, scheduled through the Student Services Office, provide an outlet to draw off these tensions.

Xavier University is experiencing a serious male-female imbalance and decreasing male enrollment. The 1988-89 entering class was particularly large and included more men (204 of 611), an encouraging trend for both the school and the larger societal concern for motivating black males to stay in school. Students and staff alike talked about how important it is to develop black male role models. Male leaders feel they are "looked up to" by students. Women students report they go to great lengths to reach out to men. Men were overrepresented in leadership roles, given the population. Student affairs staff implied that the overrepresentation was conscious in order to create positive role models. One staff member feared this practice could, over time, disadvantage women. More than one of the senior women spoke of the dilemma faced as soon-to-become black professional women worry over whether to marry, the impact of marrying "up" or "down," and the concern over the scarcity of similarly educated black men.

Conclusion

The Xavier University community, 75 years after its founding, continues to act on the beliefs of its founder, that people who face overwhelming obstacles can succeed and, indeed, excel if given the opportunities to do so. The values of achievement and excellence in the context of service to the black community permeate the institution's culture. These values shape the expectations for all who enter the community — new students, new faculty and staff, parents of students. Xavier University addresses a critical societal need to develop the intellectual and personal competence of black students who will subsequently attain positions of responsibility in their chosen professions and communities.

Xavier students often are transformed by their college experience; those whom we met displayed skill and confidence in their ability to succeed vocationally and socially while also remembering the responsibility to "bring others along." They exhibited a strong sense of identity as a black man or woman scientist, or accountant, or pharmacist, or computer scientist. The structured sequential experiences which leave nothing to chance also contributed to a high degree of competence for the white "minority students." But all of this is balanced by a special kind of involvement that again emanates from the founding and mission.

The Xavier ethos of cooperation, care, and service joined with the drive for success and achievement is manifested in a special way. In this sense, the Xavier experience merits close examination as higher education grapples with the challenges of a pluralistic society and how to share power and resources. The values of service and care seem to ameliorate the negative consequences of competition and achievement so that even when power and wealth are sought, students manage to talk about using the power and wealth "to bring others along."

To be sure, the highly structured environment and the ladders for successful involvement contribute to frustration on the part of some students. Yet, for the most part, Xavier University attracts students who can benefit from hard work, respect, accomplishment, and service in a "family environment" that "parents" students along. The "parents" (faculty, staff) let go, little by little, as students gain intellectual and interpersonal competence, enough to send students off campus to internships that prove to students that Xavier University has prepared them "to make it out there."

The students who are attracted to Xavier University, its mission and culture, and the deeply committed faculty and institutional leaders all seem to shape each other in mutually enriching and transforming ways so that out-of-class experiences contribute to excellence, achievement, and service. This mission-driven institution works well for the people who are here. And because it works so well, its history, saga, and traditions are embellished by graduates returning to the campus who weave their stories into an even richer tapestry. To a large degree, the "student-institution fit" that Xavier University enjoys is a product of the distinctive nature and qualities of the Xavier tapestry, the publications that describe the warp and woof so clearly, and the socialization processes to which assiduous attention is given.

Finally, student services at Xavier University function as part of the safety net, support network, and set of structured, sequential experiences that show students the paths to academic excellence and entry to professional service to others. Moreover, student affairs staff are committed, investing the extraordinary amount of time and energy required to keep "the Xavier way" alive.

Commentary

What Can Be Learned from Xavier University?
Rodger Summers

The *American College Dictionary* (ninth edition) defines family as "a group of related things." In reading through the Xavier case study, the word *family* immediately comes to mind. Indeed, in large measure, the success of Xavier University appears to be a product of people with common interests and backgrounds responding positively to the kind of high expectations that only parents, siblings, and other relatives can express. At Xavier University, students, faculty, and staff alike know that the sense of "family" exists because they see it in the behavior of colleagues, and they hear it from the president and others. Indeed, every facet of life at Xavier University commands its community members to honor and advance the family tradition — and they do!

Dating back to Xavier's founding, the values espoused by Mother Katharine Drexel resonated in the hearts and minds of an audience eager for the kind of nurturing and excellence found in strong family units. As the current "head of the family," President Norman Francis symbolizes strong, positive leadership by showing that even busy university presidents can find time to personally help shape student behavior using established principles for success. His belief that the "whole" student deserves to be educated suggests that the assumptions on which *The Student Personnel Point of View* (American Council on Education, 1937) was based remain important today.

From the president on down, those who work and learn at Xavier are committed to nurturing students directly and indirectly; this nurturing begins as early as the orientation program. President Francis nurtures parents by providing information important to understanding what Xavier University expects of their sons and daughters. Parents, in turn, are in a better position to help their children because they have more information about university life and are made aware of the tasks which lie ahead. Through this type of encouragement — much like that an encouraging, trusting uncle might offer — parents push their children to beat the odds, to excel.

As with many families, Xavier University has clear expectations and norms for students which are communicated early and often to students. While some members of the family may elect at some point to ignore these expectations and violate campus norms, Xavier University makes it clear what students must do to remain members in good standing.

In addition to holding students to high expectations, Xavier University recognizes the value of building high self-esteem as a part of earning the degree. That is, if students feel good about themselves, they will transfer these positive feelings into all aspects of their undergraduate education and succeed. High self-esteem at Xavier University is instilled because each student is valued as an individual and students feel that someone in addition to their family of procreation cares for them.

Mentoring has a positive effect on students by allowing them to see themselves through the experiences of their mentors, many of whom experienced the same inner struggle to succeed. As a result, students develop confidence in their abilities. They may not fully believe they have the skills to achieve at the expected levels or even at the expectations of their professors or the administrators. But through constant nurturing and confidence building, students are encouraged to achieve their educational and career aspirations. The lesson to be learned is that mentoring and building self-esteem cannot be left to chance; rather, it must be planned and carefully orchestrated to produce the expected results.

Academic and Student Affairs

The Xavier mission emphasizes academics. As a result, the social side of student life receives relatively few resources as evidenced by an inadequate student union and a shortage in campus housing. The greek system as described in the case study suggests that its values conflict with Xavier's mission and philosophy. Institutional values run too deep to be even slightly challenged by a select group of only 175 students. Without the support of the president and the rest of the academic community, the greek system's influence on the quality of the undergraduate experience at Xavier will be quite limited; indeed, fraternities and sororities may even again risk extinction because of a lack of focus and educational purpose.

The marriage between student affairs and academic affairs appears to be solid as "both partners" share in the rearing of "their children." Xavier University seems to lack the rivalry and competition in which senior administrators struggle and compete for dwindling resources that one often finds at other institutions. There seems to be a high level of trust between faculty and student affairs staff. Positive relationships between faculty and student affairs staff who were once faculty members perhaps contribute to this sense of trust. When trust exists among these groups, integrity in thought and deed will follow.

Building strong partnerships between faculty and staff is expected of everyone at Xavier University; such feelings are necessary for the institution to work as well as it does. The same could be true of other colleges and universities. Faculty may feel their goals are not understood or shared by the administration and vice versa. Consequently, faculty senates and bargaining units are often at odds with the administration because faculty want to have more input in shaping policy and influence in governing the institution. Student affairs staff, particularly the chief student affairs officer, should be certain to maintain as a high priority nurturing positive relations with faculty. Perhaps if student affairs staff devoted more time and attention to developing strong, trusting relationships with faculty colleagues, there would be less in-fighting and competition and more assistance in helping each other to graduate well-educated students. Again, Xavier's mission seems to be the key.

Ethnicity

Being treated differently because of skin color is a long-standing point of contention among some blacks. Skin color has been known to determine the acceptance or nonacceptance of a black person (Johnson, 1972). For example, during the slavery period in the United States, dark-skinned blacks did the hard, manual field work while light-skinned blacks (many of whom were sired by white fathers) were assigned easier tasks (e.g., house workers, maids). Such distinctions persist today. It is not uncommon to hear blacks at times pejoratively describe other blacks by skin color rather than other characteristics. What is surprising is that given the mission of Xavier and the role played by its faculty, staff and students continue to practice this type of class distinction. Xavier University is in the South and many racial prejudices in that region as well as other parts of the country — even within the same race — have not been eradicated.

Ethnicity may be a consideration for new student affairs professionals searching for "the ideal position" (that does not exist). Too often positions are accepted because of reasons other than a good match between an individual's expectations and values and those of the institution. At Xavier University, such a match is essential, even to the point of fitting in with the rest of the staff who believe in "the Xavier way."

New professionals must be cognizant of their values and needs. A white staff member might find working at Xavier (or at any other predominantly black institution) uncomfortable if he/she does not believe in the importance of such institutions. Some may view Xavier's philosophy as "old fashioned" or, perhaps, even oppressive. Feelings of loneliness and isolation can have a deleterious effect on a white professional at a black institution (Richmond, 1986). Also, students expect to find black role models and mentors. This may disadvantage white professionals.

This is not to say that whites cannot be role models for students of color; quite the contrary is true. But white staff members at a black college must be exceptional individuals not to allow their ethnicity to become an obstacle to building authentic relations with others. White professionals must learn about and understand the culture and climate of the black institution. Equally important, they must be willing to take risks in forming relations with students, faculty, and others because they respect and like the people and believe in what the institution is trying to accomplish.

Lessons Learned

There are many lessons that student affairs staff at other colleges and universities can learn from Xavier University. First, maintaining an institution of manageable size seems to be essential to the Xavier miracle. An institution which controls its size controls its destiny. Larger institutions can become bureaucratic and impersonal. In the context and culture of Xavier University, the personal touch — faculty knowing students by their names and students knowing and calling professors and administrators by their titles and names — contributes to academic excellence and personal success.

Second, the Xavier experience works because student affairs staff are dedicated to the values and principles on which the institution was founded. Despite problems that may exist because of insufficient funding, status issues, or other factors which affect morale, Xavier faculty and staff remain highly dedicated to turning out a high-quality student. At many institutions, collective bargaining contracts constrain staff who aspire to levels of excellence in their performance but fear that when they bust the norms of mediocrity they will be ostracized by peers. Happily, Xavier University is an exception; people feel their individual contributions make an important difference and they are valued for what they bring to the institution. That is, people view their roles as more than a job. For student affairs staff, their work is both avocation as well as a vocation. The concern for young people is based on a love for the institution and its ideals. The lesson to be learned here is that a happy staff is a productive staff. This "happiness" becomes contagious.

In the final analysis what makes Xavier University special is an enviable combination of trust, caring, high expectations, and clear direction of mission and educational purposes. Xavier University does not accept mediocrity; this ground rule is very clear from the beginning with all students. Students know what is expected of them and they work toward achieving the goal. Much like the Berlitz course in a foreign language, students live the Xavier experience each day. Soon, they begin to speak "Xavier" fluently and help others who might need assistance in understanding the language. The trust level among and between the many, different constituents is firm but also constantly nurtured in an attempt to help students.

Moreover, Xavier University knows and embraces what it is and aspires to be; it has never wavered in its mission. In an era of possible enrollment shortfalls and tight fiscal resources, it is even more important that higher education institutions clarify their purposes. Clarity of educational purpose is an area in which most institutions can improve. Much of Xavier's success can be attributed to its clear mission statement which links the founding history of the institution to the role of each of its members. Too often, a mission statement for many higher education institutions is a bland piece of obfuscation unknown not only to students but also to faculty and staff. Xavier's mission is an integral pattern in the institution's fabric of daily life. Consequently, all members of the institution are moving in the same direction to attain the institution's purposes and student aspirations. Other colleges and universities can learn a lesson from Xavier University by having a mission statement which is realistic, pragmatic in its approach, and clearly understood by the people for whom the institution exists.

Chapter Seven

A Community of Women Empowering Women
Mount Holyoke College

Elizabeth J. Whitt

Is a women's college a place for women to be protected or empowered? What is a women's college for? ...What does it mean to educate women? (Rich, 1986, p. 189)

The questions Rich asks are fundamental, reaching to the heart of the reasons for the existence of women's colleges. This case study describes one women's college — Mount Holyoke College — and the ways in which the Mount Holyoke community answers these questions. It is the case that the processes of self-examination and self-definition — of confronting fundamental questions — are continuous at Mount Holyoke.

As we shall see in this case study, the nonacademic and academic aspects of Mount Holyoke College are blurred; identifying certain roles and functions as belonging to student affairs and separating the work of student affairs from other elements of the college are not always possible or useful. Therefore, expect to find examples of encouragement and support for student out-of-class learning throughout the case, and from many sources.

History

Understanding the history of Mount Holyoke College is essential to understanding Mount Holyoke in the present. In the words of a current student affairs staff member, "What we feel is the progression of the historical moment; there's a sense of relevance of tradition, of the mission — a connection to history." A complete history of the college is not possible here, but some of the highlights of Mount Holyoke's past are offered to convey a sense of that history.

Mount Holyoke Seminary (or high school) was established in 1837 at South Hadley, in the Connecticut River valley of western Massachusetts. The school was named for one of the several hills on the edge of town. Mary Lyon founded the seminary to provide an education for daughters of New England farmers that combined religious and liberal education with a system of discipline and work. Her purpose was to develop women "capable of self-propelled action" (Horowitz, 1984, p. 12) who would use what they had learned at Mount Holyoke College to serve Christ in the outside world.

> She drew together key elements: academic subjects to train the mind as an instrument of reason; domestic work and a carefully regulated day to meet material needs and to protect health; a known, clear sequence of each day to lend order and predictability; a corps of transformed teachers who provided proper models for imitation; and a building shaped like a dwelling house as the proper setting for study, prayer, work, and rest (Horowitz, 1984, p. 12).

By the time of Lyon's death in 1849, the seminary had a building that provided classrooms, as well as living space for students and faculty; an endowment sufficient to ensure the future of the school; a faculty composed of Mount Holyoke graduates; and a student body of approximately 250 "serious, mature young women" (Horowitz, 1984, p. 25) from throughout the Northeast and Midwest. Mount Holyoke alumnae lived the lives of service Lyon envisioned. Between 1838 and 1850, 82.5 percent of the seminary's graduates taught school; by 1859, 60 had become foreign missionaries (Horowitz, 1984). Mount Holyoke alumnae were also instrumental in helping to establish seminaries and colleges modeled on Mount Holyoke College all over the United States. Western College in Oxford, Ohio, was an early example.

In 1861, the academic program was extended to four years and the students pursued a course of study much like that of the men of Amherst College. In the decades after the Civil War, the need to become a college in name, as well as in program, became apparent. In 1887, the Massachusetts legislature granted Mount Holyoke trustees the right to the name Mount Holyoke College, and the right to grant degrees. At the same time, the practice of selecting faculty from among Mount Holyoke graduates was discontinued in favor of hiring women who had broader experience in the world and stronger traditions of scholarship.

In addition, students were freed from the strict controls and domestic duties of Lyon's disciplinary system and allowed to indulge in "the pleasurable pursuits of student organizations, publications, athletics, socializing, and rituals" (Horowitz, 1984, p. 327). The college also began to look like a college with the addition of student residences (called cottages), a classroom and office building named for Mary Lyon, and a gymnasium (Horowitz, 1984). With the turn of the 20th century, Mount Holyoke College was on the way to becoming an institution respected for the quality of its students, faculty, and academic program. Nevertheless, despite the changes that have taken place at Mount Holyoke College over the past 150 years, Mary Lyon's influence and her vision of women's education survives, a point to which we will return later in the case.

Mount Holyoke College Today

Mount Holyoke College has a full-time undergraduate enrollment of 1,903 (1990-91 academic year). Graduate programs in chemistry, biological sciences, education, and psychology enroll approximately 20 students per year. Students come from 47 states and approximately 60 foreign countries. In selecting students for admission, the college looks for women who are "outstanding in intellectual ability and personal qualities...The college looks for evidence of character, originality, and maturity, as well as sound academic training" (*Mount Holyoke College Bulletin, 1990-91*, p. 42). Admissions are selective and based on assessments of the student's ability to benefit from and contribute to the Mount Holyoke experience.

In keeping with the college's commitment to creating a multicultural community, 12 percent of the student body is composed of students of color from the United States and 10 percent is international students. Lyon's commitment to educating women whose families may not be able to afford college persists in a policy of need-blind admission; that is, students are admitted to the college without regard for ability to pay for their education. Once a student is accepted, an aid package is developed to meet her full need. (Multiculturalism and need-blind admission will be revisited in the section on policies and practices.)

Mount Holyoke students are described as bright, diligent, high energy, and in some respects, driven; we were told "there aren't passive women in this place!" Almost every student we talked with said that she had not come to Mount Holyoke because it was a women's college, but she had stayed because it was a women's college and because of the opportunities and experiences that can be found "in a community that is only women." For example, students appreciated being in a setting in which women fill all the leadership roles. (The opportunities provided to women at Mount Holyoke will be described in more detail later in this case study.)

Factors and Conditions Associated with High-Quality Out-of-Class Experiences

Mission and Philosophy

Two aspects of Mount Holyoke's mission are described here: women's education and liberal arts. Bolstering the mission are elements of the institution's philosophy, "the way we do things here," including a commitment to providing challenges with support and a strong sense of community.

Women's Education

Mary Lyon's commitment to educating women continues as an underlying spirit as well as a living mission about which all community members agree: to provide an excellent liberal arts education for women. Thus, virtually all of the college's resources and class time, and all of the student leadership and employment opportunities are for women. The fact that the institution exists for women creates what students describe as "a totally affirming environment....An environment where women do everything is necessarily strengthening."

The means by which the college's mission for women's education is fulfilled include an atmosphere of challenge and support and a sense of community.

Challenge and Support. Striking an appropriate balance between challenge and support is a task shared by student affairs staff and academic administrators at Mount Holyoke College. Their common goal is to develop independent students within a nurturing environment. Therefore, they must be nurturing without fostering dependence and challenging without creating feelings of helplessness and isolation. In order to take risks, Mount Holyoke students need to feel comfortable — but not too comfortable.

The message from Mount Holyoke College to its students is clear: "You can do anything you want to do." Supporting this message are expectations that each student will work hard to discover and explore the limits of her individual potential. Self-discovery involves risk — the risk of facing the unknown, the risk of failure — but risk taking is encouraged at Mount Holyoke College. Students and alumnae refer to being "stretched" — exceeding their assumed limits while meeting demands for excellence both in and out of the classroom.

Although anticipatory socialization of students is described later in the case, it should be emphasized here that, from the first contact with prospective students, the college emphasizes challenges. In fact, the title of the Mount Holyoke viewbook is *Challenge* — printed in bold letters on the cover. Students face not only the challenges of rigorous academic expectations and the challenges of leadership, but also the challenges of taking a stand in discussions over dinner and the challenges of forming lasting friendships. Faculty push students to think for themselves, to confront their insecurities and overcome them. Out of class, students are given responsibility for developing and maintaining a healthy residence hall community and for participating in most major decisions regarding the college. Many challenges encountered by Mount Holyoke students come from other students. In interaction in class, at dinner, and during study breaks (at "M&Cs" — milk and crackers) in the residence halls, women challenge one another to examine their values, appreciate diversity in lifestyles and cultures, apply in-class learning to real life, and seek self-knowledge. Students learn early to articulate and defend their beliefs because "someone always asks 'why?'"

The result, for most students, is a sense of accomplishment. A senior stated, "We are asked to work hard and that gives us confidence in ourselves. You learn about yourself and your capabilities, and then you do more. I am stronger [as a result of] putting myself in situations that were difficult and making the best experience out of it."

Mount Holyoke College is also "a place where you can grow and not feel threatened." The pressures to perform with excellence, to take risks, and to stretch oneself are tempered with strong and extensive support systems. According to one senior, "The word [to describe Mount Holyoke] is 'embracing' — from everybody who has anything to do with the place. This is a very caring place." An academic administrator asserted, "We believe in the students even when they don't believe in themselves."

Whereas faculty are an important source of support in the academic arena, the most visible formal sources of support for life outside the classroom are members of the Office of the Dean of Students, including the dean and assistant and associate deans, counseling services in the health center, the residence life staff, and the alcohol and drug awareness project director. Peer educators who are trained in issues of alcohol and other drug use, wellness, and women's health are an important part of this support network. Support groups are plentiful at Mount Holyoke College and include groups for alcoholics, daughters of alcoholics, women with eating disorders, and lesbians. In addition, there are support groups for women of various nationalities and ethnic and racial backgrounds.

Support is also provided in informal ways, such as encouragement from friends in the residence halls. Younger students are lovingly (in most cases!) challenged by older students to "be true to yourself" and "get a grip" when overwhelmed by academic pressures.

Sense of Community. Mount Holyoke is "a community of women empowering women," a community that conveys to students "an immediate sense that you're wanted, that you're special, that 'we're so lucky you're here and we want you to think of this as your community.'" Central to the development of this sense of community are college traditions and residence halls, both of which are described later in the case. Suffice it to say here that the residence halls are the primary locus of community building at Mount Holyoke College, and the traditions create a feeling of shared experience and bonding across generations of Mount Holyoke students and alumnae. A sentiment often expressed at Mount Holyoke College is, "You make sisters here as well as friends."

Students learn early that being part of the Mount Holyoke community is a lifelong commitment. Alumnae play an important role in the life of the college, including student recruitment, fund raising, career advising and mentoring, and support networks. Class reunions begin two years after graduation so that alumnae can see their "little sisters" graduate. At that point, alumnae educate the seniors in "the facts of alumnaehood": that once you have experienced the advantages and the support of Mount Holyoke, you are expected to use those experiences in the service of others, both within and outside the college community. In other words, "Take what you have gotten here and do something important with it!"

A strong sense of community may not be shared by all Mount Holyoke students, nor do all students feel that an "embracing" community is always a positive thing. According to the Mount Holyoke Task Force on Student Life (1989), there are students who feel isolated for various reasons. For example, many international students expressed feelings of not belonging to the larger student community. African-American students perceived a lack of white student participation in their events such as Black History Month. Another potentially negative aspect of the Mount Holyoke community is that it can, in the words of a senior, "be suffocating after awhile." The small size of the college, its seemingly isolated location, and its intense academic and social life can become intolerable. Many students cope by taking advantage of opportunities to spend junior year and/or January sessions off campus.

Liberal Education

Liberal education is also central to the college mission and experience. Liberal arts are "the arts of thought, perception, and judgment, the arts that foster humanity and a civility of spirit, and it is these arts that Mount Holyoke places at the center of its life" (*Mount*

Holyoke College Bulletin, 1990-1991, p. 8). Students and faculty constitute a "collegium" based on a shared commitment to the liberal ideals of "learning, freedom, and community of purpose" (*Mount Holyoke College Bulletin, 1990-1991*, p. 8). The primary goal of liberal education at Mount Holyoke is developing an appreciation for learning as a lifelong commitment, rather than preparation for specific careers.

Interdisciplinary studies are the cornerstone of liberal education at Mount Holyoke College. An interdisciplinary seminar, Pasts and Presences, is offered to first-year students and sophomores. Interdisciplinary courses are also popular among upperclass students; a recent course, Quantitative Reasoning, was offered by faculty in physics, mathematics, biology, and history. Students perceive interdisciplinary work to foster intellectual experimentation and "help us learn about ourselves, what we can do." Many students avail themselves of opportunities to design majors that cross fields of study, such as environmental economics.

Mount Holyoke students are required to take at least one course that provides exposure to Third World perspectives, including people of color of North America. Students often point to courses in women's studies and Third World studies as having been "most significant" in fostering their consciousness of sexism, racism, hunger, and other forms of oppression; increased political awareness and activism are seen by many students as an important outcome of their time at Mount Holyoke College.

Student life out of class is perceived by the Mount Holyoke community to be integral to the total educational experience. The college bulletin asserts the belief that "[r]esidential life and the spectrum of co-curricular activities bring a richness and dimension to the student's liberal education not otherwise possible" (*Mount Holyoke College Bulletin, 1990-1991*, p. 33). (A discussion of the integration of in-class and out-of-class life at Mount Holyoke is provided in the section on policies and practices.)

Campus Environments

Mount Holyoke College is situated on an 800-acre campus. The setting is pastoral, dominated by woods, greens, and two lakes. Campus buildings are a combination of red brick, ivy-covered collegiate gothic and modern, and contain state-of-the-art library, computer, science, and athletic facilities. The campus feels peaceful and isolated — an ideal environment in which to learn and think, undisturbed by the demands of the real world. The town of South Hadley is a small, postcard rendition of New England, and is dominated by the presence of the college. In the following paragraphs, three aspects of the campus environment — the Five-College System, residence halls, and Blanchard Campus Center — are described.

Five-College System

Although the campus conveys a sense of separation from the hustle and bustle of real life, Mount Holyoke College is part of one of the largest higher education communities in the world, the Five-College System: University of Massachusetts, Amherst College, Smith College, Hampshire College, and Mount Holyoke. A college publication refers to the five-college community as "the best of two worlds. One need only travel 10 minutes from the peaceful, seemingly isolated, Mount Holyoke campus to find more than 30,000 other students" (*Times*, 1989, p. 10). The Five-College System campuses are linked by a bus system and numerous shared curricular offerings. Mount Holyoke students may, for example, take Advanced Arabic at the University of Massachusetts, Vietnam War at Smith College, and History of Twentieth-Century Africa at Amherst College. The students of the five colleges also share an active social life; Mount Holyoke students attend parties and dances at the other institutions and vice versa. The colleges influence one another in other ways as well. For example, incidents of racism at the University of Massachusetts several years ago prompted community-wide convocations and task forces on multiculturalism and diversity at Mount Holyoke College.

Residence Halls

The 18 Mount Holyoke residence halls — referred to by all as "the dorms" — are "the center of student life outside the classroom" (*Times*, 1989, p. 7). They have been kept small (60 to 135 students) to develop strong living and learning communities within the larger college community. It is in the residence halls that students reinforce their sense of ownership for the college and the importance of taking care of one another.

Residence halls range in style from the old "cottages" (red-brick houses with large front porches) to modern multilevel halls. Each has a formal living room, study rooms, a baby grand piano, a grandfather clock, original art, a kitchenette, and a dining room. Meals are served "family style" in each hall by residents; a great deal of community building seems to take place at meal times. One student asserted, "You learn more at dinner sometimes than in class!"

Members of all four classes live in each hall, a policy that is designed to provide learning opportunities for both younger and older students. Particularly important is the fact that first-year students and sophomores have role models for both academic and extracurricular involvement. Many activities connected with new student orientation are implemented in the residence halls, including Big and Little Sisters; pairing juniors with first-year students; and Elfing, in which sophomores serve as secret "elves" for new students. (Opportunities for leadership and involvement offered by the residence halls will be described in more detail in the section on policies and practices.)

It is ironic that a strong sense of residential identity may also inhibit the development of a broader sense of college community. Some students and others perceive that the emphasis on residential community encourages students to limit their contacts and involvement outside the residence.

Blanchard Campus Center

Blanchard was recently renovated to provide a central gathering place, "a living room for the campus." The college post office (where all students receive their mail), bookstore, information desk, offices of student organizations, meeting rooms, a game room, the Student Activities Office, and a snack bar are in Blanchard. Students and faculty use the snack bar to continue class discussions over coffee, and programs such as dances, comics, singers, and parties are offered every weekend. Blanchard compensates, to some extent, for the potential divisiveness of the residence hall communities by bringing students together at least once a day — to pick up mail and messages — and offering an accessible place for students, faculty, and administrators to come together for social events. The Blanchard Center manager is a member of the dean of students staff.

Culture

At Mount Holyoke, there is a strong sense of being part of history, of the continuity of shared experience stretching back in time to Mary Lyon, a shared experience dominated by shared traditions. The founder's impact continues to be felt on the campus, almost as though she were alive. The use of her words and ideas in daily conversation enhances the impression that she is a living presence.

At Mount Holyoke College, "they have a tradition for everything." Traditions at Mount Holyoke transmit what is important, who should do what, and why, and encourage feelings of membership in the college community. Traditions are handed down from one generation of students to another, and are cherished as a means to unify current students as well as create bonds of sisterhood with Mount Holyoke students of the past.

Traditions at Mount Holyoke College are an important aspect of out-of-class life. Space limitations prohibit a detailed description of all of the college's traditions, but five — three old and two new — are particularly worthy of note here.

128

Mountain Day has been a Mount Holyoke tradition for 150 years. At 8 o'clock on a morning in October, the bells in Mary Lyon Tower ring more than eight times, announcing that classes are cancelled for the day. In the past, students and faculty hiked up Mount Holyoke, then spent the night in a camp at the summit. Some students and faculty still take to the hill, while others use the free day to explore rural New England. In either case, it is a time to take a break from the rigors of student life and relive a bit of the college's past.

For many years, M&Cs (milk and crackers) have been a nightly tradition at Mount Holyoke College. At 10 o'clock, students gather in the dining rooms for a snack and to talk. This is more than a study break; M&Cs are described by students as an essential aspect of residence hall community and a place where feelings of togetherness and friendship are reinforced.

Another long-time tradition at Mount Holyoke is a tradition of service. In Mary Lyon's time, the emphasis was on being models of female service to God, through teaching or missionary work. Lyon's ethos of taking what was experienced at Mount Holyoke College and using it to help others exists today in the myriad volunteer activities in which students are engaged, including assisting pregnant teens, tutoring Southeast Asian refugees in English, serving as Big Sisters, working with the Holyoke Girls Club, and leading SADD (Students Against Drunk Driving) groups. According to a nontraditional-age student, "We are given the message that 'this is a valuable experience and you owe it to the world to pass it on.'"

A fairly new (1980) tradition is "Pangynaskeia" (the total world of women). Pangynaskeia was suggested to Mary Lyon as a possible name for her seminary; it now denotes a spring celebration of women. The event is coordinated by student government and the Student Activities Office, and includes a community picnic and a parade of decorated cars that ends at the outdoor amphitheater, where students dressed in class colors sing class songs and cheers. Student government awards for service and leadership are presented, and outstanding (or simply humorous) events of the past year are remembered. In this way, the importance of out-of-class involvement to good times and learning are emphasized and a sense of women's community is affirmed.

Another new tradition — or set of traditions — is a celebration of holidays from around the world at the end of fall semester. Mount Holyoke's commitment to becoming a multicultural learning community led residence hall staff and student governments to abandon a focus on Christmas and sponsor a variety of holiday activities that are both educational and celebratory. These events convey appreciation for all the religions and nationalities that constitute the Mount Holyoke community and highlight the contributions of each to the whole.

Thus, Mount Holyoke traditions illustrate one way in which out-of-class experiences reinforce and celebrate institutional values and community ties. They also demonstrate the evolutionary nature of those values and the need for traditions to be responsive to change.

Policies and Practices

The policies and practices described in this section are:
- blurred boundaries between in-class and out-of-class experiences
- anticipatory socialization and orientation
- opportunities for involvement and responsibility
- the presence of female role models
- efforts toward diversity and multiculturalism
- need-blind admissions
- faculty roles at Mount Holyoke College

Blurred Boundaries

An assertion was made in the introduction to the case that the line between in-class and out-of-class experiences at Mount Holyoke College is "fuzzy." Evidence for that statement is found throughout the college. According to an academic administrator, historically, the Mount Holyoke student has been "more than just a student; the focus has been on the total experience." Current faculty and administrators recognize that, without extracurricular activities, students "live only half a life" and that connections between in-class and out-of-class experiences should be made explicit to provide a full life for students. According to another academic administrator, "The institution recognizes that the involved student is happy and successful."

Responsibility for education outside the classroom is placed primarily on the Dean of Students Office, but it is a shared responsibility as well. The academic counterpart to the Dean of Students Office is the Office of the Dean of Studies, including the dean of first-year studies, the assistant dean of international affairs, the associate dean of studies and Third World affairs, and the dean and assistant to the dean of studies, who are responsible for (among other things) academic advising, addressing academic difficulties, and tutoring programs. The Dean of Students Office and the Office of the Dean of Studies work together from a common philosophical base — that is, both offices are involved in student learning and development — and a shared assumption that fostering a residential academic community is at the heart of what both are about. For example, members of both offices work together to address concerns about the quality of intellectual life in the residence halls, including creating an environment appropriate to study and creating opportunities for conversations that reinforce academic experiences.

Students themselves describe the frequency with which in-class experiences "are interwoven back at the dorm" into meaningful discussions about values and beliefs. In addition, academic advisors encourage students "to take a normal courseload — and then ask, 'what can you do then to enrich your life?'" By the way, academic advising is performed by faculty as well as members of the Dean of Studies Office.

Many out-of-class experiences have direct links to academic concerns and programs. For example, many Mount Holyoke students conduct research with faculty members. Internships are available for summers and semesters-on-leave, including the International Program, the Program on the Administration of Complex Organizations, the Washington Program, and the Science Program. The Writing Program uses student tutors and departments nominate upperclass students to serve as academic advisors in the residence halls; students must be not only knowledgeable in the discipline, but also approachable and willing to help. Faculty and administrators work together to provide a wide array of programs and events, including poetry readings, plays, lecture series, and concerts in the residence halls and elsewhere on campus. In a recent year, events ranged from a reading by a South American novelist to a performance of Japanese dance to a concert by a gospel choir.

Similarly, concerns of students out of class are reflected in the curriculum. Women's studies and Third World studies courses have already been mentioned. Sexism and racism are incorporated by some faculty into courses and class discussions. And, although many Mount Holyoke faculty do not participate in students' extracurricular activities, they are very active in matters related to their classes and disciplines. For example, in addition to involving students in their research, faculty are very willing to engage students in discussions about academic subjects outside of class.

Faculty-staff-student lunches are one way that faculty, students, and staff members maintain a sense of shared educational purpose and, in some ways, retain the spirit of a time when Mount Holyoke faculty lived near campus and shared their daily lives with students. The lunches are held every other week in a dining hall that is not usually open at noon; meal costs for faculty are covered by the dean of the faculty and meal costs for staff are paid by the dean of students. Gatherings are limited to 50 people (so far, no fewer than 35 have attended), and every group which participates must include both students and faculty or staff. The program has been very popular as a way to extend class discussions in an informal setting and to bring people from all parts of the community together to talk about topics of interest.

Mount Holyoke students describe their out-of-class activities as "the most significant" aspects of their collegiate experience: "Being really stretched here doesn't happen only in the classroom." They also see many connections between what they learn in and out of class. For example, leadership roles are perceived to be opportunities to develop assertiveness, self-awareness, political and social consciousness, as well as teaching thinking, writing, organizational, and communication skills.

Anticipatory Socialization and Orientation

According to Mount Holyoke students, "there is a strong anticipatory socialization" to what it means to be a part of the Mount Holyoke community. From the beginning of the recruitment process, the college provides extensive personal and written information about "what it's like here." Recall the earlier mention of the college viewbook for prospective students and parents with its title, *Challenge*, boldly stated, introducing potential newcomers to one of the overriding values of the college.

Alumnae play a very important role in conveying, chiefly through the example of their own lives, the impact and meaning of the Mount Holyoke experience. Mount Holyoke graduates throughout the country make contacts with prospective students to talk about the college and its values, opportunities, and outcomes. When asked why she came to Mount Holyoke, a graduating senior said, "I met alumnae who were in charge of their lives and I wanted that for myself. They seemed special, and I thought 'there must be something special about Mount Holyoke.'"

Prospective students also receive a large number of written materials about the college. In addition to *Challenge*, publications include *Times*, a booklet about student life, and *Impact*, a pamphlet describing various Mount Holyoke faculty members and the benefits of a liberal arts education. All are colorful, professional, and straightforward and the messages they convey are consistent: excellence, hard work, challenge, support, fun, service, liberal learning, and community.

One publication students feel is particularly helpful in introducing newcomers to Mount Holyoke is *A First Year Handbook*, prepared by members of the junior class for their "little sisters" (i.e., first-year students) and mailed during the summer. This little booklet is full of helpful hints (such as where to cash a check and how to cope with stress) and humorous perspectives on college life. New students are introduced to academic routines such as class schedules, and are strongly encouraged to get involved in extracurricular activities. One section describes all of the Mount Holyoke traditions and explains why they are important to the community. The segment on "Living Life" warns, "Don't be shocked when you first walk into your room. Stepping into an empty lifeless room can be slightly depressing...[but] within a few weeks the place will have its own 'lived in' look" (*A First Year Handbook*, 1989, p. 18). There is also a section entitled "Learning the Lingo," a guide to the vocabulary of Mount Holyoke College, including such terms as "the Rat" (dances held in Blanchard every Thursday) and "random" (a miscellaneous person, usually an unescorted male). This publication, like the others, assists newcomers to feel a sense of belonging in their new home from the start.

Orientation for new students strikes a balance between academic and nonacademic aspects of student life; both the dean of students and the dean of first-year studies are involved in planning the event. Because Mount Holyoke students are drawn from such great distances, all orientation activities take place in the fall. Orientation begins about five days before classes begin, with special events for international students and students of color from the United States. Students are greeted by their first names by residence hall staff and orientation advisors, all of whom assist in the moving in process. Included in orientation activities are sessions on what it means to be a member of a multicultural community such as expectations for behavior and ways to cope with differences. A panel of senior students talks about how the diversity of students at Mount Holyoke College has affected their college experience. New students also participate in "a modified Outward Bound experience" that emphasizes risk taking and relying on others for help and support. The activities give every student an immediate sense that she is up to the challenges that Mount Holyoke will present.

Opportunities for Involvement and Responsibility

A college publication asserts that Mount Holyoke is "a 24-hour-a-day adventure" in which "women are given 100 percent of every chance to grow and test themselves" and "every title and every job belongs to a woman" (*Times*, 1989, p. 1). Students are told by faculty, administrators, other students, and an array of college publications that part of the Mount Holyoke tradition of "uncommon women" includes investing oneself in some activity outside of class; thus, each student makes a contribution to community life, while also making friends and developing skills. In addition, students are given considerable responsibility for the quality and conduct of their lives.

Students willingly accept the challenge to make the most of opportunities for involvement and leadership by participating extensively in cocurricular activities. A student affairs staff member commented that Mount Holyoke students "integrate so much into their lives that's productive, and they integrate fun into their lives as well." In fact, a nontraditional-age student asserted that there may be too many opportunities to get involved given the academic demands of the college. But most students find a way to use out-of-class time that is personally meaningful.

Mount Holyoke College has over 70 student clubs and organizations that reflect the varied interests and commitments of the student body. Examples include Action South Africa, Association for Pan-African Unity, Cambodian Tutoring Program, Campus Girl Scouts, Glee Club, Intramural Sports, SAUCE (Substance Abuse/Use-Campus Educators), WASH (Women Against Sexual Harassment), and WMHC radio station (the nation's oldest continuing FCC-licensed radio station run by women). Organization advisors include faculty, student affairs staff, and the campus ministers and rabbi. If a student is interested in something that is not offered, she can start a new group with little effort. The Office of Student Activities, located in the Blanchard Center, serves as a resource for program planning and for ways in which students can get involved.

Mount Holyoke students "take responsibility for running their lives" *(Challenge,* 1990, p. 25). Student responsibility takes many forms, including Student Government Association, class governments, residence hall governments and staff, and the Honor Code.

The Student Government Association (SGA) is the representative government of the student body. SGA is funded by an SGA activities fee assessed to all students in an amount determined by the students themselves. Activity fees support SGA's work and are also allocated by SGA to student clubs and organizations. Through SGA, students are involved in decision making in nearly all aspects of college life. Students are appointed by SGA to serve with faculty and administrators on college-wide committees, such as the Academic Policy Committee and Committee on Academic Responsibility. In addition, SGA sponsors a variety of committees to address student concerns, including Committee on Student Evaluation of Faculty Teaching, Third World Advisory Committee, and Affirmative Action Committee.

Another SGA standing committee is the Advisory Committee to the Dean of Students, a group that meets regularly with the dean to advise her on matters of student life and needs. The dean has requested that this committee membership be limited to students who have no other leadership role on campus; thus, she can hear from students who do not have another forum and also provide additional opportunities for leadership experience.

Residential life at Mount Holyoke is based on principles of community responsibility, including respect for the freedom, rights, beliefs, and feelings of others, and a commitment to an environment that celebrates diversity. Students are given responsibility for maintaining these principles in the residence halls. Each hall is staffed by a hall president, assistant hall president, student advisors (peer counselors and advisors), and a head resident, a part-time staff member of the Office of Residential Life. Head residents are not Mount Holyoke students, although several are alumnae. They may be pursuing graduate study or hold a combination of positions at the college.

The student staff are selected for their leadership, communication, and helping skills, and serve without remuneration. Other students hold elected hall offices, including residential events coordinator, dorm treasurer, dorm senator, intramural representative, security representative, and energy representative. All of these students, including the student staff, constitute the Hall Committee, the group charged with forming a residence hall mission statement, planning hall programs and activities, and responding to problems within the residence. The student staff and the head resident compose the Closed Hall Committee, the body that may, if necessary, deal with violations of community standards and that meets regularly to discuss residents' problems and educational needs.

According to the *Student Handbook* (1989), "social courtesy rather than specific regulation covers most of the aspects of daily living" (p. 35) at Mount Holyoke College. A very detailed alcohol policy has been developed recently, but there are few other written rules or regulations. Instead, students are expected to behave in a manner that considers the rights and comfort of others. Undergirding community standards for conduct is the Mount Holyoke Honor Code, a key element in maintaining a sense of community within the college. The Honor Code assumes that Mount Holyoke College "is a community of scholars — teachers and students — whose collaborative efforts to attain knowledge of intellectual fields is based upon mutual respect" (The Honor Code, 1988, p.4). The Honor Code encompasses both academic and social behavior, and prohibits plagiarism, cheating, misuse of the library, infringement on others' rights and beliefs, and damage to another person or property.

Also included in the Honor Code are several sets of principles of community responsibility, including a policy on human rights; a statement on rights, responsibilities, and dissent; and a statement of multiracial commitment. The multiracial commitment statement was developed in 1973 and asserts the necessity of "an academic environment free of racial discrimination in which all individuals are treated with a common standard of decency" and which "confronts and resists" racist behavior (Honor Code, 1988, p.10).

If a student violates the Honor Code, she is on her honor to report herself to a faculty member (in the case of academic violations) or to a member of the Closed Hall Committee in the case of a social regulation. Students perceive the Honor Code to be a positive aspect of the community: "It treats all members of the community as adults and with respect; the implicit assumption here is that students are intellectually capable and responsible." For example, students are permitted to take unproctored final exams any time during final exam week.

Hall presidents deal with most social infractions of the Honor Code. The Council on Student Affairs (composed of the college president, the dean of students, three faculty, and six students, including the SGA president and the chair of the hall presidents) may hear cases of serious social violations, when suspension or expulsion may result. Student academic violations are addressed by the Committee on Academic Responsibility, whose members include the dean of the faculty, three faculty members, and five students (including the SGA president). The Committee on Academic Responsibility may also hear cases of alleged violations on the part of faculty if the faculty member requests a hearing.

Presence of Female Role Models

Some research on women's colleges suggests that the presence of female role models at these institutions may be one reason for the success and satisfaction of their graduates (Smith, 1990). Mount Holyoke College supports its assertion that "women are taken very seriously here" with the practice (which extends back in time to Mary Lyon) of placing women in formal leadership roles throughout the college. The president, Elizabeth Kennan, is a Mount Holyoke alumna. Approximately 50 percent of the faculty is female, and, in 1989, all but three of the student affairs staff members were women. Perhaps equally important is the strong and pervasive message conveyed to all faculty, staff, and students that the college exists for women. The men who choose to work at Mount Holyoke College are also role models in that they are committed to taking women seriously.

Students also point to the impact of alumnae and older students as role models. The achievements of alums, as well as their continuing commitment to the ideals of Mount Holyoke College, encourage students to believe that they really can be anything they want to be. The fact that all student leaders are women helps other students to think that "yes — I can do it, too."

The emphasis on women's achievements is perceived by some at the college as a "double-edged sword." Some students believe that excellence both in and out of the classroom is pushed to an extent that can be unhealthy. For example, several Mount Holyoke women suffer from eating disorders. In addition, there are alumnae who feel that, because they have chosen to marry, have children, and work in the home, they have not lived up to the college's expectations for them and feel they no longer have a place there.

Efforts Toward Multiculturalism

Mount Holyoke faculty, administrators, and students have made a commitment to create and sustain a multicultural community, a community in which diversity is celebrated and differences are appreciated. In the words of an African-American senior, "Mount Holyoke is truly a multiracial community," a fact that she identified as a highlight of her college experience. Other students describe having increased their understanding and appreciation of different cultures, political perspectives, and lifestyles.

Students assert that "diversity is a word you hear around here," and issues of racism, sexism, classism, and heterosexism are regularly examined, discussed, and confronted. While a diverse, even pluralistic, community is celebrated, it is also acknowledged to be a matter for constant attention on the part of all community members, not just people of color. Efforts toward multiculturalism and elimination of "the isms among us" are viewed by student affairs staff as implicit in their developmental mission, and in the college's educational mission.

At the same time, there is a recognition that, to build and maintain a multicultural community, some risk and public struggle will be required. A member of the student affairs staff stated, "If this is a goal, then what problems do we face? Someone will finally have to say 'Professor X is a racist.'" The message from administrators and faculty is, clearly, that they are willing to face the inevitable conflict that comes with change and they are willing to admit that "we make mistakes and we're willing to address them in a very public way." Nevertheless, racial incidents at the University of Massachusetts have made African-American students at Mount Holyoke College more aware of potential problems and "more cautious." Also, recall the earlier discussion of feelings of isolation and separation expressed by some students of color and international students. No one at Mount Holyoke College believes that change will come quickly or easily.

Student affairs staff play many roles in the movement toward multiculturalism. The assistant dean of students serves as a liaison between the organizations of women of color and gives voice to their concerns in meetings with staff and faculty. In addition, student affairs staff are actively involved in modeling what an inclusive world means, in their language, hiring practices, and policy decisions.

Need-Blind Admission

Mount Holyoke College currently has a policy of need-blind admission — admission of students without regard for ability to pay — and a commitment to financial aid packages that meet 100 percent of need, policies that a student affairs staff member called "the ticket to building a multiracial community." In addition to demonstrating the college's commitment of becoming a multicultural community, these policies also model the college's value of service. As a consequence, Mount Holyoke College provides full funding (over $100,000 over four years) for several hundred students, and varying amounts of aid to others, each year; approximately 60 percent of Mount Holyoke students have some form of financial aid, all of which is need-based. The college is also committed to minimizing the differences between students that can occur with a wide range of socioeconomic backgrounds. For example, computers have been placed in each residence hall so that being able to afford a computer of one's own need not create an academic advantage.

These policies result in financial obligations that are increasingly difficult for the college to maintain, and painful discussions have occurred about what funding Mount Holyoke College can afford to continue to provide for students. Mount Holyoke is not alone in confronting what some at the college call "a fundamental issue for selective, expensive schools" whose philosophical commitments depend, in part, on shrinking revenues for implementation. For example, Smith College decided last year that it could no longer continue its policy of need-blind admissions.

Roles of Faculty

Faculty roles at Mount Holyoke College have changed in the past decade, and continue to evolve. During much of this century, Mount Holyoke faculty lived in the white frame houses that surround the campus, and academic and personal involvement between students and faculty was commonplace. Alumnae from the '50s and '60s recall single female faculty members whose lives were totally focused on the campus, although their involvement with students, even then, was based primarily on academic interests and pursuits.

It is clear that professional and personal demands on Mount Holyoke faculty are changing, as they are at most colleges and universities. Many faculty are in dual-career relationships that require that they live somewhere other than South Hadley. According to current faculty, proximity of faculty homes to campus is a big factor in involvement with students outside of class. Faculty were very involved in the residence halls — especially at meal times — until six or seven years ago, but that no longer seems to be the case. The dinner hour is a very busy time for faculty members with children, as well as for students. This press of evening time commitments was one of the reasons for instituting the faculty-student-staff lunches described earlier in this section.

Scholarship — that is, expertise in a discipline, research, and publication — is of increasing importance at Mount Holyoke College, in terms of both the reward system for faculty and the professional interests and commitments of individual faculty members. Junior faculty come to the college socialized to research as an essential part of their work and with expectations that success in their disciplines requires publication of that research in national journals. In addition, there is a perception among many students, faculty, and staff that "excellence in research" (as indicated, in part, by publications) has assumed increasing importance for obtaining tenure and promotions; it has not, however, eclipsed the importance of teaching.

Some recent tenure decisions have increased student interest and concern about institutional priorities for faculty time; students are worried about the apparent valuing of scholarship over involvement with students out of class. Similarly, an academic administrator asserted that a critical issue for Mount Holyoke College in the near future will be coping with the changes that will occur as a result of recruiting noted scholars and researchers to the faculty. In his words, "we're facing reality and becoming more flexible" in expectations for faculty involvement with students, as well as trying to figure out how to involve faculty with students in ways that support the college's educational mission. Involvement based on academic endeavors is the likely pattern for the future, and faculty, and the college as a whole, will probably define involvement as primarily intellectual, rarely social.

The Role of Student Affairs Staff

Although student affairs staff and their roles have been mentioned throughout this case, two issues deserve specific attention here: the characteristics and functions of the Mount Holyoke student affairs staff and the influence on student affairs staff of changing faculty roles and changing needs of students.

Office of the Dean of Students

The formal title for the student affairs staff is the Office of the Dean of Students. The office is generally responsible for providing services to students which support the college's academic purposes and enhance the quality of out-of-class life.

In addition to the dean, staff roles include:

- Associate dean who advises student government, provides training for residence hall staff, and coordinates Wellsprings, the college wellness series
- Assistant dean who advises the Latina-American, Asian-American, and African-American student organizations and ensures that these students' needs are heard throughout the college; coordinates the orientation program for women of color; coordinates all honors and awards programs; and edits the student handbook
- Director of student activities who advises and coordinates cocurricular programs and activities
- Director of residential life who oversees all aspects of the residence halls, including room assignments, staff supervision, and educational programming
- Residential life staff, including head residents, hall presidents, and student advisors

Other staff members are responsible for managing the Blanchard Campus Center, the health center, the Alcohol and Drug Awareness Project, the Office of Career Services, and the chaplaincies.

The student affairs staff are very energetic. As previously stated, in 1989 all but three of the staff members were women, and most were not alumnae of Mount Holyoke College. They have a shared commitment to student development, particularly women's development, and believe that Mount Holyoke's institution-wide commitment to a total educational experience for students provides an ideal environment in which to "do" student affairs work. A majority of the staff do not have backgrounds in student affairs work or professional student affairs preparation programs; this may be helpful in fostering the blurred boundaries between academic and nonacademic aspects of the college.

Changing Faculty Roles

In the previous section, the changes in institutional expectations for faculty (i.e., more research and publications, perhaps less involvement with students in out-of-class activities) and in faculty lifestyles (i.e., living away from the campus, multiple family responsibilities) were described. What these changes will mean for student affairs staff is not altogether clear. The president has made providing additional resources (people and money) for student affairs a priority at the same time she has emphasized recruiting high-quality faculty who may not be interested in spending much time with students' extracurricular activities. The Office of the Dean of Students is increasingly charged with tasks related to the nonintellectual development of students. Thus, the responsibilities and visibility of student affairs staff have expanded and so has their influence.

These trends have prompted some thought and discussion among some faculty and student affairs staff about "where the faculty role stops — where the line falls between intellectual and emotional development, and whether they can, in any reasonable way, be separated." So far, student affairs staff perceive that faculty members are their partners in the process of determining how they can pool their strengths to serve the needs of students. The dean of students asserts that "there is a complementary quality to what we do that recognizes and respects different ways of helping students." For example, several faculty use class time to make links between the curriculum and the daily lives of students, including issues of racism, sexism, and classism.

Nevertheless, a concern of student affairs staff, as well as others in the college, is the extent to which students will feel — or should feel — comfortable with shifting faculty priorities. The college community is talking openly about these issues while focusing on what it means to provide a high-quality liberal education for undergraduate women.

Changing Needs of Students

Student affairs staff described their role at Mount Holyoke College as including that of "institutional observer of the changing student." That is, student affairs staff define themselves as the institutional experts on issues and problems affecting students' lives and learning. For example, a team, including the dean and financial aid staff, has been organized to identify and respond to students most at risk as a result of family financial crises. In addition, these staff help students and parents with the complex process of applying for financial aid.

Student affairs staff at Mount Holyoke College increasingly find themselves "picking up the slack from other social institutions" such as family and school. Students are coming to the college with more complex personal histories and in need of services that, in the words of the dean, "keep a person together emotionally." In the past, the college years were a time when students began to experiment with alcohol and sex, and when some students faced parents' divorce; the role of the college was in shaping students' development in these areas. Many of today's students have established patterns of sexual behavior, alcohol and other drug use, and have coped with fragmented family life. The role of the college, then, is to react to what has already occurred in students' lives. For example, the focus of alcohol and drug programming at Mount Holyoke College has had to move beyond education about effects to dealing with such topics as the role of alcohol in sexual assaults and the effect of alcohol on trust between men and women.

These trends have also raised concerns about the extensive use of peer educators (e.g., in alcohol and drug education, women's health issues, wellness) and peer helpers (e.g., in the residence halls) at the college. The extent to which students can, or should, be responsible for helping other students deal with problems of such magnitude as alcoholism, eating disorders, and abusive family relationships is a matter of serious discussion among student affairs staff. A complicating factor is, according to the dean, "the endlessly supportive nature of a women's community" in which students' perceived obligation to help one another has no limits. This perception can be particularly debilitating for student hall staff and peer educators. At the same time, there is an institutional commitment to allowing students to take ownership and have responsibility for as much of their lives as possible. The student affairs staff face "a real dilemma" in balancing these conflicting needs and priorities in a way that is ultimately helpful and healthy for students and the college. One step that has been taken is to increase the time and numbers of staff involved in the training and supervision of peer educators.

Conclusion

Self-confidence is a word that one hears often at Mount Holyoke College. Students express confidence in their ability to know, and speak, their minds; confidence in their ability to be effective leaders; and confidence in their ability to think, write, do research, and learn. They are confident of their ability to do these things in the future because they have done them, and done them well, at Mount Holyoke College. The combination of challenge and support offered within a community dedicated to the liberal education of women enables students to believe in themselves and their capabilities, even after they graduate.

This case began with the words of Adrienne Rich (1986); it seems appropriate to conclude with her words as well:

> Most of the world is not a women's place, but a women-negating place....[W]omen need a sense of what a women's place can be — not somewhere to retire to and be protected, but to become empowered, go forth from, sure of their own value and integrity...not just having beautiful residence halls and gardens, but a soul (p. 196).

   While Mount Holyoke College is certainly a lovely place, it is also a place where women — students, faculty, and administrators — are empowered by the presence of rigorous challenges and nurturance. They learn that they can, indeed, be anything they want to be. Student affairs staff play an essential role in the "soul" of Mount Holyoke College; they are the experts on students and keep the attention of the college focused equally on the heart, body, and mind.

Commentary

The Mount Holyoke Case
Daryl G. Smith

What, then, are the lessons to be learned from the Mount Holyoke case? Is there any way that institutions which are not small, are not women's colleges, and are not single-purpose institutions can learn from this case? The answer is *yes*.

It is all too easy to look at such a school and dismiss its accomplishments as having been achieved easily as a result of its size and relative homogeneity of purpose. Indeed, there are many small, single-purpose institutions which are not characterized by a high level of student involvement and a strong sense of community and which would not have been considered successful by the standards of the cases in this book.

Nevertheless, it is important to note at the outset that large, nonresidential campuses have to struggle against the disadvantages of size and proximity to achieve what smaller, residential institutions more readily can achieve. Moreover, it may be easier (though not easy) to create affirming, rather than negating, environments for women at women's colleges and for African-Americans at historically black colleges. The challenge of doing so is important. Not only are negating environments all too common for many students, but they are antithetical to the educational purposes of our institutions.

What then are the lessons to be learned, and how might a large institution or a nonresidential institution develop qualities of involvement seen in this case?

Creating a Community Ethos

One of the first lessons of this case is the degree of intentionality which exists in creating the Mount Holyoke community ethos. Nothing appears to be taken for granted. Students are socialized early on to their specialness, to the challenge for excellence, to the expectations for community standards and behavior, and to their participation and value to the community. Too many campuses assume that if they are small, then community will develop naturally. Too many campuses assume that institutional expectations and values will be transmitted easily to students. Many campuses assume that expectations for students and community are impossible to achieve. We assign students to committees without training, for example, and we leave the transmission of the history and culture of the institution to groups which are often not part of the institutional mainstream (such as fraternities and sororities). Indeed, we often abdicate teaching leadership and values, and thus miss the possibilities for creating community.

Mount Holyoke College also seems to reflect support for a body of research evidence on the impact of college; that is, campuses which have shared values but which involve students from diverse backgrounds are likely to have the most impact. The shared values are the basis on which community is built. Its dedication to educating women is certainly part of that commonality for Mount Holyoke College, but there are other values as well.

One of the most powerful is the expectation for achievement and excellence in a supportive environment. The case suggests that this value lives not just in the rhetoric of the institution but in the minds of administrators and faculty as well. As our campuses become more diverse, it is this belief that will probably have more to do with campus success than anything else. As it is now, too many campuses fundamentally do not believe in the students' ability to excel. Overreliance on tests, stereotyping, or lack of commitment leave many students concluding that they are not expected to succeed.

Students also are expected to contribute to the community through service, through exercising responsibility for healthy residential and community life, and through participation. This campus does not shy away from creating expectations for behavior and attitudes which support the community. These expectations are laid down in standards, not legalistic policies, and they are clearly supported and enforced with student participation and support. Behavioral expectations of respect for persons and property do not appear to contradict encouraging individual points of view, academic freedom, and free speech.

Ironically, even though Mount Holyoke is small, the college has found it easier to develop communities in even smaller residence halls than on the campus as a whole. Indeed, the basis of relationships is being addressed outside of the residence hall through a better designed and implemented campus center. Campuses which have small residence halls but common dining facilities can capitalize on the possibilities of developing community in the larger context as well.

This case suggests that any campus has to begin to identify natural groups which are available, or which can be developed as the locus of a reasonably sized community. As with the Holyoke case, there will also be the continuing need to develop multiple communities so that students are not isolated. This strikes me as both the potential and the liability of fraternities and sororities and athletic groups on larger campuses. Use of colleges or schools within universities, fraternities and sororities, residence halls, or

145

even residence hall floors must all be considered. Campus clubs, athletic groups, religious groups, and other smaller communities can be explored. The challenge is to develop cultures, traditions, and values which are supportive of the institution and which do not negate important institutional goals. On many campuses, the isolation and lack of connection between the larger campus and isolated groups often results in the development of group values which are antithetical to academic and intellectual values, for example. Even student affairs professionals can be perceived as unsupportive of academic values by paying little attention to those issues or by paying attention only to extracurricular experiences, thus creating a schism between the faculty and student affairs. It may be important, then, to encourage multiple memberships so that individuals are not encapsulated. Student affairs professionals who advise and students who are members of athletic groups and honor societies are all examples of multiple memberships.

Adequate Role Models

Another factor which is important at Mount Holyoke College is the presence of many women in leadership positions at the student, faculty or administrative level, so that students see diversity among women. That is, at Mount Holyoke College a woman might fail without being labelled as a failure for all women. The absence of token women (i.e., the presence of many women) gives students a range of styles, attitudes, and abilities to observe. Students can choose based on individual preferences, rather than based on inaccurate, stereotypical expectations for how women are to lead their lives. No doubt Mount Holyoke College went through periods where there was pressure for women to assume certain lifestyles, but the sheer variety of faculty, staff, and visible graduates makes simple conclusions or stereotypes difficult. The lesson is that members of historically underrepresented groups are needed in sufficient numbers at all levels of the institution so that no one person has the burden of being the representative for all. No doubt Mount Holyoke must still struggle with this for faculty and staff of color. In addition, the importance of men who strongly support women's education and leadership cannot be underestimated.

The Role of Faculty and Student Affairs

The role of faculty and the relationship between faculty and student affairs obviously is still evolving at Mount Holyoke. There are two lessons to be taken from the case in this area. The case points out that the student affairs staff often do not come from backgrounds in student affairs. The lesson is not about the content of one's background, but rather about the importance of appreciating and creating links to the academic purpose of the institution and establishing credibility in that arena. Student affairs staff must vigorously reflect the mission of the institution in its structure, programs, and attitudes.

The second lesson here is that faculty can and should be involved and (I would suggest) will be involved in activities which closely connect to their work as faculty. There are, and always will be, faculty who are interested in student life in a purely extracurricular sense. Indeed, one finds these lines being blurred more and more with faculty from fields such as ethnic studies and women's studies where the basic paradigm of the field blurs personal, intellectual, and professional lines. Nevertheless, it may be important to stress those areas which come closer to "normal" faculty responsibilities. Advising cultural programs, developing visiting scholar and lecture series, and working as academic advisors are just a few such areas.

As Mount Holyoke College is adjusting to an evolution in faculty lifestyles, other campuses never have had the advantage of faculty living in close proximity. Indeed, on many contemporary campuses, neither faculty nor students are available in the evenings. Community can be built at times of the day when people are available, academic programs can build expectations for participation (e.g., in lectures and programs) and, where possible, events can be designed to include families. As Mount Holyoke is discovering, activities which ask people to choose between family and the campus will struggle. Including the families of students and faculty can be a successful approach to ensuring student participation in these kinds of events.

To conclude that the strength of the community of Mount Holyoke is simply a function of simple institutional characteristics is to dismiss the effort, tradition, and vision of those who understand that community and involvement are developed intentionally and over time by articulating shared values and building genuine participation in the development of that community. Expectations for success and participation combined with examples of and opportunities for leadership are characteristics that can be emulated much more widely.

Chapter Eight

Checking of the Truth
The Case of Earlham College

Lee E. Krehbiel and C. Carney Strange

Earlham College is a four-year, residential, coeducational, liberal arts college founded in 1847 by the Religious Society of Friends (Quakers). It currently enrolls approximately 1,100 students (52 percent female) from 46 states and 16 foreign countries. Earlham's 120 faculty members offer a full range of traditional liberal arts majors (e.g., chemistry, French, political science), an unusual selection of interdisciplinary majors (e.g., human development and social relations, wilderness studies, and Japanese studies), special academic programs (e.g., museum studies), cooperative programs (e.g., engineering, business, and architecture), and preprofessional programs (e.g., medicine, law, and ministry). The distinctive character of this institution is a product of its affiliation with Quaker thought and ideals, and understanding the Quaker tradition is a key to understanding the mission of Earlham College.

Quakers migrated to the farmlands of Indiana from the slaveholding South, where farmers without slaves operated at an economic disadvantage. Quakers had always been leaders in education and several academies, some of college-level, were established in the upper Midwest — institutions that later served as feeder schools for Earlham College. The year 1847 marked the inauguration of the Friends Boarding School in Richmond, Indiana, which became Earlham College. The name *Earlham* dates to the ancestral home of a prominent English Quaker family, the Gurneys. Fittingly, Earlham was the meeting place of many English reformers.

Earlham College's history is best read with some knowledge of Quaker business principles and decision-making processes. Local monthly business meetings (always accompanied by worship) are combined into quarterly meetings for a larger group and these, in turn, into a yearly meeting. All meetings are headed by a clerk who records the "sense of the meeting" (i.e., the consensus of those present), which is then articulated at appropriate times during the proceedings. As a general rule, discussion proceeds until a consensus is reached on what is discerned to be the truth. Although consensus building is rarely a brief process, it has provided a foundation for the resolution of difficult questions throughout the society's history and has averted a number of schisms threatened by an inability to listen thoroughly. Remarkably, consensus pervades the society and its institutions in practice as well as language even today.

Earlham's "way of getting things done" rests on a series of rather discreet Quaker principles, among which are:

- There is God in every person, an Inner Light for guidance
- Evil is also present in each individual, and thus a battle is fought
- An imperfect perception of God renders it necessary to check the truth one perceives against that perceived by others.

Although in today's formulation of these principles the emphasis on the presence of evil in the human heart has diminished somewhat, these historic tenets of Quaker belief still make sense of much of what occurs at Earlham College.

The Inner Light referred to in these principles is seen as a democratizing influence at the institution, such that all formal or titular distinctions are downplayed. For example, in the post World War I period, a debate over wearing academic regalia at commencement ensued and the distinctions attributed to caps and gowns were thus challenged as conflicting with the Quaker emphasis on simplicity. Even Earlham's architecture reflects a functional simplicity. Other expressions of this emphasis on the Earlham campus are found in the widespread use of first names (a modern custom that is actually inconsistent with the traditional Quaker use of the full name) and a campus directory listing all persons alphabetically and in uniform style, from the grounds crew to the president.

The Quaker belief in "checking of the truth" stems from an acknowledgement of sin, an insistence on none having all the truth, and a belief in the possibility of real good being accomplished, in part, through reaching consensus as a community. The humorous saga is chronicled in the history of Earlham College about a prominent professor of math, chemistry, and botany, Professor Erastus Test, who became interested in evolutionary theory. As the story goes, in 1874, he named his newborn twin sons Charles Darwin and Louis Agassiz, respectively, after the famous evolutionary theorist and the Harvard scientist who opposed him. The professor's propriety may be challenged, but the point of the story is clear: in the Quaker tradition, minds should not be made up prior to a full hearing of all evidence or consideration of all sides of the question.

There are several features, physical as well as programmatic, that mark the history of Earlham College and lend to its distinctive character today: the centrality of the library in the life of the college; the recurring emphasis on and success in the natural sciences; and a long-standing interest in non-Western cultures and peoples, particularly the Japanese. These features have remained steady through the usual institutional cycles of feast and famine, the disputes over policy and personnel, and gallant recoveries from devastating fires or other tragedies in Earlham's history. Throughout are roots that run deep in the moral and spiritual values of a Quaker understanding of Christianity.

Earlham's library today (with generous support of the Eli Lilly Foundation) is highly ranked and is described by students and faculty as a center of the campus, in many ways the heart of the school. The librarian, Evan Farber, is an integral figure on campus and is thought of as a rich resource and a "keeper of the vision," a critical role in maintaining an institution's distinctiveness. He is perhaps best known for posting clippings from a wide range of current publications on a highly visible bulletin board in the library, challenging all who pass through to consider various issues of importance to the world. The head of the Indianapolis Public Library stated in 1926 that there was perhaps no other college in America of Earlham's size which had sent as many trained librarians into professional service.

Long tenures of librarians have been the rule at Earlham, with their dedication to student learning being perhaps more impressive than the collections themselves, although the Quaker and other special collections are noteworthy in their own right. The current library staff has a core of 5-6 persons who have been together for close to 20 years, and remain innovators. Farber and company pioneered in a cogent and transportable model for developing close ties between library staff and teaching faculty, and more recently have delved into the effect on learning (teaching and being taught) of unlimited information. A current agreement with Digital Corporation provides access to a 24-hour-a-day, on-line computer information service.

The famous Quaker historian, Rufus M. Jones, attributed to President Joseph Moore (1868-83) the vision of complementariness between the gospel and scientific inquiry, revealed and discovered knowledge. This combination of spirituality and scientific rigor, through recurring episodes of debate and even acrimony, has served Earlham College well throughout its history. As early as 1903, particularly in chemistry and geology, a tradition of involving undergraduate students in current scientific research was apparent. In the 1930s and 1940s, studies by the Association of American Colleges, among others, applauded Earlham College for its contributions to the ranks of scientists, especially in light of the institution's considerable enrollment of women in the sciences at a time when opportunities for professional involvement were often proscribed. Today, these traditions are present in joint efforts of faculty and students in science-based research projects, working toward a solution for an existing problem in the local community or beyond. Indeed, concern for and involvement in the larger community is a touchstone of Quaker spirituality. Thus, when a new science hall was dedicated in 1952, along with a new meetinghouse, the special convocation speech was entitled "The Contribution of Religion and Science to a Free Society." Earlham's influence in the sciences, the success of its graduates, and the quality of its facilities remains first-rate, a point well supported by the fact that Earlham ranks 17th among the nation's colleges in its per-graduate production of PhDs in the natural sciences.

Earlham's interest in and involvement with peoples of other cultures, most notably the Japanese, has a colorful history. In a 1915 speech, the international secretary of the YWCA noted that, of the hundreds of American colleges, she recommended Earlham to a Japanese student because she was impressed by the "clean, Christian type of students here." In 1926, the World Fellowship Group of the Christian Associations consulted with Earlham's Professor Thomas R. Kelly, resulting in a campus-wide project challenging the Japanese Exclusion Act as uncharacteristic of the American student spirit of friendliness, cooperation, and appreciation for the Japanese people and culture. In a statement of campus values, an Earlham student was subsidized through fund raisers and contributions for the cost above Earlham fees for a year of study at Imperial University in Tokyo. Friends and Earlhamites in Japan acted as facilitators, and the project was successful. Its fruits, direct and indirect, continue to the present day and included in one recent year a football contest between Earlham College and its sister Japanese institution. The World War II period saw Earlham taking in various refugees, among them Japanese-Americans (the Nisei). Up to ten Nisei students at a time came to Earlham from the western United States. A later Earlham president, Thomas Elsa Jones, was a professor at Keio University in Japan, a member of the Tokyo Mission of

Philadelphia Friends, and wrote his doctoral thesis on Japanese mountain folk. A new non-Western studies program, developed in the 1950s in conjunction with Antioch College, again featured the study of Japanese language and culture. A Professor Bailey, instrumental in developing that program, had been a member of the forces occupying Japan after World War II. He returned to teach for three years under the American Friends Service Committee and spent another year in Asia for study and research. Today the campus and many of the curricular and off-campus study opportunities reflect this interest in peoples of non-Western cultures. The Japanese concept of "shabui," a special appreciation for simplicity, is particularly resonant with the Quaker ethos and identifies much of what is deemed virtuous and admirable in both cultures.

The post World War II era witnessed the arrival at Earlham College of various new influential persons from the Civilian Public Service camps (serving as "conscientious objectors") and other institutions. This cohort included what are affectionately termed *Quakeroids*, that is, non-Quakers who are nonetheless committed to Quaker ideals and who challenge Quakers by their lives to live out their creed. One of these new members of the Earlham community was Professor Elton Trueblood, who articulated seven hallmarks of Quaker education: veracity, discipline, simplicity, individuality, community, concern, and peace. Simply put, the central purpose of Quaker education is to infuse people with these traits, a goal that continues to shape Earlham's fourfold emphasis on the worth of the individual, a sense of mission, discipline, and agreement.

Student Characteristics, Subgroups, and Cultures

Despite students' insistence that diversity prevails at Earlham College, there is a clear and consistent profile which can be drawn among them. Only about 12 percent of the students enrolled are of a Quaker background and fewer than 5 percent are African-Americans. For the most part, Earlham students tend to be middle- and upperclass, urban, second or third generation college attenders, frequently sons and daughters of university professors or administrators (about 25 percent), and typically from the Midwest (about 50 percent) or East Coast (about 40 percent). Current clothing trends among the self-described cosmopolitan student body are for a loose-fitting, earth-tone casual dress, described by one observer as the "Annie Hall" look.

The student-institution fit is very good. Students easily resonate with the kinds of opportunities Earlham offers, and the college itself benefits from the types of students who enroll, most of whom are politically active and aware, liberal, bright, and interested in collaboration. Earlham College attracts this type of student through word of mouth, reputation, self-selection, and honest recruiting based on a direct and realistic presentation of the institution's values and context. The fit is further honed through a consistently articulated and nearly universally shared "cognitive frame" comprised of a discernible core of common understandings and values. This is perhaps the most striking feature of all at Earlham College.

A large majority of Earlham students could have been successful, and probably would have been, at any of hundreds of other institutions. They view their own experience as whole and seamless, without strict divisions. They learn quickly how the institution works and indeed are a large part of the governance structures. Expectations of responsibility for personal lives and learning are taken seriously.

A key to understanding the typical Earlham student lies in the concept of *being PC* (i.e., being politically correct), a term they may use to refer to each other's point of view or action. As one senior noted, "being PC" is assured by being liberal, sensitive to social values, sensitive to the oppressed; by seeking social change; and by rejecting capitalist ideas of individualism and material consumption. From a more cynical perspective, a self-proclaimed "non-PC" student (who nonetheless appreciated the Quaker concepts of community, mutual respect, positive confrontation, and consensus) described the typical "PC" Earlhamite (an oxymoron in this student's view) as having a "Farms not Arms" bumper sticker, one tie-dye shirt, a closet full of good clothes never used, at least one Grateful Dead album, a '60s type liberalism, and as being an "outsider" to the system. In any case, Earlham students are activists in their own right, and it is not unusual to hear them acknowledge a sense of guilt if they are not as heavily invested outside the immediate classroom as someone else, or to a degree they deem acceptable.

One observer perceived that Earlham students "tend their own communities," by and large, communities that are compatible with the prevailing values of the college. Student-faculty relationships are close at Earlham College and may be initiated by either party, as often occurs in the context of various institutional structures such as the Wilderness Experience, humanities program, or various service projects. Earlham students learn from each other, from work in the larger Richmond community, and from faculty beyond the classroom settings. Finally, most student subcultures promote student involvement in activities that complement the institution's educational purposes.

Factors of Campus Involvement

Earlham College contributes to students' out-of-class involvement in educationally purposeful ways through its mission and philosophy, campus environments, campus culture, various policies and practices, and institutional agents, including faculty, administrators, and students.

Earlham's institutional mission and philosophy are both coherent and distinctive: to make a difference in human society. Earlham College seeks to develop morally and socially sensitive leaders who will be committed to making the world a better place. Faculty, administrators, and students alike have a common understanding of what the college is about, and that vision is carefully infused into writings, curriculum designs, teaching practices, administrative policies, admissions materials and, perhaps most important, the core of the institution's decision-making structures. The principal components of the institutions's philosophy include a commitment of responsibility to the betterment of the global community, a belief in the presence of the Light of Truth in each individual, and an expectation that learning entails action and must make a difference in one's life. Thus, any participant in Earlham's community is likely to be thoughtful and articulate in his or her description of the college's mission and to express a personal commitment to many of the tenets contained therein.

Earlham College is nestled on a wooded 200-acre front campus and 600-acre back campus of woods, fields, and farmland within walking distance of Richmond, Indiana, a small city of 40,000 inhabitants. The campus' 35 buildings convey an architectural and functional simplicity, in testament to the Quaker style, and include typical small-college arrangements of administrative, classroom, library, residential, and union facilities, purposely situated among native hardwoods and open lawns to preserve both privacy and space. Distinctive to Earlham's physical plant, though, is the meetinghouse, a simply designed structure where silence is respected, ideas are openly shared, and decisions are made in the time-honored tradition of consensus. Earlham College maintains five residence halls and 15 college-owned houses adjacent to the campus (including four language houses and a black cultural center) for approximately 800 residential students. In addition, the college supports Miller Farm, a nearby small-group cooperative, where students explore interdependent living in an isolated rural setting.

Institutional culture and various campus traditions also distinguish Earlham College. For example, a Vigil on the Heart refers to an outdoor meeting held near the center of campus, in an area encircled by a sidewalk, where students may gather to show support for a worthy cause or issue. If the vigil attracts an unbroken circle of persons holding hands in a demonstration of support around the entire circumference of the "heart," it is considered especially successful. Other campus events that qualify as traditions include the quadrennial May Day celebration dating from the Victorian era (known as Big May Days to distinguish them from Little May Days which are held in alternate years), when students reenact the fabled days of Robin Hood, Maid Marian (the designated Queen of the May Day) and her court, complete with jesters, shows, puppet plays, costume horses, sword fights, and "romping around" on the Earlham lawns. More recent additions to the current campus culture include: Winter Carnival, observed since the Blizzard of 1978; Sun Splash, a full day of reggae music and sunshine in May (when the weather cooperates); Air Guitar, a lipsync mime show of popular music hits; Cafe and Bread Box, both regular showcases of campus talent in the union coffee shop; and Saga Announcements from the balcony of the union cafeteria.

A particularly prominent and interesting artifact of Earlham culture is the Opinion Board, begun in 1948 as a forum for expressing views. Located in a high-traffic area of the union building, a large bulletin board provides space for posting written statements of view, usually about recent campus, community, or world events. Responses to these statements are posted in like fashion, until the wall takes on the appearance of a paper smorgasbord of opinion, fact, and interpretation. An Earlham professor's recent visit to Saddam Hussein and the Eli Lilly Company's (one of Earlham's major benefactors) stock policy in South Africa were two recent subjects of rather intense scrutiny. The Opinion Board is both a lively place and a symbol of many cherished values at the school, including the provision for an open hearing of all sides of an issue, mutual accountability (statements are usually signed), and the revisiting of important issues to keep them alive. Earlhamites, especially some concerned faculty, appear wary of institutionalizing any but those practices most fundamental to the institution's core of beliefs. Whether any of the more recent additions to the campus lore will persist, time will tell.

Several venerated heroes and heroines are quietly celebrated in the history of Earlham College. As is the Quaker custom, the lives and accomplishments of individuals do the speaking at Earlham College, and praising others is unseemly and a potential source of embarrassment. This holds true for the institution as well as those who have helped shape it, and questions must be carefully worded to uncover the litany of these principals. A reflection of this press toward egalitarianism and understatement is the use today, across the board, of first names and the rare use of titles. Movers and shakers are known, but quietly. One name mentioned frequently is that of Joe Elmore, a former dean of faculties and "Quakerized" Methodist minister who played a major role in building the faculty and encouraging both Quakers and non-Quakers to work together. Elmore is spoken highly of as a significant translator and shaper of the Earlham College experience. Others are faculty members, such as Bill Stevenson and Gordon Thompson, practicing Quakers who kept the tradition alive. To each recognition is afforded, but in a manner that outsiders must look carefully to find.

Policies and practices, both within and outside of the classroom, reflect the Quaker ethos and serve to communicate the "Earlham way" to all members of the campus community. Widespread use of consensus as the preferred means of conducting business, involvement of students in all aspects of campus decision making (including review of new and continuing faculty appointments), an emphasis on collaborative rather than competitive learning techniques, and endorsement of learning opportunities beyond the classroom through structures such as a Service Learning Program and an Office of Co-Curricular Studies are examples of how Earlham College engages students in a distinctive experience of living and learning.

Finally, the nature of institutional agents at Earlham College, including faculty, administrators, and students, is important in understanding the institution's distinction as an involving college. Students repeatedly pointed to being challenged by faculty through example. Faculty are often personally involved, especially in ways that build bridges from the classroom to the larger world. For example, a physical science class may have ties to an environmental issues group. In one case, a professor was involved in a local water quality project, which attracted the attention and the efforts of students. Thus, it is not unusual to find classes, student organizations, and research projects interconnected as one continuous experience, in large measure through the efforts of committed faculty. The traditional liberal arts goal of "knowledge for its own sake" is viewed with much suspicion in the Quaker tradition. To learn about something entails a conclusion, and conclusions entail action. An awareness of the causes of illiteracy, for example, entails the learner to do something about its contributing factors.

A related factor in understanding the Earlham professoriate is reflected in the criteria for tenure. Rejecting the current trend by liberal arts schools to consciously emulate the values of larger, research-oriented institutions, Earlham College emphasizes teaching as the single most important factor. Other criteria include "quality of mind" (a term used to refer to an individual's intellectual vitality, which may be demonstrated in a variety of ways), compatibility with the community, and service to the community. Students report that faculty assign much and encourage involvement in much. There is an apparent synergism created as students help select new faculty who will reinforce the existing norms regarding student involvement and personal commitment, which in turn adds to the institutional climate in which students repeat those types of selections. This is a self-renewing process which carries within itself the seeds of the next generation. Any change in the faculty's commitment to student involvement, personal responsibility to better society, or a collaborative learning model would pose a significant threat to the effectiveness of the student affairs division in complementing the educational purposes of Earlham College.

Academic Programs and Student Affairs

Programmatic ties between the Earlham curriculum and the efforts and goals of the student affairs division are plentiful and impressive. These programs, a sampling of which are described herein, facilitate the contribution of various student affairs offices to the educational purposes of the institution. The goals of these academic programs are clearly congruent and supportive of those shared in student affairs.

One illustration of this connection can be found in Earlham's international study programs. In the interest of cultural awareness and appreciation for diversity (values which have received a good deal of attention in student affairs recently) Earlham College has cultivated a deep and lasting relationship with the people and culture of Japan, a relationship that has spanned 100 years. Evidence of this exchange is reflected in the curriculum of the institution, in frequent cultural exhibits, in a formal Japanese garden on the Earlham campus, and in ongoing projects and trips involving faculty and students. By graduation, fully one-half of all Earlham students will have studied overseas for a semester or even a year, and almost 70 percent will have studied somewhere off campus. There are some 30 options of international study available to Earlham students, and such experiences are a major component of the institution's commitment to global awareness.

Another important illustration is found in the institution's peace and global studies program. With the help of students, Earlham College initiated this interdisciplinary major comprising a series of four courses which concentrate on disciplinary tools needed for analyzing an increasingly complex and interconnected world. A sampling of the curriculum includes one political science course, entitled Political Violence and the World Order, which looks at causes, consequences, and potential solutions to political violence at both the national and international levels. All students take at least one of the four base courses. Many of the related campus-based student organizations and activities focus on these same issues.

Finally, the humanities program is an interesting example of the complementary relationship between student affairs and academic affairs on the Earlham campus. This program is especially noteworthy because it reuses a common core of readings on an annual basis. The program is described in a carefully worded rationale discussing what the humanities are and why they are part of the college's course of studies. A preface is written to colleagues and parents explaining the course's emphasis on collaborative learning, its approach to canonicity, and the egalitarian method used for selecting faculty (i.e., without regard to rank) to participate (created and sustained by senior faculty). First-year students take a common humanities course. Classes comprise participating in a living-learning experience in a residence hall, where the trials of learning to struggle analytically with texts are paralleled by the trials of living on one's own and adapting to a new roommate. Decisions in both instances are made using consensus, the Quaker way. With papers due each Monday morning, this class serves as an extended orientation experience, a loom in which living and learning in a Quaker context are woven into a seamless fabric.

These kinds of experiences (especially the international studies and the peace and global studies programs) do for students, in terms of cultural understanding and sensitivity, what few "in-house" programs can. Even under restrictions of time, finances, or student demographics, the establishment of formal ties, student and faculty exchanges, symbolic physical plant reflections, and promotion of various credit bearing courses go a long way toward meeting these goals. The combination of a culturally rich and provocative curriculum and students returning from a variety of cultural "immersions" inevitably leads to student-initiated groups, projects, and programming which provide exactly what thoughtful activities programmers strive for — a balance between activities provided for students and those which arise through student initiative.

In summary, the student affairs' ties to the curriculum emerge from the college's culture as well as its personnel, and some have been intentionally forged to exploit a particular opportunity. The most impressive resource for student affairs personnel on the Earlham campus is a classroom faculty who are committed to students, involved in their lives and projects (often their own projects), and are concerned about their conduct and well-being. Faculty, through their assignments and expectations, contribute to a climate where heavy involvement is the norm.

The Contributions of Student Affairs

Traditional distinctions between student affairs and academic affairs are not readily applicable or discernible at an institution like Earlham College. The contributions of the student affairs division appear to be successful precisely because of practices and policies informed by the same values as the rest of the college, and because their staff efforts are generally supported by the faculty and other administrators. Involvement in campus organizations has long been an explicit feature of the Earlham learning experience as evidenced by a point system devised as early as 1912 regulating the amount of cocurricular involvement a student might undertake. The Quaker ethos and values permeate a range of divisionally sponsored programs and structures, particularly apparent in the following illustrations.

Judicial Affairs

Earlham College emphasizes positive support and contributions at least as much as adherence to rules. In doing so, the institution communicates very high expectations. In terms of judicial affairs, this means that efforts are made to settle any grievances at the lowest possible level, through direct dialogue if possible. If an incident cannot be resolved immediately, the "Hall," that is, a group of 12-15 students within a residence facility, is the first level of formal recourse. Those parts of the community most affected by a given action are engaged in the judicial process. Meetings between the offender(s) and the offended party(ies) are common where an understanding of the offense's ramifications for the broader community is pursued (e.g., its effect on trust, an essential element of community life), above and beyond any immediate considerations of property or personal damage. Reconciliation of the parties is another intended outcome of such meetings. The focus, according to student affairs staff, is on the behavior and not the person, thus providing an environment where mistakes may be accepted without the usual adversarial climate that often accompanies a formal judicial process.

Rules within the system are somewhat informal, although the Community Code delineates a series of aspirations and expectations which members of the community are to live by. According to Earlham's dean of student development, elaborate procedures, even those designed to protect due process or the signing of an honor code or behavioral contract, would in most cases be perceived as an insult at worst, a lack of trust at best or just inappropriate. Indeed, self-selection at Earlham (among other factors) is strong enough that the norm is for a guilty student to admit the same and to accept the consequences. Sanctions are linked to the offending act through this direct meeting system, and through frequent reference to the Community Code, itself an extension of the larger Quaker value system. It is commonplace for alternative sanctions to be offered, and the student is invited to discuss the more desirable of those alternatives. An attempt is made to hold hearings where an incident occurs, not at the violator's own residence, thereby strengthening personal accountability to the larger campus community.

Campus Activities and Organizations

Campus activities at Earlham College are less social and more political and issue-oriented than is usually the case on small college campuses. The Office of Campus Activities coordinates calendars and advises and assists students, but in many respects staff members act primarily as resources for students and generally remain out of their way. This intentionally demonstrates a respect for the autonomy and initiatory spirit of the Earlham student. The director's authority is purely advisory, without veto power. This orientation is best illustrated by a campus policy of attaching a rider to various performers' contracts, warning them of the likelihood of their views being rigorously challenged by the audience. Policies are enforced at campus events but the group is responsible for doing so, not the staff. Thus, the Community Code becomes the province and property of the students, and not a point of contention between students and staff.

Organizations are formed easily at Earlham College. Any group with a few interested parties may organize, have meetings, and conduct events, subject only to the Community Code. Once the group is active and visible, formal recognition, which allows access to funding and use of the college name, may be granted and normally is if the group's aims do not violate anyone's civil rights or are not contrary to Quaker traditions. No fraternities or sororities exist on campus and all student organizations are endorsed for their educational, rather than social, value. Consensus again is the modus operandi of these groups.

Prominent cocurricular organizations, among the 50 or so funded, include an FM public radio station involving fully 10 percent of Earlham's student body, as well as several faculty and staff. The Earlham Volunteer Exchange coordinates literally hundreds of students' efforts in various community service projects within the Richmond community. A final example is the Earlham Food Cooperative, initiated, organized, and run by students. A variety of home-grown, organic, or otherwise "desirable" foods are sold, largely in a self-service style. The operation is increasingly sophisticated and, as so many of the other ventures on the Earlham campus, demonstrates a melding of activity and issue, of philosophy and action. Perhaps not surprisingly, organized sports such as football, baseball, and basketball do not occupy an exalted or elite position on campus. If anything, there is a conscious effort to see that such activities represent no more than just another option for students.

Both the extent and style of student involvement in campus governance and leadership are important features of the organization of Earlham College. Students are full participants on the Committee on Campus Life, the Student Faculty Affairs Committee (which oversees faculty personnel decision making), and the Administrative Council (a governance body that meets every other Friday over lunch). Students also hold an "All Student Meeting" every other week on Wednesday morning, opposite the Faculty Meeting, to discuss various aspects of campus life. In accordance with the Quaker tradition, the meeting begins and ends with a period of silence to insulate the proceedings from the often frenetic pace of the world. Another interesting reflection of these values is found in the student government elections. One student relayed that candidates who run as a team (e.g., co-presidents or co-chairs) are almost always preferred over a solo candidate. Not surprisingly, from their perspective "four eyes are better than two" and "two minds are better than one," a statement of practicality as well as Quaker value (i.e., such an arrangement allows students to accommodate their busy schedules).

Career Planning

The career planning center at Earlham College looks much like any other typical college career center. But there too are found signs of the "Earlham way," as observed in a prominently advertised Peace with Justice Day on the center's walls. Consistent with Earlham's philosophy in which careers are treated as much as a means to address issues in society as they are a means to earn a livelihood, this planned day offered a series of interview options with organizations whose missions are congruent with the goals of peace and justice in the Quaker tradition. Such events are clearly an expression of the institution's dominant cultural values and help shape and renew it, both in the short run and in the long run, as Earlham's tradition of sending its graduates into service-oriented careers continues.

Office of Co-Curricular Studies

Effective student affairs divisions are sensitive to the distinctive values of their institution and generally are respected by cabinet-level officers. There is much discussion on the desirability of bridging students' out-of-class life and their academic programs. Earlham College has successfully avoided the need for such bridging by creating a web-like experience in which each facet of the collegiate experience is tied to a core of beliefs and values about the world and to the espoused characteristics of a productive life. Desirous of being even more explicit about the curricular and out-of-class connections, the institution created an Office of Co-Curricular Studies in 1988. There, academic resources are drawn upon to enrich students' out-of-class experiences. For example, one of the first major programs, sponsored by the office during a presidential election year, used Plato's *Gorgias* to raise students' political consciousness and their ability to analyze political rhetoric. In the 1990 academic year, seminars included the topics of free speech and effectiveness in organizations. The participation of the president and prominent faculty members symbolically reinforces the seamlessness of the experience and Earlham's determination that life be a whole and, as John Calvin put it, all of life is religious. Cocurricular transcripts are an option available to students who wish to document their various campus involvements and leadership roles.

Residence Life

Typical of many small colleges of Earlham's size, the residence halls and surrounding theme houses form a system that is critical to the sustenance of the campus culture and community. At Earlham College, residences are divided into "halls," usually a group of 12-15 students, supported by a "convener" or a resident counselor (both paraprofessionals). It is at this level that many living environment decisions are made and where students are first introduced to the principles of consensus (by a pamphlet, *Making Sense out of Consensus*) and are put to an immediate test of how they function on a day-to-day basis. Emphasis is placed on students creating their own place (including any specific rules they wish to endorse) through consensus and application of the Quaker business principles.

The balance between individual rights and community values is an open agenda in these halls. Students are encouraged to arrive at their own resolutions rather than respond to an intervention, and collaboration and community are benchmarks of a group's success. Vandalism, while not unheard of, is not tolerated by students. The Community Code, a general outline of both rules and aspirations of caring for oneself and the larger community, is a constant referent for students and staff alike. Upperclass students (although such distinctions are not that important) are dispersed throughout the system and are seen as important socializing agents in the halls (especially those returning from an international experience). A single hall will usually house students from different classes. In addition, residence hall staff play a critical role in the early socialization of new students to campus, familiarizing themselves with new students' names and faces before they arrive and greeting them personally with an offer to help with their belongings.

Campus Union

Runyon Center, the campus union, is a very busy place on most days at Earlham College. The building houses, among other facilities, the radio station, bookstore, coffee-shop food service, meeting rooms, the opinion board, and the student dining service. All students gather several times a day to share meals together in a large dining hall with the usual array of cafeteria selections and salad bars. What is striking about this dining hall, though, is the large number of banners draped on the walls and from anything that will hold them, announcing various campus events or addressing a current issue. In addition, dining tables are usually replete with handouts and table tents about campus activities and descriptions of political action issues and concerns of all sorts. Some attempt to teach students and the campus community about world issues (e.g., official positions of parties within the Israeli parliament), while others may exhort students to action (e.g., boycotting certain products) or call for understanding and support of campus events and observances (e.g., Pink Triangle Week in support of the gay/lesbian community at Earlham). Once again, the campus union, like all other facilities at the institution, serves as another stage upon which the Earlham "orthodoxy" is scripted and played.

Service Learning Program

Earlham College is a member of Campus Compact and COOL (Campus Outreach Opportunity League) and sustains a growing, active interest in community service among students through the Earlham Volunteer Exchange. The Service Learning Program was established in 1987 to revitalize the campus' interest in civic responsibility to the local Richmond community. Over half the student body joins in this effort (although interest and participation wanes occasionally under the press of time demands), participating in various agency and community projects. This program is a direct extension of the Quaker ethic of service and is presented by Earlham (and, indeed, visibly encouraged by the provision of campus vehicles) as an alternate means for students to gain valuable skills and experiences while, at the same time, providing much needed support to the community.

At Earlham College, learning is always a whole experience where classes, either via content, methodology, pedagogy, or some combination, are regularly tied to events ongoing outside the class. Thus, a community-service project may involve faculty and students, be directly related to an academic class, and lead to student involvement in relevant research. This constellation of connections is not uncommon or out of place at Earlham College.

New Student Week and Wilderness Orientation

As early as 1925 Earlham College, in conjunction with other colleges, requested new students arrive five days early for orientation. The legacy of that investment is now Earlham's New Student Week, part of an extensive anticipatory socialization process organized by the college, which includes a program of campus visits and mailings to students. Three aspects of the Earlham program are especially instructive: the collaboration of the student affairs and academic affairs staffs in the content and delivery of New Student Week; the use of student co-conveners (group leaders in the Quaker tradition); and the Wilderness Experience. Meetings with academic advisors are liberally sprinkled throughout the week, as are other activities such as a picnic with the advisors at the president's home. Parents have a scheduled time to meet the academic advisors. There are overviews given of international programs, the humanities program, and the Honor Code. Two volunteer students are chosen to act as co-conveners of New Student Week and, with guidance from the dean of student development, they plan and execute the week largely on their own. Real responsibility is given and these positions are highly respected. Thus, another core value — that of peers teaching and leading one another — is enacted and publicly reinforced.

An optional experience for incoming students is a one-month wilderness orientation. Organized around backpacking and hiking in Utah's Uintah Mountains or canoeing in Ontario, Canada, the trip provides a forum for social integration and an introduction to Quaker decision-making or consensus. An intense environment is inevitable, composed of challenging physical demands, proximity with fellow Earlhamites (students, faculty, upperclass guides), and even a reflective solo experience. This ferment yields a firsthand knowledge that academic and cocurricular life at Earlham College are terms which simply look with different lenses at a closely knit whole. Academic credit is earned as readings, writing assignments, and group discussions all form parts of the total experience. The required individual observation project entails reflection on the impact of the wilderness trek on their personal lives, and the expression of that learning in an essay. Students form strong friendships, establish ties with at least one upperclass student and faculty member, gain confidence in knowing "the way things are at Earlham" is gained, and enter the year with an earned academic credit. For these students, the notion of a dichotomized student life (i.e., in class vs. out of class) probably appears inappropriate. A significant portion of each first-year class (25-30 percent) participates in the Wilderness Experience at one time or another. Trips are primarily targeted toward entering students but are open to all.

The key to a successful orientation experience is the process of anticipatory socialization, or making it possible for entering students, prior to and upon their arrival, to gain a broad, consistent, and accurate knowledge of campus life, expectations, mores, traditions, history, and opportunities. While espousing simplicity of life, though not of mind, Earlham College has created and disseminates an impressive array of documents and publications describing itself, its mission and philosophy, and its special emphases. Indeed, in response to a few rather lean recent recruiting years, a marketing consultant firm was engaged and an approach was designed to focus on the basic principles of

Quakerism without the strong attachment to the "Quaker" name. Apparently this labeling was being misunderstood as referring to a different perhaps more narrow denominational commitment than is actually present at Earlham. A review of a few of these documents as they relate to student life is instructive.

One small pamphlet draws an intentional parallel between what "the experts say" about a high-quality institution and what Earlham College has to offer. The key points are drawn from the recent Carnegie Commission report, *College: The Undergraduate Experience in America* (Boyer, 1987), and are visually accented on each page with a different piece of a puzzle. The final page shows a completed puzzle spelling *Earlham College.* The various pieces of the "Earlham puzzle" include, among others, a clear and vital mission, investment in teaching, a coherent general education core, a high priority on learning resources outside the classroom, the measurement of all parts of student life by high standards that see the relatedness of the academic and nonacademic functions, and an emphasis on the worth of service and involvement in campus governance.

Making a Difference . . . Reflections on Earlham College is another publication which articulates many of the core values of the institution under three major headings: curriculum, community, and careers. Some of the values and opportunities identified in this communique include: community, collaboration, a mandate to commit one's life to something, career goals beyond affluence, service to society, the value of learning from cultural differences, clubs and activities which promote service, advocacy and political content, and the interrelatedness of various areas of knowledge. Under the subheading, "Curriculum," Elizabeth Kirk '59 (now professor of English at Brown University), offered a powerful testimonial: "Earlham offers an education that elicits from the student the making of connections between one class, one problem, one discipline and another, an education that will not let one rest in an understanding of separate problems and modes of experience, shut off from each other or from their implications for living one's life." In the subsection on "Community," President Richard Wood said that "many colleges talk about developing leadership, about effective participation in the human community, but few structure their total experience and co-curricular experience to do much about it." Wood continued, "Diversity is not a good in itself, but a means to further the search for truth, to see the world through the eyes of others, to overcome self-centeredness." Such values and assumptions offer a clear and important invitation to all members of the Earlham College community, including the student affairs staff, to respond in ways that are supportive of that vision.

Observations and Conclusions

Earlham College is an open, socially aware, and cohesive community with a powerful environmental press toward conforming to the dominant Quaker values. That which is the strength of this institution, however, may also give rise to some concerns. The coherence and constant press to be involved in social issues is, for certain individuals, smothering. Consensus itself may be perceived by some as an oppressive process, leading to excessive discussion and a lack of decisiveness. While the expressed openness to a diversity of ideas is a positive dimension of the campus community, it tends to be afforded, by admission of institutional agents and multiple observers, primarily to ideas left of center. Conservatives, both politically and religiously, may have a difficult time at Earlham where there is such public accountability. Although some ranking of acceptable views is inevitable, if real values are affirmed, a danger at Earlham is to define liberal views as open, all others closed, and thus to create a new orthodoxy in place of the alleged one being challenged. Simply put, there is a clear need for Earlham students, as well as staff and faculty, to be carefully selected for "fit" and to self-select carefully as well. The challenge for Earlham is not what to do with the true believers, but how to respond to the doubters and those who, for whatever reason, take issue with any of its tenets.

As a final point of concern, it is conceivable that the sheer intensity of life at Earlham College, even toward involvement, may engender a simple lack of fun, of the joy and exuberance often associated with undergraduate life. Others perceive this same phenomenon as a lack of triviality or foolishness. The reality may encompass both, but the danger of taking oneself too seriously, of "missing the life that is lost in living," is genuine.

Nevertheless, Earlham College is a distinctive institution whose character, culture, and mission send out an unmistakable beacon to those who find its doors a welcoming entrance. One of the most important factors in the college's mission is that it not only drives specific practices and policies, but points toward a way of conceiving of and implementing the policies as well. The concept of consensus is inextricably bound up with a constellation of Quaker values, and is not as simple as a cursory glance might imply. It is at the very heart of the college's high levels of involvement and is worthy of careful consideration as a model from which to draw. A mission which combines content and process, if it is recognized as a shared commitment, is a powerful tool. Specifically, at Earlham College the way of doing business is focused; it constitutes a common way of thinking and, also of considerable importance, a common or shared language.

Earlham College thrives on the type of students, faculty, and staff it attracts; and those who come to learn from, work with, and participate in the Earlham community clearly benefit from what the institution has to offer. Students arrive with characteristics amenable to the process and values of the college. Faculty, administrators, and staff are socialized through such intensive scrutiny and collaboration that, again, a good "fit," in terms of style, content, and community values, is as nearly assured as could possibly be hoped for. Earlham is not hard to read; there are few if any secret pockets. Visits to the college, publications, and word of mouth, all set forth honest and fairly comprehensive appraisals of its way of life.

Finally, student affairs at Earlham College functions as a set of "experts" in functional areas (e.g., career planning, counseling, student activities), seemingly more in response to specialization and time restraints than to any desire on the part of faculty to rid their hands of these areas. Thus, another Quaker ideal, collaboration, is evidenced in the institution's academic affairs/student affairs relationship. Student affairs on the Earlham campus supports a number of initiatives contributing to the high level of educationally purposeful cocurricular involvement at the college. Such involvement, and other "student affairs goals," are realized in large measure as a function of their not being "student affairs" goals but rather warp and woof of the culture of the place. Student affairs is a part of a larger whole, and its offices have been faithful in aligning their own mission and practices with those of the college. While Earlham College presents unusual opportunities for student affairs to be integrated into the core of the institution — the "shared vision" is pervasive and tight — the selection of staff committed to that mission and willing to order their own activities and operations accordingly is essential.

Commentary

What Can We Learn from Earlham College?
Frances Lucas-Tauchar

The case of Earlham College offers rich examples of programs, practices, and principles that warrant consideration by student affairs professionals in similar coeducational, residential, liberal arts colleges. Many concepts and practices may be used by other institutions to achieve a much needed sense of community and regard for shared values in higher education. Earlham is, indeed, an "involving" college and was well selected for inclusion in the College Experiences Study.

Positive living-learning environments are characterized by shared values. Earlham College faculty, staff, students, and graduates know and understand the values and mission of their college. When an accreditation team visits a college, they first explore the degree to which the educational purposes and values of the institution are understood by all involved. Clarity is power. In the case of Earlham, the clarity of values and the degree to which they are shared is unusually high. The traditions fit with those values and the self-selection of both students and faculty depends on those values. Student affairs professionals at other colleges should assess the degree to which the values are clear on their own campuses and how they could be better communicated and shared.

Not only is the clarity of the mission noteworthy, but also the mission content. It is clear to all campus community members that students are there to learn how to make a difference in the greater society. Developing leaders who will commit to enhancing the world is central to Earlham's mission. Some would argue that ethical and sensitive leaders are in short supply. Nonetheless, Earlham College attempts the difficult task of developing those attributes and values in each student.

Most student affairs professionals learn in their graduate study that student involvement is the key to enhanced learning and satisfaction with the college experience. They are also taught the importance of encouraging students to make their own decisions as much as possible and claim ownership for their experiences. In practice, however, those concepts are particularly difficult to achieve. Many student affairs professionals were student leaders themselves and have trouble relinquishing control in certain situations. Additionally, there can be a low political tolerance throughout the institution for student error. Earlham College models what many student affairs professionals believe, but may have difficulty implementing. Earlham student affairs professionals are seen as valuable resources and the students are viewed as the critical decision makers. These dynamics are ideal for maximizing student development.

The fact that Earlham students feel ownership of the Community Code is another noteworthy feature. The title itself denotes the importance of caring for oneself and belonging to a community that shares in creating guidelines for coexistence. Resident students are encouraged to design by consensus their own codes, rules, and aspirations for their smaller living groups. Ownership for oneself and the community can be one of the greater lessons taught in higher education today, in light of the "look out for number one" mentality of the 1980s. Ironically, the '80s mentality did not bring the desired side effect of increased self-esteem for most students.

Among the developmental needs of new students are to fit in to a group, to belong, and to integrate their experiences. At Earlham College, orientation is designed with these needs in mind. New Student Week and the optional Wilderness Experience are planned and executed by both student affairs professionals and faculty. Students begin their college career seeing both sets of educators working together. They also get acquainted with the administrators and faculty right away. This approach helps to begin the "seamless" experience which is critical to both a liberal arts philosophy and a student affairs philosophy of educating the whole student. Far too many institutions have chasms in the teachings between the out-of-class experience and the in-class experience. Some colleges try to build helpful bridges, but few can proudly point to a design without a gap in the curricular and cocurricular programs.

Earlham College also is praiseworthy for its strong commitment to student development. From the beginning, the college emphasizes the ultimate goal for all students is to commit their lives to some good cause or action. Commitment to a set of positive values is the desired developmental goal. By Quaker tradition, it is not enough simply to learn about a problem but, rather, one must help in its solution. Far too much education is spent on problem identification and more should be spent on problem solving. A call to action and a model to learn how to act are experienced throughout the undergraduate activities in the curriculum and cocurriculum. This principle is applied by involving students in a variety of activities from participation in scientific research in the classroom to a substantial emphasis on volunteerism outside the classroom.

Furthermore, student involvement in decision making is evidenced by both the freedom they are given to regulate their own community and their presence on key college committees. Close student-faculty and student-administrator relationships are critical to making such a climate effective because far too often students are token voices in college decision-making arenas. Students may be invited to serve on a committee, but without the strength of networking and relationships, their voices can be lost. Student affairs professionals should serve as watchguards to ensure that students are taken seriously on their representative committees.

Consensus decision making is highly effective in building a strong community and ownership of values. However, for those students who come from extremely different points of view, it can be dangerous and devaluing. Earlham College apparently tries to balance that hazard by teaching about diverse people and cultures. The Japanese presence is celebrated, global understandings are encouraged, and overseas study is made available to help educate students about the beauty of difference. Pink Triangle Week in support of gay/lesbian issues also must help in insisting on tolerance and encouraging the celebration of diversity. In its pure form, consensus decision making would take into consideration all points of view on an issue.

A word of caution should be given to the student affairs professionals who are inspired by reading about Earlham College to rush from their office, relocate their earth shoes, and begin to abolish structures and establish many more vehicles for student input. First of all, Earlham College has a distinct population that does not need much structure.

Most colleges have a more diverse student population which would include many students who need and want more structure. Structure often is seen as a form of support and it makes students feel more secure. Some students can not handle the challenges of college without numerous support structures. Moreover, in the current legal environment, it can be dangerous not to identify specific procedures for judicial action and community living standards regarding safety. It would be a confusing and disappointing environment for many students to be given so little direction and low structure.

As the work force becomes increasingly multicultural, it is important that students be exposed to people from different cultures while in college. Though it is admirable that students are exposed to certain foreign students, the lack of exposure to African-American, Hispanic, and socioeconomically deprived students appears to be a vital missing piece of the Earlham experience. Programs about people of color, for example, are helpful but understanding comes from authentic relationships with those from other backgrounds. Understanding does increase when a student works on a civic project with economically depressed people in a town of 40,000, but it does not substitute for a shared experience with underprivileged students in a living-learning environment. Earlham graduates may be unpleasantly surprised how far from the mainstream of life they have existed for four years.

Moreover, the Earlham concept of "being PC" (i.e., being politically correct) also may be far from the norms in most work environments. Students may meet with harsh contrasts to their undergraduate experience upon graduation. The intent of "being PC" is to establish sensitivity regarding language about oppressed groups. However, when taken to an extreme, it can be used like a club to admonish those who are either not current with the latest "appropriate" word or those who are simply conservative and have traditional values. The liberal haven Earlham students enjoy is refreshing and exciting. On the other hand, without a contrasting, substantive backdrop against which to weigh and argue other points of view, the Earlham experience could lack the challenging contrast needed to broaden thought. In fact, the search for truth and light is only as complete as the representative points of view in the discussion. Earlham College may, indeed, attract a narrow range of backgrounds and viewpoints.

The fact that all student organizations must be endorsed only for "educational value" and not for social value should be challenged. Social skills are vital in developing the whole person. In fact, developing those skills has educational value. Having a good time and learning to have fun in positive ways is a part of the human wellness model that should not be ignored.

Volunteerism is an exciting part of the Earlham experience and, it is hoped, will become a more integral part of the ethos of all colleges and universities. Certain social issues must be observed and experienced to be understood. Volunteer efforts can greatly enhance learning. At the same time, some students at other institutions are so busy working two and three jobs to pay for their tuition that they barely have time to study, let alone give hours to volunteer efforts. Wealthy young students have extra resources and extra time to give to others. Older students with many responsibilities and poorer students simply are unable to give much time to such efforts, though they may really want to volunteer. Nonetheless, student affairs professionals should deliberately broaden volunteer organization efforts to enhance learning in a provocative and meaningful way.

All in all, it is no wonder that approximately 25 percent of Earlham students are sons and daughters of college and university administrators and professors. For those who have chosen higher education as their life's work, Earlham College is able to put into practice the theories and dreams of many professionals in the field. The Earlham model deserves our attention. One or more of the college's approaches and principles could possibly be adopted by other colleges.

Chapter Nine

An Eclipse of the Usual
The Evergreen State College

James W. Lyons

The Evergreen State College was established more than two decades ago to seek alternative, better ways to teach undergraduates than the commonly accepted approaches. The distinctive approaches that evolved have worked well and are as vital and effective now as they were when Evergreen was founded. In this time when so many colleges and universities are recognizing a renewed need to commit themselves to undergraduate education, The Evergreen State College offers some ideas that work. If an institution is looking for structural models that will enhance their teaching missions, The Evergreen State College is a good place to begin. It is a "class" educational act in "sheep's" clothing.

For student affairs professionals, the lesson offered by The Evergreen State College is that history can repeat itself. Most of what is done by student affairs professionals today was once done by the faculty and the students themselves. That is the way it is at The Evergreen State College. The lines between in class and out of class, curricular and extracurricular, and even teachers and students are blurred. Many of the usual divisive boundaries have been made very permeable. For example, the faculty's role as developers of students' intellect vs. the student affairs role as nurturers of the students' affect are not so tightly drawn at The Evergreen State College. Faculty tend to be genuinely concerned about the whole experience of students, about their orientation, about their career paths, and about individual situations that hinder academic achievement. The usual functions of student affairs are evident in abundance and are a valued part of the Evergreen experience. What is different is that the responsibility for these functions is shared by faculty.

The Evergreen State College is all the more interesting because it is a public college. It feels like a private or independent college; there is a dogged independence of philosophy and spirit that sets it apart from the more typical public institution. Its director of planning and research reported to the president and deans about the results of the ACE Freshman Survey to which 55 percent of the Evergreen first-year students responded. He found that,

> Our freshmen (had responses that) are most similar to those of freshmen entering highly selective, private, liberal arts colleges. Our freshmen tend to be more liberal in their views, hold the value of a liberal arts education above the value of landing a well paying job and to have parents with higher levels of education.

Yet Evergreen is not private, and it is not selective. What goes on here?

The college has evolved into a highly respected liberal arts institution that is relatively free of constricting politics, educationally choking external controls, and demanding constituencies. As we will see, The Evergreen State College is not without its critics and a history of rocky times. But it is animated, nurtured, and sustained by a distinctive mission to which a superb faculty, students, and staff have committed themselves. Somehow, it has managed to insulate itself from the understandable public pressures for it to be all things to all people. To the contrary, Evergreen knows what it is about and regularly reaffirms its educational mission.

Overview

The Evergreen State College is a relatively young four-year, state-supported, liberal arts college. The name of the school is *The Evergreen State College* — not Evergreen College, nor Evergreen State College. "The" is part of the formal title. The friendly term for the college is *Evergreen*, and the students are *Greeners.*

Although the campus has a rural and even remote geographical feel to it, it is only about 20 minutes by car from Olympia, the capital of Washington, and the edge of urban sprawl. The college occupies 1,044 thickly forested acres that extend upward from Puget Sound where it has a shoreline and more than 3,000 feet of beach front. One small hidden part of the beach is regularly used by some students for nude swimming and sunbathing. On the edge of campus is a 13-acre organic farm that makes possible a regular program in small-scale organic agriculture. The farmhouse there is also the site of retreats, pitch-in suppers, and other social events. The roads surrounding the campus are very rural and extend through heavily wooded areas. The main entrance road, Evergreen Drive, also winds through heavily wooded areas and connects with a busy freeway, Highway 101. Actually, there are two campuses: the main campus in Olympia and a branch program in Tacoma.

Most of the information in this chapter was collected during the 1988-89 academic year. Since then there have been changes. For example, there has been turnover in the institution's leadership; the president and all but one of the vice presidents (that being the vice president for student affairs) have changed. While some particulars of the college are different today, the basic mission and approaches of The Evergreen State College remain unchanged.

The Main Campus — Olympia

The Olympia campus is partially residential: 33 percent of the students live on the campus in 11 residences and 19 modular duplexes. Many other students live nearby in Coopers Glen Houses, a contiguous private housing complex developed with HUD funds in the 1960s. The rest live in the nearby communities of Olympia, Lacey, or Tumwater. There is regular bus service between the campus and Olympia.

The student body of approximately 3,000 students is diverse and brings to the college a broad array of ages, learning skills, and educational backgrounds. Eighty-five percent are full-time. Students are diverse by age: 51 percent are between 18-24 years of age; 34 percent are 30 or older. The median age is 25. There is an uncommonly high level of self-selection involved in the application process. The Evergreen State College's distinctive qualities are recognized by prospective students; thus, a good deal of matchmaking occurs even before application to the college.

Evergreen's students and faculty are infectiously enthusiastic about their academic and intellectual pursuits. They have an approach to learning that is so old it is regarded by some as non-traditional, experimental, or even radical. In fact, the Evergreen approach is quite traditional; students should receive as much individual attention as possible. Further, students are expected to assume responsibility for their own education. A related organizing belief is, according to one of the founding faculty members, "...that anybody can learn anything given the right circumstances and encouragement!" Faculty hold that belief closely and are excited about what they do, and with good reason: it works for them.

The academic structures are unusual and determine the kind and quality of student life. They are marked by collaborative teaching and learning, an interdisciplinary curriculum, extensive evaluation but with an absence of grades and traditional academic departments, and opportunities for individual study and research as well as internships and other field experiences. There is an absence of competition, of status, of cliques, and the kind of imperiousness all too common in colleges and universities. A visitor senses immediately that the college is socially and politically conscious. It shows on college bulletin boards and in many student organized activities. Yet The Evergreen State College is marked by collaboration, an unusual and functional kind of egalitarianism, and a special level of caring and community.

The Tacoma Program

The Evergreen State College also has a program in Tacoma. As with Olympia-based programs, the same forms of curriculum (i.e., interdisciplinary approaches and team teaching) are used although tailored for an older and predominantly evening student body. The Tacoma program had a unique beginning, explained in one of their publications:

> It began when Evergreen Faculty Member Dr. Maxine Mimms agreed to hold small seminars around her dining room table at convenient times for working adults in Tacoma. When the seminar outgrew Dr. Mimms' home, community organizations generously volunteered meeting space. The Tacoma Community House, the Tacoma Association of Colored Women's Clubs, the Tacoma Urban League and the Tacoma Opportunities Industrialization Center have all housed the seminar group in past years....Since 1972, more than 500 adult learners have graduated from the Tacoma Program. In addition to upper-division offerings, the Tacoma Program also offers a lower-division Bridge Program in conjunction with Tacoma Community College for students who have less than 90 credits.

Evergreen's History and Mission

While The Evergreen State College is young compared with most four-year colleges in the United States, it has a very distinctive character and is cluttered with traditions that support its founding mission. Founded in 1967 by the Washington State Legislature, The Evergreen State College opened in 1971 with the dual mission of being a liberal arts college and a regional institution. There is a deep commitment to the founding academic purposes which are acted out and organized in much the same way as they were conceptualized 20 years ago. Recently, the state removed the regional mission because it conflicted with the liberal arts mission and created curricular expectations that a liberal arts college could and should not meet.

Critical and Criticized Early Years

Until The Evergreen State College was acknowledged by the higher education community nationally as being an effective institution, it was regularly criticized by many in Washington, especially legislators. Seven times during its brief history Evergreen learned of bills being drafted or discussions in the legislature that would have closed the college or significantly altered its character. Hence, The Evergreen State College developed a kind of siege mentality that probably gave it added strength. Greeners then, as now, liked to be and be seen as different. They do so with an almost "secret knowledge" of how unlike their image they really are. They know their college works. Students and faculty share a quiet confidence that they are a college that employs a very traditional form of learning akin to Mark Hopkins on a log.

Nearby Olympia also feeds the siege mentality. It is the capital so the legislators and their generally conservative social attitudes are just 20 minutes away. The "shaggy, baggy, unkempt, '60s" appearance of the Greeners invites some ridicule, occasional caustic comment, and some anger. These perceptions began to change, however, when *U.S. News and World Report* identified The Evergreen State College as being among the very best schools. Soon thereafter a reporter from the Olympia daily newspaper commented, "When that came out, attitudes changed almost overnight. It was as though many realized that maybe there was something actually good happening there!" Indeed, there is.

Mission

Evergreen's mission and philosophy were established in the 1960s through dialogues between a key consultant, Joseph Tussman, and many of the key figures writing about higher education at the time. That was a lively era in American higher education; a time when educational ideals and aspirations knew no boundaries; anything could be done. It remained, however, for Evergreen's first president, Charles J. McCann, to give the mission meaning in practice.

McCann, who continues to serve on the faculty, was a powerful advocate of individualized education and shaped many of the college's qualities and structures that continue intact. McCann wrote in 1977 while reflecting on his presidency:

> My ideas for Evergreen were composed of a list of negatives (no departments, no ranks, no requirements, no grades) accompanied by a vaguer list of positives: we should have cooperative education (internship) options for students, we should be interdisciplinary, there should be as little red tape as possible among the faculty members and students and what's there to be learned, freshmen — everyone — should have the opportunities and

177

obligations presented by seminars, evaluation should be in narrative form, library and computing services should have disproportionately large shares of the budget, students should be able to study on their own when they're capable of it.

In 1989 Evergreen's Assessment Study Group identified six explicit teaching and learning goals that made up an important core of its mission. These were expressed in terms of skills, attitudes, and abilities the college expects will be the results of its teaching and learning processes:

- To study interdisciplinary themes
- To develop the capacity to judge, speak, and act on the basis of reasoned personal beliefs, understandings, and commitments
- To link theory and practice
- To create and share work within a cooperative, noncompetitive context with mutual respect for diversity of perspectives, abilities, and experiences
- To develop a capacity to elucidate and appreciate differences of culture and gender in order to live in an increasingly diverse world
- To continue to develop reading, writing, computation, critical thinking, speaking, listening, and computer skills.

The Assessment Study Group's subsequent study, incidentally, determined that Evergreen's alumni believed these objectives were met. They were supported by their employers (or faculty, in the case of graduate students) who reported that Evergreen graduates succeeded in these areas beyond the levels achieved by graduates of other institutions.

The successful education that Greeners experience is, however, more than just a function of the mission of The Evergreen State College. As Charles McCann wrote in his reflections, how Evergreen approaches and organizes teaching and learning is at least equally important. It is here that we find the truly distinctive qualities of the college.

Key Aspects of Evergreen's Learning Culture

A Teaching Faculty

When we studied The Evergreen State College there were 153 full-time regular faculty and 30 adjunct faculty who taught part time. The student/faculty ratio was 22:1.

The faculty is deeply committed to the liberal arts, to teaching, to working collegially in an interdisciplinary mode, and to the academic processes that are distinctive and central to The Evergreen State College. They are also intellectually alive and vital and have a visible dedication to learning — something that, once again, is fueled by the form and substance of Evergreen's special curricular approach.

In an era of a narrow, often suffocating, focus on research championed by research universities and emulated throughout higher education, one might speculate that it would be difficult to recruit faculty who are fully committed to a teaching career. That is a particularly important question as the founding faculty ("old dinosaurs" as they are affectionately referred to by some) approach retirement age. Can equally dedicated and effective replacements be found? Evergreen's recent searches have resoundingly answered that question in the affirmative. There are ample numbers of scholars who seek a situation like that offered by The Evergreen State College where one can be fully invested in interdisciplinary teaching, unencumbered by the politics and constraints of departmental structures. The absence of departments and their many encumbrances is regarded by faculty as a key strength of The Evergreen State College.

Administrators Who Support and Not Dominate

Charles McCann was a key leader who set the stage for what The Evergreen State College was to become. But it was a stage marked by a profound faith in faculty and students to organize their own learning, to work cooperatively, and in interdisciplinary ways. It was also a stage where red tape was kept to a minimum — where administrators were to know and keep their place; to support and not dominate.

The second president, Daniel J. Evans, became president after leaving the post of Governor of Washington and was instrumental in providing The Evergreen State College with the political protection needed to give it time to establish itself. He was also a forceful advocate for its educational mission. The college was, after all, young and without the usual constituencies that older and more established schools count on. Evans is now one of Washington's two senators.

The last president, Joseph Olander, left the college after less than five years of service. His was, by necessity, a different role. His agenda included creating and implementing a strategic plan, stabilizing the relationships between the college and the state, implementing administrative procedures (something quite foreign, even now, to the Evergreen way of doing things), and clarifying its mission. These were some realities of institutional administration that many at The Evergreen State College found distasteful.

An interim presidential appointment was made in the 1990-91 academic year while the search for a new president was begun.

The Evergreen State College is a college that is likely to resist any sort of top-down corporate style administration. The faculty and students are convinced that good educational ideas percolate upward from the active learning community and that those ideas and undertakings should be supported by the administration who should otherwise stay out of the way. The Evergreen State College, as an organization, cannot be understood by looking for any kind of pyramidal paradigm.

Governance and Community

Community is an important concept at The Evergreen State College, yet many of the trappings often found in a community-oriented campus are not present. The governance structures of The Evergreen State College are certainly evident, but are less prominent than usual. After all, minimizing administration was one of the founding ideals that has survived the first 20 years.

The administration is more the keeper than the leader of the community. The community (or better said, the communities) virtually lead themselves. There is more a sense of place, of common mission, of membership, than a sense of citizenship. The academic vice president and many of the deans are not making their jobs a career. For them it is understood that they are "taking time away from their faculty duties" to do their share to organize and "keep the complex academic systems running." Many will return to the faculty after a 3-6 year stint.

There is no form of community-wide governance, although students at times wish there was. Some wish their "membership privileges" that include a high level of participation in academics would also include participation in college governance. This is not the case. Students have their association, the faculty have theirs, and the staff have theirs (a union). Each seems limited to an advocacy role for the special concerns of the constituents.

Some things that are commonly centralized and coordinated at most institutions (such as standard class hours) are not at The Evergreen State College. Instead, the faculty who band together to teach a program set the class times and settings for that program. After all, what difference does it make when students have committed their quarter or even their year to that program?

There seems to be an aversion to institutional governance, to structures that get in the way and, to some extent, become more important than the academic activities in which all participate. One example of this are the Disappearing Task Forces (DTFs). These are committees established to deal with issues (there are committees for nearly everything) which operate in an open and participatory way and then disband. There is an institutional ethic that wants to avoid permanent committees that outlast their usefulness.

Although the college seeks to avoid too much administration, it designates part of one day each week as a College Work Day to tend to the needs of its educational community. This is a time when no classes are scheduled, and in which projects and Disappearing Task Forces do their business. It is the day when many at The Evergreen State College participate in the governance of their college.

Admissions

The Evergreen State College is clearly not for everyone. A student's "fit" at Evergreen could be more of an issue than may be the case at more traditional schools. For example, students who expect and count on a traditional approach to scholarship could have difficulties adjusting to its curriculum. So would students who are passive learners, i.e., students who expect to arrive and be pleasantly filled with knowledge and expend no personal energy. The college knows the importance of fit and does a particularly good job in its preadmissions publications; it is unerringly clear about its student life and learning expectations.

Some of the specialness of the student experience at The Evergreen State College is related to the presence of many nontraditional students. Evergreen historically has reserved spaces in each class for students who have not done well in the traditional routines of high school (or college in the case of transfers), but who show promise of being able to do well in Evergreen's supportive, noncompetitive, interdisciplinary academic environment. The independently minded student is often drawn to an arrangement like Evergreen's, in which students assume the major responsibility for their own education.

As mentioned earlier, the student body is older than usual. One of the current worries among students and faculty is that the average age of the student body is decreasing. That may be partly due to pressure from the state to be more selective in admissions — a policy that often discriminates against older students who may have a weak or different high school experience but who, because of maturity and readiness to learn, may be especially able to contribute to and benefit from The Evergreen State College. Many people believe older students are important to the educational success of the college. Younger and older students complement each other and enrich the learning environment.

The educational success of the college probably contributes to the pressures to have a more traditional (or at least traditionally competitive in admissions) student body.

Increased applications for admission are related to the college's enviable educational success. Ninety-four percent of graduates succeed in entering the jobs and graduate programs of their choosing; 93 percent of the graduates who apply to medical and law schools are accepted. And, as we have already mentioned, surveys of graduates and their employers show that Evergreen graduates are better prepared than their counterparts from other schools for work and advanced study.

The Organization of the Curriculum

Certainly the most distinctive characteristic of The Evergreen State College is its academic program. It centers the interest and energy of faculty and students alike. Let us examine the basic components of the program — coordinated study programs, individual learning contracts, group contracts, and internships — and some of its additional features.

The Coordinated Study Program

The coordinated study program is the main feature of the Evergreen curriculum. A program usually requires the full-time participation of the student, often spans the entire academic year, and is made up of a team of faculty numbering from two to five and 40 to 100 students. The ratio is usually one faculty member for twenty students. For all practical purposes a program is Evergreen for the students as long as they are in it. It is where their orientation occurs, it is their primary affinity group, it offers social support and enrichment, it offers opportunities for leadership, it fosters both social and intellectual interaction, it is where they will establish many of their friendships, and it teaches how to care and be cared about. The relationship between the student and the faculty of the program is intense. At the beginning of a program, time is set aside to allow students to get to know one another and their faculty "senior learners." One of the regularly mentioned and highly valued Evergreen traditions is the potluck dinner. Everyone pitches in for these events that are commonly held in faculty homes. The students and faculty in a program occasionally have organized retreats to do the work of the program and to build a healthy sense of community within the group. An early task of the student assistants in a program is to collect information and publish a directory of the students and faculty in the program.

What are these programs? Most are offered for a full year, some are offered for only one or two quarters. Illustrative titles of the 1989-90 core programs included:

- Great Books
- Pursuit of Virtue

- Ways of Knowing
- Ourselves Among Others: Cultural Perspectives in Arts
- Rags and Riches: U.S. at End of 20th Century
- Reconstructing the Past
- Earth, Wealth, and Democracy's Promise

There are also programs in other areas such as applied social theory with titles such as: Mass Media, Popular Culture, and Folklore; Making a Difference: Doing Social Change; and Teacher Education.

Environmental studies is one of the more popular areas of study, due undoubtedly to the geography of Washington and the Puget Sound. Programs in this area had such titles as Habitats: Marine, Terrestrial, and Human; Principles of Biology: Cells and Organisms; Ecological Agriculture; and Tribal Resource Development. Additional areas of studies include expressive arts (music, theater, and studio arts), humanities, language and culture, management and the public interest, Native American studies, science-technology-and-health, Center for the Study of Science and Human Values, and political economy and social change.

The program is best described in a chapter in a 1989 report for its accreditation activities, *Constancy and Change at Evergreen — A Self-Study Report to the Northwest Association of Schools and Colleges:*

> From a faculty point of view, the main structural features of a coordinated study include: the Program theme or problem and the faculty seminar. The organizing principle of a coordinated study has two dimensions — the program concept and what Evergreen has called the "Program Covenant." The Program concept refers to the central matter, or questions, or problem to which the year's reading, lecturing, seminaring, and writing will address itself. The Program Covenant refers to a contract among the faculty team for how the central matter of the study will be collaboratively presented. This Covenant functions as insurance against the very understandable tendency to drift toward one's disciplinary strength as against the will required to exercise one's interdisciplinary responsibility in such a program.
>
> A second faculty-centered aspect of the coordinated study is the Faculty Seminar. This arrangement is designed to make it possible for faculty members to teach with each other across their disciplinary specialties by providing them with a time each week for their discussion of the material as it bears on the Program theme for that week. This Seminar occurs prior to their meeting with students on the same material and is the glue for collaboration.

From the students' perspective the important structural features of coordinated study include the Program idea and the Faculty Seminar, but also book seminars, lectures, workshops, the assigned reading and writing, individual conferences, and evaluation. Coordinated study may also include internships, group projects, special interest seminars, examinations, program retreats, business meetings, and what Evergreen locals call "down days," usually one day a week when faculty prepare to teach and/or attend college meetings, giving students the opportunity to do likewise.

Because the programs are interdisciplinary, they bring faculty together in ways that make things exciting for both students and faculty. As several put it, "At Evergreen many of the things that separate students and faculty just don't exist. Here there are only younger learners and older learners."

Core Programs

Core programs are coordinated study programs that are planned especially for first-year students. While each core program has a theme, they all expose students to interdisciplinary learning, to certain learning skills, and to the Evergreen approach which places so much responsibility on the individual student to both learn and teach, to work collaboratively, and to shed any need for competitiveness when it comes to scholarship.

Individual Learning Contracts

Individual learning contracts are examples of how a student and faculty member work on a one-to-one basis. The contract may include reading, writing, painting, photography, research, field studies — any activity that involves the student in what he or she will need to study. These are more common for more advanced students with well-defined goals.

Group Contracts

Group learning contracts are like individual learning contracts except that a group of students, rather than an individual, arrange with a faculty member to take what often turns out to be a course. Such group contracts are occasionally taken in conjunction with a program. For example, to develop a film or video about ecosystems of Puget Sound, students may realize they need to know much more about film making and arrange to learn. Or some in that same group may decide they would like to learn more advanced biology than that which is a part of the program.

Internships

Internships are similar to individual learning contracts. There is a one-to-one relationship with a faculty member and with a field supervisor, usually the student's sponsor on the work site. Internships range from students working in nearby state agencies as legislative assistants to doing biological field work in remote places in Alaska to doing anthropological field work with Native Peoples.

Constant Change and Innovation

The curriculum is always being invented. Although a program may be offered annually, it is never twice the same. The teaching team changes; an interdisciplinary team will never teach the same program twice. As a new faculty team prepares to teach a core or coordinated program, the content and often the basic approach invariably changes; so might the academic disciplines represented on the faculty teaching team.

The Organization of the Faculty

Faculty are quick to point out that Evergreen's academic organization makes possible their distinctive curriculum and approaches to teaching. They believe strongly that the traditional departmental organization inevitably results in narrowness of intellectual view, nonproductive departmental politics, and promotional and appointment rituals that consume time and energy that could be better spent with educational matters. Other characteristics include the absence of: tenure (faculty have term-renewable appointments that provide points for evaluation and which seem to provide sufficient security), designated ranks such as assistant, associate, or professor, and accountability primarily to one's academic discipline. To the contrary, faculty are encouraged in the interdisciplinary mode to learn to conceptualize broadly, contextually, and in relation to current issues.

Avoiding Chaos

How faculty form an interdisciplinary team to offer a program is worth describing. Published each year is *The Geoduck Cookbook of Program Planning Among the Evergreens.* It is essentially a recipe for curriculum planning which explains the roles and responsibilities of members of the college community, guidelines for submitting proposals, criteria used in selecting programs, a flow chart of the planning process and a planning timetable, an overview of the curriculum, and tips on planning. It also includes a large chapter about faculty interests and academic backgrounds that helps faculty members find each other. One typical example is that of Rudy Martin:

In 1990-91, in terms of teaching, I am uncertain...I may be involved part-time with National Faculty. I'd like to work in coordinated studies (I like this best!), or teach alone in a group contract, or teach in the individual contract mode. If I ran the zoo and could teach anything I wanted, it would be: (a) humanities, arts, science — something like "Space, Time, & Form" (b) a writing, music, visual art program (c) global studies in Africa or Asia (d) broad-based American studies in Latin America. My current major interest is "the politics of knowledge." I'd like to work with some of our expressive artists, other faculty of color, and most of those I've taught with before. I think this "writing center" idea should be continued — I'd do it part of the time. I have high standards. Students say I'm "a warm friendly hard-ass." Mainly, I inquire and critique, still trying to discover and understand the "right questions."

(Subjects: Afro-American studies, American studies, composition, creative writing, English literature, ethnic studies, American history, literature, novel, poetry, prose fiction, Third World studies, social agency work, communications [publishing, editing, etc.], humanities. Biography: A.B., English Literature, U of California, Berkeley, 1957; M.A., English Literature, San Francisco State College, 1961; Ph.D., American Studies, Washington State U, 1974.)

Rudy Martin's listing, like all others, included his picture, current assignment, and discipline — in his case, American Studies/English Literature.

Students and the Curriculum

One of the factors that contributes to the students' sense of involvement in, indeed almost ownership of, the educational program is their role in curriculum development. There are specified bulletin boards throughout the college where curricular ideas are constantly submitted for public view. Students participate by putting ideas (on a 3 x 5 card!) on the boards, and reacting to ideas placed there by faculty. Students also give counsel to the deans and faculty about the overall shape, scope, and content of the curriculum. More important, they often work directly through specialty areas or individual faculty members to develop program proposals.

Students Take Charge of Their Own Learning

The program becomes the context for many different activities. Students regularly organize and conduct book seminars where they read and discuss a book related to their program. The purpose is to examine a reading assignment in relation to the program theme. But there are other purposes: they help students learn how to work together as a group by paying attention to issues of equivalent participation and relating to implied faculty authority. The seminars are small, and students customarily take responsibility for certain parts of the reading and discussion. They are designed to be truly interactive and give students practice in articulating ideas with increasing precision, to be responsible for coming to the seminar prepared, and to become both independent and interdependent with the group.

Evaluation

Evaluation is another special part of the academic structure and student/teacher relationship. At the beginning of each program or learning contract, the student and the faculty member each identify their expectations of the course and each other. These become the basis for later evaluations. Although there are no grades, there are regular individual evaluation sessions where the teacher and student share and discuss a written evaluation of the student's activity in the course. The student also prepares a written evaluation of the faculty member. The dean receives the evaluation after it has been discussed by the student with the faculty member.

The evaluations are thorough and sensitive to the needs, abilities, and special circumstances of each student. Yet, there are clear academic expectations. The very process of such an evaluation is heralded by both students and faculty as an important step in taking responsibility for one's own learning and for helping others, and in setting the stage for collaborative learning instead of competition.

Given these attitudes about evaluation one can understand why The Evergreen State College balked when the Higher Education Commission Board's Master Plan passed in the 1988 legislative session. This plan mandated standardized testing of students in Washington. Against that background, the following text appeared in a draft of a proposed student governance "background paper" (144 pages!) for new students:

The Master Plan's first step into Evergreen sent waves throughout the campus. Although less than twenty protesters showed up outside Lecture Hall 5 on the cold April morning of the first standardized test, only six students showed up to participate in the study. Two of them then refused to take the test (and the $35 remuneration) after talking with the demonstrators. The role of participation in the test reflected Evergreen's widespread opposition to the Plan, and the resentment against its newly legalized imposition.

Technically, the April tests were only a pilot examination, to be used in a two year study of the effectiveness of standardized testing. This two year "grace time" was only allowed after college provosts objected to the hasty implementation of the Plan's assessment component. However, many feel that standardized testing should be rejected on principle; serious study lends an undeserved legitimacy to the fundamentally flawed method.

The full paper represents an effort on the part of student leaders to pass on the distinctive culture of Evergreen.

The legislative history of this plan was not studied by our research team. However, it was allegedly based on the need for fiscal accountability and focused on the "efficiency," "unit costs," and "feasibility" of higher education. One political analyst wrote that "the state legislature has been increasingly anxious that state programs . . . produce measurable outcomes that allow for quantitative comparisons of programs in terms of production, and tangible results." One student critic later wrote, "The legislature wants to make sure that students coming out of college are prepared to work for Weyerhauser."

The Evergreen State College understandably chose not to administer the College Student Experience Questionnaire portion of the College Experiences Study. To have urged that would have discredited the study in their eyes. How, it would have been argued, could one possibly understand and reflect the distinctiveness of Evergreen's educational missions and culture on the one hand, and suggest such a questionnaire on the other? They had a point. The questionnaire uses words and frames of reference that are largely foreign to them. The Evergreen State College is, after all, an alternative college and to suggest that somehow the students could be made to fit in such a standardized context would only offend.

Students and Student Subcultures

There is a remarkable absence of the more usual subcultures such as fraternities, sororities, marching bands, and intercollegiate sports. But there are subcultures.

Greeners — More Than Meets the Eye

Greeners appear to be a politically active and socially conscious student body that is more liberal than conservative, more casual than formal, and clearly not interested in the more usual careers (e.g., business, engineering, medicine). Their dress is casual to the extreme and modeled on the countercultures of the 1960s. Yet, their core of values and attitudes may be different. One senior who sought to distance himself from the normative group of political activists noted, "They play the part but don't actually do it!" This was an older student with a long record of social and political activism, mostly around environmental issues. He had been arrested repeatedly for civil disobedience.

Another senior described herself as "a closet Christian" to distance herself from the perceived norm. She was, in fact, quite conservative in many ways, but culturally advanced in others. The point was, however, that she felt the need to distinguish herself from the more usual "Greener image."

After failing to connect with us on our first visit, one senior wrote us to describe the student culture. She wrote, "On Valentines Day, two girlfriends and I staged a protest to the sexually repressed, ultra-feminist, 'politically correct' dictums of Evergreen, which is otherwise a vital place." They published a pamphlet entitled *The Under-the-Counter Culture* in which each of them presented themselves by nickname, measurements, likes and dislikes, ambitions, hobbies, and personal pictures with quotes such as "Born to eat toast," "The girl your mother warned you about," and "Men take heed." On Valentine Day they wheeled a piano into the student activities building and, clad in tight evening gowns, they invited other students to "try our wares" and distributed the pamphlet. On the last page of the pamphlet was the following:

> ...Spring is nearly upon us....There is an interesting dialogue going on behind the closed doors of homes peopled by lonely college students. It seems that a general sense of alienation has set in, and even here at a progressive, unique alternative school we have not escaped the effects. The question is, what does one do when even being friendly has become some sort of political event?
>
> We, The Under-the-Counter Culture, have decided to join in. We have organized so that you might meet us and talk to us. Find out what we want. Find out who we are. We don't bite (unless you want us to).
>
> Our plight has been discouraging. We have observed sad faces and lonely eyes for too long. At a place where we are able to be spontaneous and original in our education, we ask, whatever happened to flirting? If you would like more information, there are no meetings, no literature, no central phone list. You'll just have to be creative and take your chances. We're willing, if you are.

What they were doing, of course, was urging students to get out of their cocoons and have fun with dating, with flirting, with traditional gender roles, and dressing nicely. Put differently, they were saying that not everyone at Evergreen "fits the mold." Not surprisingly, their effort resulted in a flurry of letters, more often than not critical, in the weekly paper, *The Cooper Point Journal.*

The Residentials

To some extent, the students housed in campus dorms are a subculture. Their regular interactions with each other in the residences and in their cooperative dining room tend to set them apart. They also tend to be underclassmen. Individual residences, however, are not as important to the students' social and intellectual experience as is often the case. The program is the main event — not the residence. Nevertheless, the residences are relatively small, organized on a truly human scale, and are located in pleasant wooded settings.

The Environmentalists

Another identifiable group is the environmentalists. Evergreen and many of its students have active environmental concerns: Organic Farm, the curriculum, individual study and research projects students often arrange, and internships. The main lobby area (three stories high) in the College Activities Building was full of posters. Many trumpeted environmental matters: "Help Blockade a Logging Operation," "Our Nevada Test Site Action: Train for Non Violent Action," "Adopt-A-Forest Program: Workshops on 'Quality Wood and Sustainable Forestry,'" and "Help Save the Ancient Forest." Aluminum and glass are routinely recycled. Plates and cups in their food services are paper and not plastic.

Evergreen's "Fraternities"

There are no fraternities or sororities at The Evergreen State College; the idea would be nothing short of heretical. But on the narrow roads that surround the campus, roads that are bounded by dense evergreen forest on both sides, one encounters occasional clearings with a house or two on them. These houses look dilapidated — partly because of the woodsy, rain forest quality of their surroundings, but also because they are, indeed, run down! Students have lived in most of them for nearly as long as the college has existed. They get passed down from one student generation to another and, like most student residences elsewhere, have developed qualities and personalities of their own. To a large extent, all offer students a challenge in cooperative and self-sustained living. Each has its own "culture" that may range from partying, to introspection, to environmentalism, to political action of one sort or another, and to serving as the key location of one "fringe element" or another. Some of the more well-established of these houses include: Yogurt Farm, Whitehouse, Pinkhouse, 7 Cedars, Turquoise House, Evergreen Shack, Sunny Muffin, Erma Goldman, Red House, and Brandywine Forest.

Students of Color

Evergreen students are ethnically diverse: 9 percent of the students are of Native American, African, Asian, or Mexican/Latino heritage. Nearly all at the college are aware that the relatively low minority population in Washington makes Evergreen's efforts to recruit more students of color a special challenge.

Students of color speak highly of Evergreen. The college has institutionalized its diversity and there are regular activities, events, and organizations that help students of color help each other discover and celebrate their cultural heritages and offer them a sense of space and full membership in the institution. Their subcommunities exist with a full repertoire of social and service activities, big sibling programs, social and political action, and community outreach and service programs. Seniors of color whom we interviewed repeatedly pointed to the good effects they received because of participating in these programs. Students are at once challenged and supported, work collaboratively but not competitively, and are taught in an environment in which there are unusually high levels of respect for the worth and dignity of the individual. They report that faculty are accessible and helpful. Students talked freely about coming to The Evergreen State College with many self-doubts, but soon learned to "trust yourself" and to have confidence.

Students of color have formed a very effective coalition of several ethnic groups which they call the First People's Coalition. It is a support group in which both individuals and groups can find friendship, common cause, and mutual support. They see themselves as also helping the college understand issues associated with racism, such as lack of respect, and ethnic matters with which other students tend to be unfamiliar. The absence of stridency or anger was striking. The First People's Coalition expressed a refreshing faith in the college's mission and in its unusual forms of learning. They liked the absence of competition and were acutely aware of one of the underlying (and founding) assumptions of the college: that all students, regardless of ability or background, can and will learn given the right environment and encouragement.

Student Parents

When the college was being organized in the late 1960s, but before it opened its doors, the first service the dean of students organized was child care. "It was," he said, "key to their need to attract a diverse student body." Now there are two day-care centers on the campus. One is run by the college and the other is a co-op on college property. Because of the number of non-traditional age students, the day-care centers are a base for social and other activities for students who have children. The single parent group especially appreciates these contacts and the resulting networks.

No Athletic Subculture!

Athletes are not a distinctive subculture at The Evergreen State College, primarily because there are few intercollegiate teams. On the other hand, the sports facilities are in constant use — the gymnasia, playing fields, pool, and workout areas. Recreational sports are popular and student participation seems high.

Traditions and Centerpieces of the Campus Culture

Although still very young, The Evergreen State College boasts a set of traditions every bit as distinctive as its history. For example, it takes some quiet pride in being able to laugh at itself. The college's motto is *Omnia Extares*, which roughly translated from Latin means, "Let it all hang out!" The college mascot is the Geoduck (pronounced Gooey-duck), a giant clam native to Puget Sound. Their intercollegiate teams — men's and women's soccer, swimming, and diving — call themselves the "Fighting Geoducks!" The film shown to prospective students and visitors is student made and begins with a scene of a young man rowing a small dory across Puget Sound toward Evergreen Beach. There he is met and given a tour by an 8-foot-tall Geoduck.

Students and graduates spoke affectionately about the potluck dinners. These are the initial cement of the programs, a time when students and faculty get to know each other, when friendships are crafted, and when the bonding that is so much a part of the Evergreen program begins. Retreats serve much the same function as the potluck dinners, and are often held at the farmhouse (really a small lodge) at Organic Farm.

One of the most interesting symbols of The Evergreen State College is the Freebox, just opposite the entrance to the cafeteria on the bottom floor of the College Activities Building, where students discard clothes they no longer want or need, and occasional items like ski wax, frying pans, walking sticks, belts, and shoes. Not all items are old, but most are. While standing by the Freebox one of our team members asked passersby whether the box was used. Almost to a person the answer was, "Of course!" followed by pointing to something they were wearing at the time. There is no doubt that the Freebox accounts significantly for the wild array of colors, sizes, and styles of clothes that adorn students. By ordinary standards, most items of apparel are ill-fitting, colors clash, and styles run the gamut. But after all, that is part of playing and living the role of a Greener.

Super Saturday arrives every year just after the end of the academic year. Begun by the former dean of students, Larry Stenberg, it is an event designed to thank everyone for another year, and simply to celebrate and have fun. It now draws nearly 25,000 people for a street fair, three stages with entertainment, two beer gardens, barbecues, and a Friends of the Library book sale. The event has created goodwill between the college and its community, its students, and its alums.

Why So Much Involvement?

There is a virtual seamlessness between in-class and out-of-class life. Evergreen's viewbook states "Social life at Evergreen begins in the academic community." They mean it! It is this condition that made The Evergreen State College so special a discovery during the College Experiences Study. It challenges the usual rhetoric and provides a most interesting example of how a truly academic community can be a balanced experience for students. There is a marvelous interconnectedness of all experiences.

First Things Easily First

Residential life, clubs, and sports are no competition for the time and attention that students devote to their program. It is not as though students don't play and relax. They do; and they are most likely to do those things with friends they have made in their present or past programs. One must understand the immense power of the program and how it affects students to appreciate the significance of the virtual seamlessness between academic and nonacademic life. Most students and faculty did not have the slightest idea what our research team was talking about when we used terms like *out-of-class* and *in-class life*. They see themselves in a powerfully integrating learning community — Evergreen is one experience.

Having noted the above, one can find few examples of things that compete with the academic. Because many of the students are of traditional age, it is not surprising that they, and especially the counselors and some faculty, report that relationships are high on students' agendas. All of the learning and trauma that ordinarily accompanies this age group is there in full measure as they learn about making, sustaining, and ending relationships. As one faculty member put it, "Around here one does not casually greet a student with the query, 'How are you doing?' unless you are prepared to invest at least 45 minutes to hearing and discussing the answer!"

College on the Human Scale

The program (which is in reality akin to a small college of 40-80 students with less than a handful of faculty) is the basic affinity group of the college; it ensures that students are known. As one faculty member commented when questioned about how well she knew her students, "You really end up knowing more than you want to. After all, I am with them, and only them, for at least 18 hours a week!" The students, for their part, talk frequently about the significant bonding that takes place within the program. These are the fellow students they know best, interact with, often live with, and develop significant relationships with.

A Facilitating and Interactive Physical Environment

The College Activities Building forms one of the parameters around Red Square. The building is the community center and crossroads of The Evergreen State College. It is the communications center — where bulletin boards and posters abound with abandon (no neat bulletin boards here!). On the way in there are the ubiquitous craft tables where the sellers are in their "uniforms" of the '60s. There is a health food co-op, a nicely stocked bookstore, a cafeteria run by an outside caterer (not a popular concept with students) that features a terrific salad bar plus several cafeteria and sandwich counters, and private dining rooms. Students rarely sit alone; most eat in groups that are presumably an extension of their seminar or study group. There is a faculty dining area, and one untitled large table for the faculty dinosaurs, a group of the founding faculty; part of that area is for the dinosaurs who smoke.

The *Cooper Point Journal*, the weekly newspaper, is also in the building, along with the college radio station, a student-run environmental resource center, the student activities office, an information center, an automated post office, and the Geo-voice, Evergreen's name for their fledgling student government.

Just outside of the College Activities Building is Red Square, a plaza paved with red bricks that is the campus crossroads, a place everyone must pass when going from residences to most classroom buildings, from the parking lots (screened by woods) to the College Activities Building or to the library, or for that matter, going just about anywhere. It is the place to post announcements, to meet friends, and hang out which, of course, means sitting around, doing little or nothing, and doing all of that with others. On sunny days (there are relatively few) students emerge from their "caves" (i.e., residences, classrooms, library, or labs) and celebrate life. Seniors speak fondly of Red Square on sunny days — music, dancing, smiles, blowing bubbles, political talks, and soapbox oration. Red Square is surrounded by green grass and trees with benches and other sitting places. In front of Red Square is the bus stop — where buses to and from Olympia and environs stop regularly. The stops are covered, of course, because of the rain and heavy mists.

The library is another boundary of the square. It is a building with many purposes, a kind of community center. Here are located many student services (e.g., admissions, financial aid), some student organizational offices, including the First People's Coalition, and the vice president for student affairs, the provost and academic dean's offices where there are full corridor walls devoted to the activities that result from *The Geoduck Cookbook of Program Planning Among the Evergreens*, the faculty's manual of planning and staffing the curriculum. Along the walls are large boards on which are pinned dozens of 3 x 5 cards called "trial balloons" which are just that — ideas being flown for comment by students and faculty colleagues. There are also books — a fairly extensive collection given the short history of the college. What stands out, however, is the "user friendly" environment that characterizes the catalog and check-out areas. Many helpful notes from one student to another, volunteered student reviews of new (and old) books, and the usual "Charlie, meet me tonight at 6 in the Deli" notes are scribbled and tacked to a board. The computing center, also in the library, is quite extensive with large clusters of personal computers with the capacity to interact with a mainframe and each other. The ever-present staff are there to help, consult, and swap the latest in software and hardware tales. In the library basement is the wood shop, a well stocked shop with good ventilation, generous worktable and storage space, and saws, lathes, planers, and shapers galore. It was here that Seawolf, a 38-foot seagoing sailboat designed to be a floating lab, was built by students and faculty a few years ago. It is not uncommon to see smaller craft being built there. Nearby is the prop shop for the theater and performing arts.

The college pool, dance studios, weight rooms, and exercise room are used frequently. And there is an abundance of outdoor activities. The director of recreation and athletics reported that her job was most likely unparalleled anywhere else. "Where else," she asked, "Would the AD occasionally have to call an intercollegiate competitor to report that the Evergreen team decided to forfeit because 'they were too busy to play' that game, match, or meet?"

The Common and Uncommon Roles of Student Affairs

There is wide agreement that the nature of a student affairs program in an institution is influenced by the special character of that institution (National Association of Student Personnel Administrators, 1987). Hence, it should not be surprising that student affairs work at Evergreen has distinctive qualities.

Unlike some of their colleagues elsewhere, Evergreen's student affairs staff are regarded as full partners in the educational mission of the college. Indeed, they do many of the same things as their professional counterparts elsewhere. But at Evergreen they are not devalued or regarded as irrelevant. The services they administer are recognized as necessary for the college to work.

Faculty at The Evergreen State College deal with the whole student; not just the student learning some special discipline during some set class hours each day. Caring for the affect is not shunted off to the side for specialists in student affairs to deal with. Rather, these are matters of genuine concern to the faculty and student affairs provides faculty with some backup: support, technical knowledge and experience, advice, and even some training.

The main student affairs practitioners at The Evergreen State College are the faculty. That is the key difference here. It is the difference that erases the usual seam between student and academic life.

Some student affairs activities can be seen as serving institutional as well as student needs. Many of these are typically organized at Evergreen. There are the usual essential services such as admissions, registration, counseling, financial aid, health care, housing, and placement. Student affairs professionals assume leadership in student crises, and serve as a resource to faculty in their work with individual students. And they participate in the governance of Evergreen and share responsibility for decisions.

Some activities, however, are atypical. Supporting and explaining the values, missions, and policies of Evergreen are especially important. The admissions processes, for example, always seek the best fit between the institution and the educational expectations of potential students. The Evergreen State College simply cannot comfortably use the educational terms commonly found in the admission materials of most schools. Its expectations and scholastic forms differ significantly from the norms. Students, for example, must really be prepared to assume significant amounts of intellectual initiative and to take charge of their own scholastic and social experiences. So too must they be open to uncommon forms of collaboration, evaluation, and learning styles. Explaining the college and its ways, then, takes on special importance for those in student affairs. Evergreen is not an ordinary college and it cannot be adequately explained in the ordinary ways.

Other common activities of student affairs are less important at Evergreen. There really is no need to encourage student-faculty interaction in programs and activities. Evergreen's educational forms (the program and individual studies) guarantee strong and genuine student-faculty interaction. Indeed, this is one of the major strengths of The Evergreen State College.

There is another array of programs and services that student affairs staff usually provide directly to students. It is here that one finds a significant difference in student affairs roles at Evergreen, primarily because they are carried out by the faculty. What are some of these programs and services? Assisting students in their transition to college; helping students explore and clarify values; encouraging friendships among students; creating a sense of community; teaching students how to resolve conflicts; helping students understand and appreciate racial, ethnic, gender, and other differences; and helping students to clarify career objectives and options for further study — these are activities that occur naturally within the context of the program. Curiously, these are roles that historically were played by faculty in early American colleges and universities. To the lament of many in higher education, faculty generally no longer assume such roles. But that is not the case at Evergreen; there they do. These are activities that are regarded as appropriate, if not essential, to the basic academic process.

Finally, we are reminded that Evergreen's model is not necessarily that of a single collegiate community. It is less one college than it is a collection of many small ones numbering from 20 to 100 — each of those being a program where students and their faculty conduct their scholarship together full time. The program is, in many ways, largely independent. This is a paradigm that challenges student affairs to foster a limited but real sense of overall community in ways that do not weaken the independence and power of the program. It was not surprising, for example, that student government (a central activity on most campuses) was just struggling to get organized during our visit. Nor do residential communities assume the importance that would be the case in a college without such preemptive affinity groups as the program. Student affairs, as a consequence, must be especially sensitive to the need to strike a balance between centralized and decentralized activities; a balance that will be very different at Evergreen from that found on most other campuses. At Evergreen, the default condition will almost always be toward the program and not to some "all-college" perspective. For it to be otherwise will serve only to weaken the educational strength of the program.

Summary

The Evergreen State College leaps out to even the most casual observer as a truly distinctive college. There are not many others like it. It is young. It has a clear and forceful purpose. It has a faculty who celebrate their teaching and their learning, and who are intellectually alive and wish to share that with their students. It is a college that puts first things first — and in their case those things are learning in an interdisciplinary mode. It provides an integrated experience. What could be more personally scaled than their basic academic process — the program? Evergreen deliberately avoids the usual institutional tendency to carve students into intellectual (or cognitive) beings on one part, and feeling (affect) human beings on the other — and then dividing the college's labors along those lines. To the contrary, Evergreen gives meaning to the idea that students are whole persons who at once think and feel. Consequently, students are recognized and responded to as individuals, take responsibility for their own education, and become autonomous learning partners with their faculty.

The Power of Permeable Boundaries

Why is the quality of out-of-class student life at The Evergreen State College wonderful? Because the concept of "out-of-class" is much less relevant than elsewhere. There is only student life, and collaborative learning by both students and faculty (the senior learners) is the unequivocal focus of Evergreen. It is not a school that a student attends with the attitude, "Well, here I am — ready to have others fill me up with wisdom and knowledge." Rather, every signal that Evergreen sends is that it is a place where active learning is genuinely prized, where everyone cares, and where everyone is encouraged, helped, and expected to become involved. It should not be surprising that so many are so involved.

Commentary

Evergreen: Prototype or Dinosaur?
David Dodson

When a conservative state with one of the most socially regressive tax structures in the country, no income tax, and 8 percent sales tax continues to support a public college, reputed by some to be a breeding ground for radicals, that institution must offer an especially effective educational experience or disaster is imminent. At The Evergreen State College supporters claim both are true.

Those of us who have followed the fortunes and foibles of this remarkable college have witnessed the excitement, humor, courage, human frailty, and educational innovation which have characterized its first two decades. But the underlying question remains: Is there something in the Evergreen experience which can provide guidance to other colleges, or is it a noble but short-lived educational experiment? More important: Is there a prototype here for student affairs practitioners, or is Evergreen's unique wedding of academic and student affairs a vestigial remnant of a bygone era?

Evergreen's Uniqueness

The optimistic experimentalism which inspired American higher education in the '60s continues to thrive in some quarters of the Evergreen campus, in a manner which might stun those who founded similar experimental ventures like the University of California at Santa Cruz or Redlands or Johnston College. But is that the primary basis for its uniqueness? If so, why hasn't Evergreen succumbed to the same moderating influences which robbed these other "radical alternatives" of their singularity?

A review of the fundamental assumptions which were the foundation of the experiment provides a ready answer. The Evergreen State College is perhaps a more radical alternative than these others (if by "radical" one understands its derivation from the Latin radix or root), because Evergreen incorporated changes which were simple but so fundamental they resulted in an absolute transformation of the educational experience. Some examples are illustrative:

- Elimination of tenure and academic rank. By abolishing academic departments, faculty rank and tenure, turf wars do not disappear, but they take on a different cast. Struggles tend to focus more on fundamental pedagogical issues than on the petty squabbles for priority and status which frustrate the educational objectives of so many academic institutions.

- An all-encompassing academic mission. Although many institutions give lip service to a mission which encompasses the "education of the whole person," very few colleges are organized so that the main business of the institution ensures this integration of in-class and out-of-class learning. Evergreen's focus on the program as the central feature of instruction requires faculty to be invested in students' nonacademic lives in a manner unlike that of other college faculty. Because so much of the program's success depends on the quality of the interaction between faculty and students, and because that interaction occurs in tremendously varied formats from lectures to book seminars to informal meals, faculty must be committed to students' development as whole persons. The success of the program depends on it!

- An inclusive educational philosophy. Many open enrollment institutions are founded upon the assumption that equal access to higher education is a right from which society should benefit. However, assuming, as Evergreen does, that all students will learn given the right environment and encouragement takes that notion one step further. In committing to that assumption, Evergreen is radically different from these other institutions which employ an open door as a means of ensuring that economically and educationally deprived students have access to the professional job market. Evergreen's insistence that all students will learn transforms the open door commitment into an assurance which eliminates all vestiges of elitism or any hint of intellectual social Darwinism; influences which can be contravening factors in open enrollment institutions and serious barriers to achievement for the educationally deprived in selective colleges. In place of elitism, Evergreen's program encourages students with different learning styles and time schedules to collaborate in the pursuit of common educational objectives. It also prompts students with undirected creative gifts to gain the discipline necessary to make the most of their talents. This remarkable curriculum also ensures that graduates are well equipped to confront both personal and professional challenges. Perhaps that is one reason why Evergreen graduates do so well in medical school admissions, graduate study, and the job market.

But these are only the most obvious organizational factors of Evergreen's uniqueness. The human factors are undoubtedly more important. The bold and perceptive way in which its founders defined and implemented its mission must be a significant reason for Evergreen's uniqueness. In an era when too many institutions tried to manufacture appeal by promising to be all things to all comers, Evergreen insisted on doing only a few things but doing them well. Moreover, it flaunted this uniqueness (to some Washington citizens in a perverse way) by coining an inflammatory college motto, *Omnia Extares* ("let it all hang out") and developing traditions which poked deliberate fun at traditional collegiate culture. An interesting consequence of this institutionalized tomfoolery is that the college refuses to take itself too seriously, a helpful antidote to too much overblown praise when times are good, and no small blessing otherwise, when financial constraints seem overwhelming.

Clearly, Evergreen's most important asset, which continues to make it a unique alternative in American higher education, is the quality of its faculty and staff. In addition to the founding vision of Charles McCann, the first president, it would be unfortunate if the guiding influence of Joseph Shoben, one of the architects of its student affairs program, or Larry Stenberg, its first dean of students, were overlooked. These individuals as well as the "founding mother," Gail Martin, until July 1991 the vice president for student affairs, developed programs and founded traditions as the needs arose, often under daunting fiscal constraints. The quality of the relationships which these faculty and staff developed with one another and with their students provides lasting proof of Evergreen's dramatic success.

By any measure, however, the truly remarkable feature of the achievement these founders institutionalized was the success they accomplished in wedding some of the most central commitments of the student affairs profession, embodied in documents like *A Perspective on Student Affairs* (National Association of Student Personnel Administrators, 1987), to the academic organization of the college. Many would argue that accomplishment is the primary reason why Evergreen continues to provide such a successful educational experience when other colleges with similar initial objectives have compromised their founding commitments or disappeared altogether.

Evergreen as Prototypic

If Evergreen provides a model for others, especially for student affairs practitioners who might wish to have a more pervasive influence on the direction of their institutions, what lessons can be learned? The evidence is readily available. To wit:

Pay attention to process. It is a truism that student affairs professionals are more concerned about process than anyone else in academe. But how many college student affairs officers stop to consider how a concern for process could be institutionalized, made an expected step in the established routine? Several Evergreen innovations provide excellent examples.

Developing College Work Days when all other commitments are set aside and faculty and students are free to invest their entire energy in maintaining and improving the quality of campus life is an important, if simple, innovation. It directly addresses the fundamental problem most institutions face of finding time to meet as a community to clarify and resolve issues.

Utilizing language, titles, and designations which maintain a distinctive ethos and minimize bureaucratic red tape and obstacles to personal interaction is another. Instead of "Blue Ribbon Commissions" Evergreen has "Disappearing Task Forces." That name communicates a refreshing approach for faculty who resent the time taken by committee work. It also quickly establishes the task orientation of group. There can be few bastions of ongoing political influence when task groups evaporate when their work is done.

Wise use of titles led members of the student affairs staff and others to develop a name for students of color at Evergreen which undermines attempts to marginalize those students. Since much of the early focus on ethnicity during the founding of the college was placed on Native Americans, students of color came to be known as "The First People." When other ethnic groups began to organize they developed "The First People's Coalition," an important symbol of the priority assigned to the appreciation of pluralism in the Evergreen community.

Another variant on intelligent titling can be seen in the way Evergreen's founders employed geographic proximity to reinforce interdisciplinary connections. How many scientists would engage in vehement denunciations of their humanist colleagues if they shared the same coffee rooms? At Evergreen the art studios abut the physics labs. Biochemists and literature scholars share the same coffee rooms and space for seminars. Another interesting example of creative designation of space is presented by the completion of Evergreen's new physical education facility. Instead of calling the building a "gymnasium" or "field house," names which risked triggering Evergreen's traditional antipathy toward overly enthusiastic jocks, the new addition became the "Multi-purpose Building."

The point made by all of this attention to process is that an institution which cares about the total education of its students must be vitally interested in the quality of the human interactions which go on there. That interest in process yields frustration occasionally. The current search for a new president has now consumed nearly ten months in discussion of the process alone. An acting president has been appointed in the interim, with the proviso that he will not be a candidate for the permanent position, so that these important process issues could be carefully examined and conflicts resolved before announcing the vacancy and beginning the formal presidential search.

The lesson for other institutions is that attention to process takes time and significant energy, but it yields rich rewards in providing the ground for establishing restorative personal relationships and developing campus groups which work synergistically.

Establish traditions which support institutional mission. How much energy is wasted in maintaining traditions and campus rituals whose sole purpose is letting off steam or providing inexpensive entertainment? Relief of stress may be a periodic necessity in academe but why nurture traditions which seem to run contrary, as so many do during fall football season, to the fundamental academic mission of a college?

Here the influence of student affairs staff in the creation of the Evergreen ethos perhaps is most visible. In an exemplary fashion the founding student affairs staff developed events and symbols which helped the college to understand and celebrate its sense of itself. The founding dean, Larry Stenberg, is probably more responsible than any other person for creating Evergreen's spring fling, Super Saturday. No one could call it a serious academic occasion. Nevertheless it symbolizes to the Evergreen community, alumni, and friends, the quality of the relationships established during the preceding academic year. It also provides an opportunity for Greeners to reward those who have made significant contributions in the past year, to hear faculty musicians perform, to dress up in medieval garb, for some alumni and friends to sell their wares, and for everyone to meet and just have a good time.

Another important tradition is the Academic Fair held near the end of each quarter. Anyone wishing to offer a course or to take one gathers at a central point on campus. Faculty who have committed to leading programs for the coming year are present as well. Students or faculty who have an idea they would like to pursue offer "trial balloons," actually a preliminary course prospectus. In casual conversations, students and faculty talk about their intellectual interests, competencies, and commitments. Decisions are made, individual and group contracts established, and plans for months or a full year of academic study confirmed. What a contrast to the inhumane and mechanistic process of class registration at most institutions!

These traditions in addition to the potluck dinners, book seminars, and other activities are only a few of the annual events of Evergreen life. Nearly all share an integrative function which helps to ensure that life within and without the classroom is a seamless web. Evergreen will ever be indebted to the student affairs staff who knew so well that when campus traditions reinforce the fundamental academic mission of the college, the medium really is the message.

Make student affairs staff educators. During times of fiscal crisis student affairs staff have attempted to parry threats to their survival by campaigning for their essential functions as retainers of students, crisis solvers, and ombudspersons. Essential though those functions are, a college faced with fundamental fiscal constraints must decide to retain only those who are integral to the educational process. That fact explains why student affairs staff have continued to be viewed as central to Evergreen even when budget constraints have been most severe.

But a more important reason why student affairs staff need to be viewed as educators has to do with the important insights they bring to the endeavor of educating students as whole persons. The old dictum frequently espoused elsewhere that the most important lessons in life are learned outside the classroom simply does not obtain at Evergreen. The expertise student affairs staff have in connecting the affective with the cognitive, or demonstrating how to make educational capital by reflecting on implications of a profound personal experience, become important skills all faculty must learn to utilize. That is a lesson the former vice president for student affairs, Gail Martin, taught faculty repeatedly. When difficulties arise in a program between faculty, or between faculty and students, often it is the student affairs professional who is called to help to sort out the issues or to enhance the educational process.

More than any other, this influence Evergreen student affairs staff exercise in helping to transform the educational experience from a purely intellectual exercise to deeply affecting personal experiences is an institutional role which student affairs professionals should understand, appreciate, and seek to emulate.

Evergreen as Dinosaur

One reason why the Evergreen community has taken nearly a year to begin searching for a new president is related to concerns about the college's viability. Some feel that the last presidential choice took a serious toll on the institution. They are convinced that must not happen again. Others are anxious about the ever-present threat of legislative budget-cutters. At a time when 20,000 Washington teachers are threatening to strike because of concerns about the quality of elementary and secondary education, conservative politicians are eager to effect economies at the expense of an institution with a radical reputation. Evergreen's cause was not advanced during student protests against the Gulf War in January of 1991 when several hundred Evergreen students stormed the doors of the state Capitol and actually held a sit-in in the vacant chambers of the House of Representatives!

So, questions about the college's viability are real. But perhaps the more serious threats are internal. Because the success of the college turns upon the quality of the education experienced in the program, faculty who are not interested in educating the whole student, or who lack a sincere commitment to interdisciplinary learning, or who are not skilled in team-teaching, can undermine Evergreen's distinctive character. During a time when graduate education is becoming more intensely focused upon the discipline and when interdisciplinary education is viewed with increasing skepticism, finding replacements for the superb faculty who founded the institution will be increasingly difficult. More worrisome is the toll institutional stress has taken upon some faculty and even some student affairs staff. During the last few months some of the founders of the college have articulated plans to leave. Even if new faculty and staff can be found who are prepared to continue Evergreen's exemplary traditions, how can they be directed if the institutional knowledge embodied in these founders is lost?

Another threat is posed by a change in the student body. In part because of its very success in attracting a large applicant pool, Evergreen has been required to adopt a more selective admission process. This means that its commitment to an open admission policy has been modified. It has also resulted in lowering the average age of the student body, a change which could have devastating consequences for Evergreen's future. It must be acknowledged that a certain portion of the institution's success has been attributable to the natural intellectual curiosity and educational persistence of its more mature student body. Can these same expectations be retained when the majority of new students are recent high school graduates? What kind of safety nets are required for students who lack motivation or need more structure than the traditional Evergreen program format allows? What prevents students with little motivation from so frustrating faculty energies that faculty abandon their commitments to educating the whole student? How can these changes in student body be accommodated without seriously altering the college's unique mission?

These are indeed fundamental challenges which require imaginative responses or they could become grave threats to Evergreen's future. Certainly extraordinary care needs to be exercised in selecting a president who can help to restore an enthusiastic commitment to the brilliant educational vision which crafted such a remarkably singular innovation on the American educational scene. The times demand a college which provides a living example of vibrant and relevant education of the whole student, not a rapidly deteriorating vestige of an appealing but bygone era. Let us hope our Evergreen friends are successful!

Chapter Ten

Conclusions and Recommendations

George D. Kuh and John H. Schuh

The seven involving colleges featured in this book reflect in many ways the diversity of American colleges and universities. Four of the institutions (Earlham, Mount Holyoke, Stanford, Xavier) are independent while the others (Evergreen State, Iowa State, Louisville) are state supported. Some are located in or near urban areas, others are geographically isolated from a major population center. Some have less than 3,000 undergraduates while two (Iowa State and Louisville) have approximately 20,000. Some are highly complex research universities, others offer a comprehensive array of academic programs, and still others are single-purpose liberal arts colleges. Admission to several is highly competitive; others admit virtually anyone who applies. The missions and philosophies of these institutions (including the other seven institutions in the College Experiences Study mentioned in Chapters One and Two) also are very different from one another. As a result, it is difficult to make definitive statements about the role and contributions of student affairs staff that apply to all of them.

Involving colleges do have one thing in common: none has enough resources to support all the worthwhile initiatives suggested by faculty, administrators, and students. Even at the time of this study (and the situation has since gotten worse), several institutions were dealing with budget cuts. Against this backdrop, in this chapter we draw conclusions about the role, characteristics, and contributions of student affairs organizations, staff, programs, and services at involving colleges. When appropriate, suggestions are made for graduate programs in student affairs and higher education.

What We Know About Student Affairs at Involving Colleges

Nine conclusions about the role and contributions of student affairs in involving colleges are warranted. None of the recommendations that follow from the conclusions requires additional resources to be implemented other than those already present: energy, ingenuity, and a desire to excel. These recommendations are merely starting points. Student affairs professionals surely will discover additional actions to take on their own campus consistent with their institution's mission, philosophy, and student characteristics that will promote student learning and personal development.

Conclusion #1: Student affairs staff at involving colleges understand and value their institution's mission, philosophy, and educational purposes.

As reported in Chapter Two and in *Involving Colleges* (Kuh et al., 1991), no institutional characteristic is more important to encouraging students to take advantage of out-of-class learning and personal development opportunities than a clear, consistently expressed institutional mission. An institution's mission determines what is and is not appropriate within a particular college or university. It can be a yardstick for evaluating the success or failure of learning opportunities. Much like the navigational equipment aboard an aircraft, an institution's mission can provide guidance for how to proceed in uncertain times.

Student affairs staff at involving colleges are advantaged because their institutions, by and large, have relatively clear and consistently expressed missions and educational purposes. For example, if an involving college expects students to behave like adults, then students are held accountable for their actions, not only by the institution but also by their peers.

Recall that an institution's philosophy is made up of assumptions, beliefs, and values and is manifested in the manner in which policies and programs are implemented (Kuh et al., 1991). Every institution, division of student affairs, and student affairs office, program, or service has a philosophy although it may not be obvious to all or discussed frequently. An institution's philosophy is more than its espoused values and beliefs about, for example, under what conditions students learn best or institutional statements about what is expected of students ("students are considered capable of making their own choices and behaving appropriately"). Often enacted assumptions and beliefs contradict or conflict with those espoused by an institution or student affairs division in, for example, the catalog or student conduct code. For this reason, any attempt to discover the institution's philosophy should obtain evidence about existing programs

208

and services that manifest enacted assumptions and beliefs rather than those that are espoused by student affairs professionals or other institutional leaders.

Suggestions were made in *Involving Colleges* (Kuh et al., 1991) for how institutions can assess the clarity and consistency of their mission, philosophy, and educational purposes. Suffice it to say here that student affairs staff must be active collaborators in this continuing process and be able to persuasively articulate their institution's mission. Additionally, they must design programs and services consistent with the mission and educational purposes. As we shall see later, knowledge and understanding the mission also are critical because an institution's mission provides the moral authority for student life policies and codes of conduct.

Recommendations:

(a) Conduct a systematic study — perhaps an audit — to discover the espoused and enacted values and beliefs that are at the core of the philosophy of the institution and student affairs. To be effective, any effort to discover espoused and enacted values must include the participation of students, faculty, graduates, and others.

(b) Use the mission and philosophy as a test to determine whether existing programs should be continued and proposed programs supported. A good place to start is by determining if student affairs staff and students understand and can explain the mission. When in doubt about how to begin a program evaluation, the mission is always an appropriate springboard.

(c) Focus staff development on activities that more closely link student affairs personnel, programs, and services to the institution's educational purposes. Staff development programs often emphasize current issues facing the student affairs profession (e.g., health, alcohol abuse, legal issues, student development theory). As important as these issues are, staff development activities that focus on, for example, Eastern religions, great books, or new scientific discoveries are closer to the primary purpose of a college or university and more likely to promote intellectual development of student affairs professionals. By becoming engaged in the intellectual life of the community through, for example, attending a distinguished lecture series, student affairs staff model behavior similar to that expected of their students.

(d) Organize a staff development session to review current catalogs and promotional videotapes to see if they are consistent with what staff believe is the espoused institutional mission and philosophy. Discussion of what a college says it is about and what actually takes place on a day-to-day basis can be quite revealing and prompt staff to rethink policies and priorities.

(e) Make certain all staff members, including paraprofessional staff such as resident assistants, understand the institution's mission, philosophy, and educational purposes and the values and aspirations from which expectations for students originate. Without a grasp of what the institution stands for, what it aspires to be, and its preferred way of doing business, staff members lack the moral authority to persuade students to modify their behavior in a manner consistent with the institution's values and aspirations. Such an understanding is required for staff to articulate the institution's need for student conduct codes and sanctions and explain to students why it is important that members of communities who enjoy such privileges as independence and autonomy must also respect the rights of others.

(f) Emphasize in preparation programs the importance of student affairs roles and functions that complement an institution's mission and philosophy. At a minimum several weeks of concentrated study should be devoted to examining how an institutional mission gives (or ought to give) direction to student affairs programs and services. The implication for student affairs and its relationships to other campus organizations also warrant special attention.

Conclusion #2: The personal values of student affairs staff at involving colleges are compatible with the institution's philosophy and educational purposes.

The philosophies of involving colleges range from egalitarian (Earlham, Grinnell, Evergreen State) to meritocratic (Miami, Xavier). The point here is that student learning and personal development can be fostered no matter what the institution's philosophy, provided the philosophy is compatible with the institution's educational purposes and the characteristics of students, and that policies, programs, and practices are consistent with the philosophy. Equally important, the values of student affairs staff must be compatible with institutional values that comprise the core of its philosophy.

It is unrealistic to expect staff to change their personal values to become more congruent with institutional values. It is relatively easy, however, for staff to acquire technical competence in such areas as the law, governmental policies regulating alcohol and financial aids, and other aspects of student life. For this reason, the match between a prospective staff member's personal value system and the institution's ethos is far more critical for selecting new staff than the traditional indices of professional competence. This is particularly important at colleges with salient missions (e.g., Berea, Earlham, Evergreen, Grinnell, Mount Holyoke, Xavier).

210

Recommendations:

(a) Clearly articulate the institution's values in contacts with potential employees. It may be prohibitive financially to include statements of institutional values in job announcements in national media (e.g., *The Chronicle of Higher Education*). But early in the selection process, and certainly when candidates visit the campus, a candid exchange of institutional values and expectations (not only for the vacant position but for students and faculty as well) and the candidate's values is in order. This assumes, of course, that institutional values and expectations are clear and understood by student affairs staff.

(b) Hire new staff members with values that are compatible with the institution's philosophy and espoused aspirations. This does not mean student affairs should seek only compliant, risk-aversive personalities; quite the contrary. Creative, independent-minded colleagues willing to challenge the status quo usually enrich campus life and the student experience. However, creativity that springs from values inconsistent with the institution's philosophy almost certainly will result in conflict. This is a complicated matter, one which warrants far more discussion than the purposes of this chapter allow. Suffice it to say here that we recognize such value conflicts may be unavoidable in many institutions if they are to become more hospitable to members of historically underrepresented groups. We shall return to this point later.

(c) Be sure orientation for new staff includes an appropriate emphasis on the institution's mission and philosophy. To have the desired effect, orientation events for new staff should make use of examples of how institutional mission and philosophy shaped the development of currently existing programs and services. Perhaps case studies and role plays also could be used to illustrate how institutional values guide decision-making processes and policy development.

Conclusion #3: Organizational patterns of student affairs programs and services vary in involving colleges.

No one "best model" of organizing a student affairs division can be distilled from the institutions in the College Experiences Study. That is, as with other colleges and universities, student affairs organizational patterns and the complement of programs and services administered by student affairs at involving colleges are disparate. At some institutions, student affairs organizations were "tall" (many layers of administration and supervisory personnel); at other involving colleges the organizational chart was relatively "flat" (many staff reported to only a few administrators). Some chief student affairs officers performed more like executives while others were very much hands-on administrators. Yet, as will be discussed later, student affairs professionals at all the institutions enjoyed excellent relationships with faculty and academic administrators. Although the functions of student affairs were not always well understood by faculty, student affairs staff were respected for the quality of their contributions.

In general, the characteristics of student affairs staff were a function of institutional complexity, including the level of professional or academic preparation of other institutional agents (e.g., percentage of faculty and administrators with terminal degrees) and the degree of specialization in academic programs and student affairs functions and services. The larger and more complex the institution, the more likely it was that student affairs staff had graduate preparation in student affairs, counseling, or a related field. For example, at Iowa State University and the University of Louisville, professional preparation in student affairs or higher education administration often was a requirement when seeking new staff.

But even in those institutions as well as others (e.g., Earlham, Mount Holyoke, Stanford), a "grow your own" tradition often permeated the student affairs division. That is, it was not unusual for graduates of the institution to be appointed to professional entry-level or support staff positions. Over time through hard work, demonstrated institutional loyalty, willingness to further develop one's own talents, and responsibility accrual (i.e., adding tasks to one's job description, Miner & Estler, 1985), people were promoted from within based upon exemplary service to the institution. In other words, inbreeding in student affairs divisions at involving colleges seems to have enhanced the capacity of student affairs to offer mission-driven programs and services compatible with the institution's educational purposes and philosophy.

Compared with their counterparts at some of the smaller colleges, student affairs staff at larger universities tended to sponsor more "traditional" programs and responsibilities and were expected to take more responsibility for the supervision and development of out-of-class learning opportunities for students. This may be in part a function of the increasing importance of the research mission of the larger institutions where faculty were expected to spend a substantial portion of their energy and research in creative activities whereas at the small colleges teaching and institutional governance were the highest priorities for faculty.

Recommendations:

(a) Be skeptical of consultants or proposed reorganizations that promise to improve student learning outside the classroom. There is no one best organizational model. Indeed, Pascarella and Terenzini (1991) concluded that the impact of college on students is more a function of environmental and contextual conditions than of organizational or programmatic variables. What is important is that the student affairs organizational structure adequately serves the students' needs and complements the institution's mission (National Association of Student Personnel Administrators, 1987).

(b) Adapt your organizational structures, services, and structured out-of-class learning opportunities to the needs of your students rather than to what is in vogue or trendy at other campuses. What works best is that which addresses the needs of your students and the institution's educational purposes.

(c) Adopt a "hunter" mindset (Whetten, 1984) by constantly looking for potential staff from among students and others on your campus (e.g., support staff, faculty) as well as elsewhere. If need be, "grow your own" by, for example, recruiting student leaders for entry-level jobs or by recommending graduate study with the expressed purpose of luring them back to work at their alma mater. This may be a particularly effective way of increasing the number of people of color among student affairs professionals.

Conclusion #4: Student affairs staff at involving colleges have diverse backgrounds and preparation.

Several chief student affairs officers did not possess terminal degrees. Many student affairs staff did not have graduate-level preparation in student affairs, higher education, counseling, or an allied area; indeed, a wide variety of degrees and disciplines were represented among student affairs personnel at involving colleges. In addition, some staff were highly involved in professional organizations, others were not.

The diverse academic preparation of student affairs staff did not seem to limit their effectiveness. Apparently graduate education in student affairs work is not essential to understand the value of student involvement to learning and personal development or to develop campus environments and policies and practices that foster student involvement in campus life. Similarly, while involvement in professional associations is considered useful for advancing one's professional career and "giving back" to one's profession (Carpenter, 1990; DeCoster & Brown, 1991), such involvement did not seem to be related to the quality of student affairs programs and services at these institutions.

Recommendations:

(a) When hiring staff, give considerable weight to a candidate's philosophy and vision in addition to technical expertise. It is much easier to teach or acquire the latter than the former.

(b) Expand the pool of potential staff members. Some student affairs professionals are apologetic when hiring people without professional preparation in student affairs or higher education. On balance, professional preparation is preferred, particularly when a candidate's understanding and appreciation of the institution's mission and philosophy are strong. But such an understanding and practical competence in human and organizational skills are not limited to people who come from the "student affairs rainforest" (Schroeder, Nicholls & Kuh, 1983). Spouses of faculty and staff, people working in related areas in the local off-campus community, and others can become, with appropriate socialization, excellent staff members.

(c) When hiring people from nontraditional student affairs backgrounds, make certain that early socialization experiences (e.g., staff orientation, meetings) and subsequent staff development programs emphasize student development philosophy and theory as well as areas of technical expertise specific to the job.

Conclusion #5: Student affairs staff at involving colleges competently perform the routine — albeit nontrivial — activities by which the work of the division and the institution gets done.

Student affairs staff at involving colleges "stick to the knitting" (Peters & Waterman, 1982). That is, they emphasize service to their primary "client groups": students whose needs and interests they know very well and the institution, the "best interests" of which are determined by its mission and philosophy (National Association of Student Personnel Administrators, 1987). To ameliorate obstacles to student learning, they take leadership in creating and maintaining early warning systems and safety nets, and expand these invisible structures by recruiting faculty, other staff (e.g., custodians, secretaries), and students.

It is no accident that telephones and mail are answered promptly and courteously, the mission and philosophy of the institution are well understood and communicated to students in various ways throughout the year, details such as accounting and recordkeeping are handled efficiently and effectively, and oral and written communications use clear, nontechnical language (i.e., void of professional jargon). A work place culture has been created wherein people perform competently what appear to be insignificant but nonetheless indispensable tasks and duties that reinforce the ethics of care and membership common to involving colleges.

Recommendations:

(a) Maintain a balance between advocating for students and the institution's needs for order and stability. On the one hand, emphasizing student life policies and practices may be necessary for promoting civility and decorum. On the other hand, an emphasis on control may stifle student creativity (Heist, 1968) and send inconsistent messages (e.g., "you are expected to behave like adults and here is a long list to govern your behavior"); neither extreme encourages student learning. Knowing one's students is a key to determining the right amount of structure in campus policies and practices. We shall return to this point in the next section.

(b) Frequently monitor the institution's early warning systems and safety nets to make certain the needs of all students are being addressed. It is not unusual for student affairs staff to devote a disproportionate amount of attention to specific groups or certain types of students. Early warnings and safety nets (Kuh et al., 1991) function best when faculty and staff acknowledge that the education of every student enrolled at their institution is the college's primary business.

(c) Do not overemphasize routines so that doing things right becomes more important than doing the right thing. The larger the institution or division of student affairs, the greater the tendency to emphasize efficiency over effectiveness (e.g., routinize functions, focus on deadlines). While efficiency is important, this must not become the preordinate goal of student affairs. Every student is unique and presents a different constellation of needs, aspirations, abilities, and interests. In institutions where an ethic of care is operating, allowances are made for individual students in ways that are consistent with the institution's philosophy. Moreover, this type of faculty and staff behavior toward students is routine and nontrivial at institutions that value student learning and personal development.

Conclusion #6: Student affairs personnel at involving colleges know their students.

On first blush, this conclusion may seem trite and condescending. Are not student affairs professionals everywhere knowledgeable and expert about their students? It is fair to say that some student affairs staff at involving colleges were familiar with the current literature on students and their experiences; others, however, were not. But, by and large, student affairs staff did have an accurate understanding and appreciation of their students and what students wanted from their college experience. Therefore, wittingly or unwittingly, student affairs staff at involving colleges were, indeed, "campus experts on students" as the National Association of Student Personnel Administrators (1987) recommended. Moreover, student affairs staff recognized that student learning and personal development was the *raison d'etre* for all personnel, programs, and services.

Recommendations:

(a) Spend time talking with and listening to students individually and in small groups. Such interactions — often spontaneous and almost always informal — produce current, relevant information about the student experience and communicate to students that the institution is interested in them as individuals. These contacts, albeit intermittent, usually are ripe opportunities for student affairs staff to socialize students to institutional values. At an involving college, spending time talking and listening to students is considered to be as important as planning programs or attending professional meetings.

(b) Spend less time developing or programming opportunities for students and more time teaching students how to take advantage of learning opportunities that already exist in the college environment. Recall the proverb which advises that giving a person a fish only feeds that person for a day, while teaching a person how to fish prepares an individual to obtain food for a lifetime. Developing learning opportunities for students outside the classroom is a variation on that same theme. At some institutions staff spend a disproportionate amount of time developing new, "trendy" programs that expand the inventory of out-of-class learning opportunities rather than adding depth to opportunities that already exist. When students know how to take advantage of existing programs and how to learn from their own experiences, they will benefit immeasurably and be able to apply these skills over a lifetime. Hence, the challenge for student affairs staff is to break the habit of doing things for students — what Argyris and Schon (1978) call "single-loop learning" — and begin to teach them how to do things for themselves (double-loop learning). Examples of double-loop learning at involving colleges include the TULIP program at Iowa State University where students who had not been leaders in activities prior to college can acquire leadership skills, and the partnerships formed between "senior" (faculty) and "junior" (students) learners at The Evergreen State College wherein every person is responsible for his or her learning in the context of a supportive group. Principles such as these and the others common to involving colleges underscore the kinds of initiatives on which student affairs staff should focus in order to encourage students to take advantage of learning and personal development opportunities that naturally occur in collegiate environments.

(c) Periodically collect information about student characteristics and student subcultures. At some institutions, information about the changing characteristics of student needs and interests may be best obtained by participating in such annual data collection activities as the Cooperative Institutional Research Program (CIRP) directed by Alexander Astin (UCLA) on behalf of the American Council on Education. In other settings, such instruments as the College Student Experience Questionnaire (Pace, 1987) may be more helpful in understanding students and their experiences. Quantitative data produced by these types of instruments seemed to be of greater utility at institutions with

216

many thousands of undergraduate students. Of course, whatever information is collected becomes valuable only when it informs policy and practice.

(d) Determine whether the students' ability to balance freedom and responsibility is consistent with the institution's espoused mission and purposes and with observed behavior. Student affairs staff are responsible, along with faculty and other administrative colleagues, for continually reexamining whether their institution's mission is viable and understood by students and other constituent groups (e.g., graduates, people in the surrounding community, parents and relatives of prospective and current students).

Conclusion #7: Student affairs personnel at involving colleges know how their institutional cultures and various subenvironments influence — positively and negatively — student behavior.

The preceding chapters have underscored the importance of cultural and environmental influences on student behavior. Culture is the glue that holds institutions together (Kuh & Whitt, 1988). Each institution's culture differs in some ways from other colleges and universities. Indeed, staff at involving colleges know that the core of values that undergirds their campus culture is like a flower garden with a wide variety of blooming plants; both require constant attention if they are to elicit the desired response. As a result, understanding the culture of one's institution is essential to effective performance in that setting.

Not all student affairs staff at involving colleges were "experts" on campus environments as the National Association of Student Personnel Administrators (1987) recommends. But most had an intuitive, perceptive understanding of the advantages associated with human-scale physical and psychological environments. Moreover, they were cognizant of their role in helping students annually (and sometimes more frequently) create living and learning environments that discourage anonymity and encourage responsibility for self and others. Creating such environments is emphasized in the "community-building" activities (DeCoster & Mable, 1980) that have become staples of residence life programs during the first few weeks of the fall semester at residential colleges. But it is not the number of programs provided in student residences or targeted for commuter students that seems to be the key factor. More important is the amount of time staff spend encouraging students to create subenvironments and affinity groups that are consistent with the institution's values and purposes.

Recommendations:

(a) Encourage every student affairs staff member to become acquainted with the history of their institution. Higher education institutions are products of their histories;

hence, knowledge of the institutional history is critical to understanding how a college or university became what it is and what makes it special. Heroes and heroines have shaped institutional values; their contributions often can be used to illustrate institutional values. For example, Mount Holyoke College invokes Mary Lyon with fondness and respect during numerous ceremonies; the statue of Supreme Court Justice Louis Brandeis at the University of Louisville symbolizes an institutional commitment to racial equality.

(b) Devote at least one staff development session annually to examining present circumstances in the context of the institution's history. For example, organize one or more staff development activities around trends in student behavior and attitudes distilled from the campus newspaper over the years. Invite "official" as well as the "unofficial" historians (e.g., a long-time faculty member or perhaps a graduate from many decades ago) to a staff development session or division meeting once every few years to talk about the history of the institution with a particular emphasis on student life or events in the institution's past that symbolize the importance of blurring in-class and out-of-class learning.

(c) Make certain that newcomers learn early on about the institution's history, traditions, and other cultural artifacts that create expectations for student behavior and encourage learning and personal development. Perhaps a copy of the institutional history and other documents can be sent before the new staff member begins work.

(d) Examine whether various programs and services (e.g., admission materials, orientation) effectively use anticipatory socialization mechanisms to introduce newcomers to the institution's cultures and expectations. Every two or three years a senior student affairs staff member might participate to determine whether important values are being communicated and what participants seem to be getting from orientation efforts. This person can attempt to make the familiar strange by adopting the perspective of a visitor to a foreign land (Whitt, forthcoming). A similar approach could be used to evaluate new student orientation.

Conclusion #8: Student affairs staff at involving colleges are campus catalysts for multiculturalism.

Multiculturalism is one of the watchwords of the 1990s. In involving colleges, multiculturalism is a state in which cultural, ethnic, racial, gender, and other differences are understood, protected, respected, and celebrated throughout all aspects of the institution, including the curriculum, student life and residences, and governance. Multiculturalism promises to enrich campus life when a tapestry of traditions, lifestyles, and values of different groups is woven as persons from varied cultural, ethnic, and racial backgrounds share their experiences and history (Bagasao, 1989; Giddings, 1990; Madrid, 1988; Oliver & Johnson, 1988). To foster multiculturalism, all those on a college campus must discover ways to engender respect, appreciation, and cooperation among student groups so that a sense of ownership and belonging permeates the campus while preserving the important contributions of various groups to the learning and development of their members (Smith, 1989).

> It means doing more than inviting outsiders to be included — it means listening to their views about what it would take for them to feel included....It means considering the preconditions for participation — the preconditions for assuring that every member of the community feels like a member of the community (Minow, 1990, p. 25).

Currently, we know of no institution — including involving colleges — that is satisfied with the degree to which it has become a multicultural learning community. Because student affairs is often on the front line in dealing with difficult issues related to understanding human differences, student affairs staff must accept, and become proficient as campus catalysts for, multiculturalism.

Recommendations:

(a) Support the establishment of multiple student subcommunities, some of which are organized around themes of race and ethnicity. For many students, learning about their ignorance or biases toward people who are different requires articulating and sharing their thoughts and feelings, debating and challenging stereotypes, and dealing with their uncertainty about cultural differences in the presence of peers. Such encounters with one's own and others' culture, beliefs, and attitudes is risky, often intense and, perhaps, most effectively achieved in one's subcommunity of choice, such as an ethnic or academic theme house where students usually enjoy a sense of security. Paradoxically, subcommunities — particularly those organized by race and ethnicity — can both facilitate understanding, sharing, and learning as well as create barriers between their members and the rest of the institution. Indeed, in the eyes of some (Finn, 1990; Short, 1988), the existence of such houses and centers fuels the divisive conditions their critics fear. Even if the institutional mission and espoused values support multiculturalism, additional steps must be taken to bring the members of various subcommunities together across subgroup lines.

(b) Use anticipatory socialization and induction experiences to underscore the importance of multiculturalism. A quarter to a third of the students at a college or university each year are newcomers; hence it is inevitable that many newcomers will not understand what the institution expects of itself and of its students in dealing with a wide range of topics including multiculturalism. Involving colleges use both formal and informal means to communicate to prospective and newly matriculated students their norms, values, and expectations — "what it's like to be a student here."

Included in those messages are statements about the institution's commitment to a multicultural faculty and student body. Be sensitive to the possibility that when an institution aspires to become a multicultural learning community, expectations may be created that, when not met, can lead to disappointment, resentment, and bitterness.

(c) Determine the extent to which institutional language and traditions embrace and affirm, or exclude and obstruct, full participation by members of certain groups in the life of the institution. An institution's language gives expression to institutional values and conveys feelings of belongingness or exclusion for people within the institution (Kuh & Whitt, 1988). Analysis of speeches and other public statements by institutional leaders can reveal much about a college's commitment to multiculturalism. Such statements, while important, may be counterproductive if the everyday language and behavior of the campus ignores members of historically underrepresented groups or makes them invisible (Kuh et al., 1991).

Similarly, campus ceremonies and traditions affirm or ignore the presence of students from different racial and ethnic backgrounds. Student affairs staff are advised to discover the messages communicated by institutional traditions and develop strategies to revise or eliminate those that are inconsistent with efforts to establish an ethic of membership. In some instances when a critical mass is reached (Smith, 1989), a group of students establish separate events such as homecoming or commencement to celebrate their achievements. It is not clear whether such separatist events should be discouraged or acknowledged as a "natural" phase in the evolution toward multiculturalism on campus. In either case, student affairs staff must be sensitive to the possibility that the expressed need for such events may reflect a growing frustration with an institution's inability or reluctance to send messages of inclusion to certain groups of people.

(d) Use teachable moments to educational advantage. Taking advantage of teachable moments means using incidents of misunderstanding, ignorance, disagreement, protest, and conflict to enhance understanding among all parties and the community as a whole about the issues, feelings, and beliefs involved. The rationale for taking advantage of teachable moments is that, through a series of small but arduous steps, the nature and quality of relationships among community members can be changed. Constant attention to teachable moments also can keep an institution focused

220

on what it should be, what it stands for, and what it can become (Kuh et al., 1991; Mathews, 1989).

(e) Introduce students in student affairs preparation programs to cultural aspects of higher education institutions that influence student learning and personal development, aggressively seek students from historically underrepresented groups (Kuh & Komives, 1990), and address systematically issues of multiculturalism and other human differences in all student affairs-related coursework. It is not sufficient to offer one course focused exclusively on issues of pluralism and multiculturalism. While such courses are important, the content of most courses in higher education and student affairs programs has implications for the multiculturalism imperative. Given the race and ethnicity of student affairs and higher education faculty, this will mean that in the majority of programs white faculty members must become prepared to address these issues.

Conclusion #9: Student affairs staff, faculty, other administrators, and students at involving colleges enjoy mutual respect.

Mutual respect across these groups is both a proximate cause as well as a result of institutional expectations for student responsibility and trusting students to take appropriate risks consistent with their institution's educational purposes. Certainly the history and cultures of these institutions are significant factors. But, as with values, mutual respect can dissipate over time unless assiduous attention is given to maintaining connections and open channels of communication between and among various campus constituencies. Hence it is no surprise that the chief student affairs officer and her or his principle assistants are visible at faculty and student gatherings and routinely report on the state of student life at appropriate gatherings of faculty and administrators such as fall retreats, faculty senate meetings, and various student groups (e.g., student government, Interfraternity Council, and Panhellenic).

Student affairs is a key partner in the educational enterprise when it cultivates good working relations with faculty and others, links programs and activities across the academic and out-of-class dimensions of campus life consistent with the institution's educational purposes and cultures, and removes obstacles to students' pursuit of their academic and personal goals. Ironically, student affairs often is most effective when its contributions are invisible to the casual observer. Some of the more important but typically unnoticed contributions mentioned throughout this book include safety nets, early warning systems, and the many small gestures (perhaps hundreds a week!) that encourage and support students in doing and learning things for themselves.

Recommendations:

(a) Reconceptualize the role of student affairs as a linking agency. According to Pascarella and Terenzini (1991), higher education institutions have the greatest influence on student learning and personal development when their social and academic environments are integrated or complementary. Involving colleges encourage student learning and personal development by blurring the boundaries between what are in many institutions visible, time-honored demarcations between the academic program and out-of-class experiences of students (e.g., the program at The Evergreen State College, the residential experience at Stanford). In involving colleges, student affairs programs and services bring together students and the numerous learning and personal development opportunities that exist in a college or university. This is a perennial challenge, one that must be addressed on an annual basis.

(b) Create a vision for student affairs consistent with the institution's mission, philosophy, educational purposes, and student characteristics. As with other institutional leaders, senior student affairs staff must be "keepers of the vision" who are committed to sustaining precious institutional values while simultaneously challenging policies and practices that either become obstacles to student learning and personal development or relegate certain groups of students to second class citizenry. Included in such a vision is what sort of education the institution should provide its students, what behaviors are expected from students, and what qualities characterize a healthy and effective academic community. Senior student affairs staff have been able to create a shared reality out of multiple, competing realities and the ambiguity that characterizes most colleges and universities. The long tenure of some chief student affairs officers, such as James Rhatigan at Wichita State University, has left an imprint on how student affairs is viewed by faculty and the messages that continuing student affairs staff send to newcomers about how business is to be conducted here and what the student affairs division considers important.

Concluding Thoughts

At involving colleges, the confluence of institutional history, mission, and philosophy; the strengths and interests of faculty, academic administrators, and student affairs staff; emerging priorities; and changing student characteristics shape student affairs organizations, programs, and services. But, by the same token, such factors as institutional characteristics (e.g., size, philosophy, curriculum), the backgrounds of student affairs staff, or the amount of available resources seem to have little influence on the number of educationally purposeful out-of-class learning opportunities.

222

Moreover, the extent to which students take advantage of these opportunities is unrelated to institutional affluence.

Taken together, the results of the College Experiences Study and the conclusions of Pascarella and Terenzini (1991) about the conditions that encourage student learning and personal development indicate that any college or university has the potential to be "involving." But involving colleges do not just happen. That is, a president or chief student affairs officer cannot simply assert that the institution will become — tomorrow if not sooner — an "involving college." Nor can student learning outside the classroom be directly controlled by any one institutional agent or agency, including student affairs. Rather, fostering student involvement requires deliberate behavior by individuals and small groups of administrators, faculty, and students working together over a long period of time.

To create an "involving college" in an era of shrinking resources, a vision is needed of what the institution will look like when students are taking responsibility for their learning and are actively engaged in educationally purposeful activities outside the classroom. The role of the chief student affairs officer is to persuade faculty, staff, and students that the vision has merit, keep people focused on this vision, and expend the effort necessary to maintaining a commitment to attain the vision. Integral to any vision of how student affairs can promote student involvement must begin with the institution's mission, educational purposes, and philosophy. There simply must be congruence among the values and expectations of faculty, student affairs staff, and students and all aspects of the campus environment, including student affairs policies and practices. Within the framework of an involving college, student affairs professionals make significant contributions to the quality of campus life and the range and depth of student learning and development.

References

Adelman, C. (1990). *Light and shadows on college athletics: College transcripts and labor market history.* Washington, D.C.: U.S. Department of Education.

American Council on Education (1937). *The student personnel point of view.* Washington, D.C.: author.

Argyris, C., and Schon, D.A. (1978). *Organizational learning: A theory of action perspective.* Reading, MA: Addison-Wesley.

Astin, A.W. (1977). *Four critical years: Effects of college on beliefs, attitudes, and knowledge.* San Francisco: Jossey Bass Publisher.

Astin, A.W. (1984). Student involvement: A developmental theory for higher education. *Journal of College Student Personnel, 25,* 297-308.

Astin, A.W. (1985). *Achieving educational excellence: A critical assessment of priorities and practices in higher education.* San Francisco: Jossey Bass Publisher.

Bagasao, P.Y. (1989). Student voices breaking the silence: The Asian and Pacific American experience. *Change*, 21(6), 28-37.

Blum, D. (1991, January 23). A national professor of the year who helps Xavier's students on the road to medical school. *The Chronicle of Higher Education*, p. A3.

Boschmann, E. (1990, December). Report on the visit to Xavier University of Louisiana. Indianapolis: Indiana University-Purdue University at Indianapolis.

Bowen, H.R. (1977). *Investment in learning the individual and social value of American higher education.* San Francisco: Jossey Bass Publisher.

Boyer, E.L. (1987). *College: The undergraduate experience in America.* New York: Harper & Row Publishers.

Boyer, E.L. (1990). *Campus life: In search of community.* Princeton, N.J.: The Carnegie Foundation for the Advancement of Teaching.

Bragg, A.K. (1976). *The socialization process in higher education.* ERIC/Higher Education Research Report, No. 7. Washington, D.C.: American Association for Higher Education.

Burrell, G., and Morgan, G. (1979). *Sociological paradigms and organizational analysis.* Exeter, NH: Heinemann.

Carnegie Foundation for the Advancement of Teaching, The (1990). Trendlines — Are liberal arts colleges really different? *Change, 22*(2), 41-44.

Carpenter, D.S. (1990). Developmental concerns in moving toward personal and professional competence. In D. Coleman and J. Johnson (Eds.), *The new professional: A resource guide for new student affairs professionals and their supervisors* (pp. 56-72). Washington, D.C.: National Association of Student Personnel Administrators.

Challenge (1990). South Hadley, MA: Mount Holyoke College.

Chickering, A.W. (1969). *Education and identity*. San Francisco: Jossey Bass Publisher.

Chickering, A.W. (1974). *Commuting versus resident students: Overcoming educational inequities of living off campus*. San Francisco: Jossey Bass Publisher.

Clark, B.R. (1970). *The distinctive college: Antioch, Reed, and Swarthmore*. Chicago: Aldine.

DeCoster, D.A., and Brown, S.S. (1991). Staff development: Personal and professional education. In T. Miller and R. Winston, Jr. (Eds.), *Administration and leadership in student affairs* (pp. 563-613). Muncie, IN: Accelerated Development.

DeCoster, D.A., and Mable, P. (Eds.) (1980). *Personal education and community development in college residence halls*. Cincinnati: American College Personnel Association.

Dobbert, M.L. (1984). *Ethnographic research: Theory and application for modern schools and societies*. New York: Praeger.

Feldman, K.A., and Newcomb, T.M. (1969). *The impact of college on students*. San Francisco: Jossey Bass Publisher.

Fenske, R.H. (1980). Historical foundations. In U. Delworth and G.R. Hanson (Eds.), *Student services: A handbook for the profession* (pp. 30-24). San Francisco: Jossey Bass Publisher.

Finn, C.E. (1990, June 13). Why can't colleges convey our diverse culture's unifying themes? *The Chronicle of Higher Education*, p. A40.

First year handbook, A. (1989). South Hadley, MA: Mount Holyoke College.

Giddings, P. (1990). Education, race and reality: A legacy of the 60s. *Change*, 22(2), 13-17.

Giroux, H.A. (1983). *Theory and resistance in education: A pedagogy for the opposition*. South Hadley, MA: Bergin & Garvey.

Glaser, B.G., and Strauss, A.L. (1967). *The discovery of grounded theory: Strategies for qualitative research*. Chicago: Aldine.

Grobman, A.B. (1988). *Urban state universities: An unfinished agenda*. New York: Praeger.

Heist, P. (Ed.) (1968). *The creative college student*. San Francisco: Jossey-Bass Publisher.

Herndon, S. (1984). Recent findings concerning the relative importance of housing to student retention. *The Journal of College and University Student Housing*, 14(1), 27-31.

Honor Code, The (1988). *The honor code: Academic and community responsibility*. South Hadley, MA: Mount Holyoke College.

Hood, A.B. (1984). *Student development: Does participation affect growth?* (ERIC Document Reproduction Service No. ED 255 105). Bloomington, IN: Association of College Unions — International.

Horowitz, H.L. (1984). *Alma mater: Design and experience in ten women's colleges from their nineteenth century beginnings to the 1930's*. Boston: Beacon Press.

Horowitz, H.L. (1987). *Campus life: Undergraduate cultures from the end of the eighteenth century to the present.* New York: Knopf.

Johnson, K. (1972). The vocabulary of race. In T. Kochman (Ed.), *Rappin' and stylin' out* (pp. 140-51). Urbana: University of Illinois Press.

Keegan, D.L. (1978). The quality of student life and financial costs: The cost of social isolation. *Journal of College Student Personnel, 19,* 55-58.

Kennedy, D. (1989, January). *Reflections on racial understanding.* Stanford, CA: Stanford University.

Kuh, G.D. (1991a, Winter). Snapshots of the campus as community. *Educational Record, 72,* 40-44.

Kuh, G.D. (1991b). The role of admissions and orientation in creating expectations for college life. *College University, 66,* 75-82.

Kuh, G.D. (in press). Teaching and learning — after class. *Journal on Excellence in College Teaching.*

Kuh, G.D., and Komives, S.B. (1990). "The right stuff": Some comments on attracting interesting people to student affairs. In R. Young and L. Moore (Eds.), *The state of the art of professional education and practice* (pp. 1-21). Alexandria, VA: American College Personnel Association Generativity Project.

Kuh, G.D., and Lyons, J.W. (1990). Greek systems at "involving colleges": Lessons from the College Experiences Study. *NASPA Journal, 28,* 20-29.

Kuh, G.D., and MacKay, K.A. (1989). Beyond cultural awareness: Toward interactive pluralism. *Campus Activities Programming, 22*(4), 52-58.

Kuh, G.D., Schuh, J.H., and Whitt, E.J. (in press). Some good news about campus life: How "involving colleges" promote learning outside the classroom. *Change.*

Kuh, G.D., Schuh, J.H., Whitt, E.J., and Associates (1991). *Involving colleges: Successful approaches to fostering student learning and development outside the classroom.* San Francisco: Jossey-Bass Publisher.

Kuh, G.D., and Whitt, E.J. (1988). *The invisible tapestry: Culture in American colleges and universities.* ASHE-ERIC Higher Education Report, No. 1. Washington, D.C.: Association for the Study of Higher Education.

Lyons, J.W. (1990). Examining the validity of basic assumptions and beliefs. In M.J. Barr and M.L. Upcraft (Eds.), *New futures for student affairs* (pp. 22-40). San Francisco: Jossey Bass Publisher.

Madrid, A. (1988, June). Quality and diversity. *AAHE Bulletin,* 8-11.

Mathews, D. (1989, Fall) . . . afterthoughts. *Kettering Review,* 82-84.

Miner, A.S., and Estler, S.E. (1985). Accrual mobility: Job mobility in higher education through responsibility accrual. *Journal of Higher Education, 56,* 121-143.

Minow, M. (1990). On neutrality, equality, and tolerance. *Change, 22*(1), 17-25.

Moffatt, M. (1988). *Coming of age in New Jersey: College and American culture.* New Brunswick, N.J.: Rutgers University Press.

Mount Holyoke College Bulletin 1990-1991: The catalogue issue (1990). South Hadley, MA: Mount Holyoke College.

Mount Holyoke Task Force on Student Life (1989). *Mount Holyoke in the 1990s: Strategic planning task force report.* South Hadley, MA: Mount Holyoke College.

Mueller, K.H. (1961). *Student personnel work in higher education.* Boston: Houghton Mifflin.

National Association of Student Personnel Administrators (1987). *A perspective on student affairs.* Washington, D.C.: author.

National Association of Student Personnel Administrators (1989). *Points of view.* Washington, D.C.: author.

Oliver, M.L., and Johnson, J.H., Jr. (1988). Introduction: The challenge of diversity in higher education. *The Urban Review,* 20, 139-145.

Pace, C.R. (1979). *Measuring outcomes of college: Fifty years of findings and recommendations for the future.* San Francisco: Jossey Bass Publisher.

Pace, C.R. (1987). *CSEQ: Test manual and norms.* Los Angeles: University of California, Los Angeles Center for the Study of Evaluation.

Pascarella, E.T., and Terenzini, P.T. (1991). *How college affects students: Findings and insights from twenty years of research.* San Francisco: Jossey-Bass Publisher.

Peters, T.J., and Waterman, R.H., Jr. (1982). *In search of excellence: Lessons from America's best-run companies.* New York: Harper & Row Publishers.

Rich, A. (1986). *Blood, bread, and poetry.* New York: W.W. Norton.

Richmond, D.R. (1986). The young professional at the small college: Tips for professional success and personal survival. *NASPA Journal,* 24(2), 32-37.

Rodgers, R.F. (1990). Recent theories and research underlying student development. In D.G. Creamer (Ed.), *College student development: Theory and practice for the 1990s* (pp. 27-79). Alexandria, VA: American College Personnel Association.

Sanford, N. (1962). The developmental status of the freshman. In N. Sanford (Ed.), *The American college* (pp. 253-82). New York: Wiley.

Saufley, R.W., Cowan, K.O., and Blake, J.H. (1983). The struggles of minority students at predominantly white institutions. In J. Cones, III, J. Noonan and D. Janha (Eds.), *Teaching minority students,* New Directions for Teaching and Learning, No. 16 (pp. 3-15). San Francisco: Jossey-Bass.

Schroeder, C.C., Nicholls, G.E., and Kuh, G.D. (1983). Exploring the rain forest: Testing assumptions and taking risks. In G. Kuh (Ed.), *Understanding student affairs organizations,* New Directions for Student Services, No.23 (pp. 51-66). San Francisco: Jossey-Bass Publisher.

Schuh, J.H., Andreas, R.E., and Strange, C.C. (in press). Students at metropolitan universities: Viewing involvement through different lenses. *Metropolitan Universities.*

Schuh, J.H., and Kuh, G.D. (1991, Winter). Evaluating the quality of collegiate environments. *Journal of College Admission,* 17-22.

Schuh, J.H., and Laverty, M. (1983). The perceived long-term effect of holding a significant student leadership position. *Journal of College Student Personnel, 24*, 28-32.

Short, T. (1988). A 'new racism' on campus. *Commentary, 86*, 46-50.

Smith, D.G. (1989). *The challenge of diversity: Involvement or alienation in the academy.* ASHE-ERIC Higher Education Report, No. 5. Washington, D.C.: School of Education and Human Development, The George Washington University.

Smith, D.G. (1990). Women's colleges and coed colleges: Is there a difference for women? *Journal of Higher Education, 61*(2), 181-197.

Steele, S. (1989, February). The recoloring of campus life. *Harper's*, 47-55.

Student handbook 1989-1990-1991 (1989). South Hadley, MA: Mount Holyoke College.

Study Group on the Conditions of Excellence in American Higher Education. (1984). *Involvement in learning.* Washington, D.C.: U.S. Department of Education.

Times: Student life at Mount Holyoke (1989). South Hadley, MA: Mount Holyoke College.

Tinto, V. (1987). *Leaving college: Rethinking the causes and cures of student attrition.* Chicago: University of Chicago Press.

University Committee on Minority Issues (1989, March). *Building a multiracial, multicultural university community: Final report of the university committee on minority issues.* Stanford, CA: Stanford University.

Walsh, E. (1989, April). An in-depth look at ethnic concerns. Special report: Building a multiracial, multicultural, community. *Stanford Observer, 9*.

Whetten, D.A. (1984). Effective administrators: Good management on the college campus. *Change, 16*, 38-43.

Whitt, E.J. (forthcoming). Making the familiar strange: Discovering culture. In G. Kuh (Ed.), *Using cultural perspectives in student affairs work.* Alexandria, VA: American College Personnel Association.

Will, G.F. (1990, June 18). The journey up from guilt. *Newsweek*, 68.

Wilson, E.K. (1966). The entering student: Attributes and agents of change. In T.M. Newcomb and E.K. Wilson (Eds.), *College peer groups* (pp. 71-106). Chicago: Aldine.

Zemsky, R., and Massey, W.F. (1990). Cost containment: Committing to a new economic reality. *Change, 22*(6), 16-22.